GOD MADE MAN,
MAN MADE THE SLAVE

GOD MADE MAN,
MAN MADE THE SLAVE

The Autobiography of George Teamoh

F. N. Boney,
Richard L. Hume,
and *Rafia Zafar*

MERCER

ISBN 0-86554-368-2

God Made Man, Man Made the Slave:
The Autobiography of George Teamoh
Copyright © 1990
Mercer University Press
Macon, Georgia 31207
Printed in the United States of America

The paper used in this publication meets
the minimum requirements of American National Standard
for Information Sciences—Permanence of Paper
for Printed Library Materials, ANSI Z39.48-1984.
♾

Library of Congress Cataloging-in-Publication Data

Teamoh, George, 1818–1883?
God made man, man made the slave : the autobiography of George Teamoh /
[edited by] Nash Boney, Rafia Zafar, and Richard L. Hume.
x + 219pp.   15 x 23cm.
Includes bibliographical references.
ISBN 0-86554-368-2
1. Teamoh, George, 1818–1883? 2. Slavery—Virginia. 3. Reconstruc-
tion—Virginia. 4. Virginia—Politics and government—1865–1950. 5. Slaves—
Virginia—Biography. 6. Legislators—Virginia—Biography. 7. Afro-Ameri-
cans—Virginia—Biography.   I. Boney, Nash.   II. Zafar, Rafia.   III.
Hume, Richard L.   IV. Title.
E185.93.V8T438   1990
975.5'0049607302—dc20   90-26719
[B]   CIP

CONTENTS

DEDICATION

This entire project would have been impossible without the love and encouragement of three Teamohs: LETHIA TEAMOH WALKER, my late grandmother; her sister, MARGARET TEAMOH HAITHCOX; and their brother, GEORGE TEAMOH of New York City, who gave his blessing to this work as well.

—R.Z.

PREFACE

This volume is truly a joint effort. Professor Boney, an authority on the antebellum South, edited Teamoh's autobiography for the period when he was a slave in Virginia and a fugitive in the Northeast; he also wrote that part of the Introduction. Professor Hume, an authority on Reconstruction in the South, edited Teamoh's autobiography for the period after he returned to Virginia at the end of the Civil War to take an active role in government as a citizen; he also wrote that part of the Introduction. Professor Zafar, a young scholar of African-American literature and a descendent of George Teamoh, applied her expertise throughout the manuscript and contributed a special essay as well.

Thus, each editor handled the part of the autobiography covering his/her area of expertise. We have used endnotes extensively to document the whole story, but in the actual text of the autobiography we have kept editorial intrusions to a minimum. Only an occasional spelling or grammatical adjustment is added in brackets, and not a single [sic] clogs this very personal narrative. We have not corrected or revised such things as Teamoh's inconsistencies in closing quotations (." and/or ".), his capitalization, his spelling of some compound (and other) words (such as "in deed"), his sometimes very lengthy paragraphs, and his digressions in sections of his diary written after 1874. We have instead tried our best to allow Teamoh to be Teamoh in this unusual manuscript, which the author began late in life (with no specific plans for publication) at the request of friends.

Yet Teamoh's offering belongs in the general category of published black reminiscences of the complex passage from slavery to freedom. A few of his early slave experiences parallel Frederick Douglass's, especially his laboring in a shipyard as a carpenter and caulker. Some of his other adventures in slavery and freedom were shared by other blacks who told their stories. But basically Teamoh's story is unique, the odyssey of an individual black man who learned to survive and sometimes even to prosper in nineteenth-century white America. He had his own particular strengths and weaknesses, his own challenges and opportunities, his own destiny. His autobiography is the story of an exceptional person, and it is best read as he wrote it more than a century ago.

This story has never been told before. His autobiography, handwritten in eighteen inexpensive notebooks (there are nineteen "parts" to the story, with the first two "parts" in one notebook), rests quietly in the Carter G. Woodson Collection at the Library of Congress. It is occasionally cited in footnotes of scholarly works, but it has never been used fully to tell the story of a slave from Norfolk and Portsmouth, Virginia, who fled to Bremen, Germany, and later lived in New York City; Providence, Rhode Island; and New Bedford and Boston, Massachusetts. Then, after the Civil War, he returned to his original home and served in the state constitutional convention of 1867–1868 and in the Virginia Senate. Events after this time took a darker turn for Teamoh, who struggled—until his death—as many others did in the postwar era.

• • •

Verifying this story and elaborating on it took us to many scattered libraries and archives, and everywhere we received fine cooperation. We are especially indebted to the patient, professional staffs at the Sargeant Memorial Room, Norfolk Public Library; the Ester Wilson Memorial History Room, Portsmouth Public Library; the Marshall W. Butt Library, Portsmouth Naval Shipyard Museum; the Office of the Circuit Court, Portsmouth, Virginia; the Virginia State Library in Richmond; the Library of Congress and the National Archives in Washington, D.C.; the New-York Historical Society; the New York Public Library; the Municipal Archives of the City of New York; the Boston Public Library; the Massachusetts Historical Society; the New England Historic Genealogical Society; and the Registry of Vital Records and Statistics, Department of Public Health, Boston, Massachusetts. Finally, we wish to thank our home schools—the University of Georgia, Washington State University, and the University of Michigan, Ann Arbor—for steady support of our research, which covered a lot of time and distance before this volume was completed.

INTRODUCTION

Radical Reconstruction ended quickly in Virginia. Its demise began in 1869, when Conservatives took control of both houses of the state legislature in an election in which several "radical" provisions of the new constitution were also stricken from that document. Symbolically, the final nails were driven into its coffin in the spring of 1870, when the Virginia Supreme Court of Appeals settled a bitter dispute that had caused bloody street fighting in the city of Richmond. This case, in which the court turned the city's municipal government back over to conservative whites, was heard on the second floor of the state capitol, in a room where Virginia's state senate had met during the Civil War.

Designed by Thomas Jefferson and completed in 1789, the impressive classical building had served the state government well over the years while receiving only perfunctory maintenance. When the Confederate government moved from Montgomery, Alabama, to Richmond in June 1861, the old capitol was renovated extensively to serve both the new national and the old state government. Partitions were removed and rooms were rearranged for the wartime emergency; and by the time General Lee surrendered at Appomattox, the old structure was showing the strain. Although it survived the fire that ravaged much of Richmond when Confederate troops evacuated their capital city in the spring of 1865, wartime service had taken its toll. Five years later the building would finally pay the full price for its Confederate adventure.

The second-story room, where the state senate had met while the Confederate House of Representatives used its old quarters, had developed a noticeable sag in its floor by 1870, when Virginia's highest court prepared to render its decision about Richmond's government. At 11 A.M. on Wednesday, 27 April, hundreds of men, black and white, packed the courtroom, restlessly awaiting the arrival of the justices. The state legislature was in session at this time, but the House and Senate were not scheduled to convene downstairs until noon, so a number of lawmakers squeezed in among the crowd as the floor groaned under the pressure.

Suddenly two loud cracks, which sounded like pistol shots, echoed through the room and the floor collapsed, plunging tons of debris and hundreds of screaming men down to the main floor. Clouds of white dust poured from smashed windows and up into the sky to signal the disaster as rescuers rushed in from every direction. More than sixty people died and hundreds more were injured. Around a dozen legislators sustained injuries, and one black senator, J. W. D. Bland, died. Other spectators—including some legislators who had fallen through to the main floor—simply got up, brushed themselves off, and walked away unscathed. Still other politicians, including state Senator Teamoh, were even more fortunate. They had not been in the courtroom at all. Thus, George Teamoh survived this tragic day to complete his term of office in the twilight of Virginia's reconstruction, and he later would write out in longhand reminiscences of his long and eventful life.[1]

• • •

From the beginning cities developed very slowly in agrarian Virginia. On the coast Norfolk led the way with Portsmouth following in its wake, more a satellite than a twin. Both developed just inland from the Chesapeake Bay and beside the waters of Hampton Roads, where all the navies of the world could anchor safely. This two-city urban area with its splendid natural harbor was thus hardly a typical environment for Southern slaves. Though local legend held that early colonial planters bought the first imported Africans on the riverside where Portsmouth later developed, Norfolk and Portsmouth bore little resemblance to the isolated farms and plantations where most slaves toiled in Teamoh's time.

Joined as well as separated by half a mile of salt water, Norfolk and Portsmouth soon fell behind other colonial seaports, such as Boston, New York, Newport, and Charleston. Not until 1740 did Norfolk's population approach 1,000, and only a few brick structures gave a hint of permanency among its crude wooden wharves, shops, and muddy streets. In the last colonial decades, however, growth finally accelerated. Shipbuilding expanded rapidly, and much of Virginia's sizable export trade began to flow out through Norfolk: lumber from the Dismal Swamp, tobacco and other agricultural products from the interior of the state, and tar, pitch, turpentine, beef, pork, and other produce from northeastern North Carolina, which lacked an adequate port. Portsmouth, nonetheless, continued to lag behind somewhat, even after Andrew Sprowle established a flourishing little shipyard. It became a federal installation in 1801 and eventually developed into the sprawling Norfolk Naval Shipyard, though it in fact remains today where it began, on the Portsmouth side of the river.

Norfolk and its nearby satellite did finally begin to prosper. In 1775 Norfolk alone boasted a population of 6,000 and more than 1,000 houses.[2] But then came the American Revolution and disaster. Vulnerable to the mighty British navy, Norfolk, the Gosport shipyard across the river, and the inland town of Suffolk were burned, and Portsmouth suffered the humiliation of military occupation under the traitor Benedict Arnold.[3]

With the coming of peace and independence, however, Norfolk managed to rise phoenixlike from its ashes. The first federal census in 1790 recorded a population of 2,959—1,604 whites, 1,294 slaves, and 61 free blacks. In contrast, Portsmouth had a total population of only 1,702—1,039 whites, 616 slaves, and 47 free blacks, even though it had annexed the Gosport area. By 1800, hundreds of French refugees from the 1793 slave insurrection on Santo Domingo helped Norfolk to surpass its prewar population and to become Virginia's largest city, with almost 7,000 inhabitants—3,850 whites, 2,724 slaves, and 352 free blacks.[4]

During the War of 1812, the British navy again strangled American trade, but this time Norfolk and Portsmouth were not actually attacked, although the nearby village of Hampton was ravaged. After the war economic recovery came slowly to the two cities. Only the revived Gosport shipyard, now a federal installation, showed much vitality, with construction of a few large warships, including the *Delaware*, launched in 1820, two years after Teamoh's birth. A few years later, one of the new nation's first stone drydocks began operations at Gosport, further stimulating the region's sluggish economy. The improved Dismal Swamp Canal also increased trade with northeastern North Carolina, but inadequate railroad connections increasingly handicapped both Norfolk and Portsmouth. Not until the late 1850s, with the completion of the Norfolk and Petersburg Railroad, did the two cities gain adequate access to the interior of the state; even then they were to remain subservient to inland rail centers, such as Richmond, where oceangoing packet ships still docked after bypassing their fine natural harbor.

Still, the population of the two Tidewater cities grew steadily if rather slowly. In 1820 the city of Norfolk had 8,608 people—4,748 whites, 3,261 slaves, and 599 free blacks; the rest of the county of Norfolk, including Portsmouth (the county seat), could not equal the population of Norfolk city alone. By 1850, when Teamoh had a wife and children, the pace of life in the two communities had quickened. The city of Norfolk had 14,326 people—9,075 whites, 4,295 slaves, and 956 free blacks; Portsmouth's population had reached 8,122—5,859 whites, 1,751 slaves, and 512 free blacks.[5]

Then, in June 1855 (two years after Teamoh had fled to freedom in the North), disaster struck again. Like other seaport cities, Norfolk and Portsmouth had endured yellow fever attacks and other epidemics, but this time the dreaded disease decimated the two communities. Brought by mosquitoes on a cargo ship docked at Portsmouth, it first swept through tenements inhabited by poor Irish immigrants. Then it spread into the rest of the city and jumped the river to Norfolk. The fever raged through the summer and only faded away with the coming of cold weather in October. By then 10,000 had been stricken and more than 2,000 had died.[6]

Norfolk and Portsmouth recovered gradually, strengthened in 1859 by the completion of the Albemarle and Chesapeake Canal, which brought even more trade with northeastern North Carolina. By 1860 both cities had matured and their white populations had risen to old levels, although the number of slaves remained diminished. Permanent brick buildings faced paved, gas-lighted streets. Norfolk's towering, domed City Hall and the federal government's elaborate classical Naval Hospital, just north of Portsmouth, drew the attention of every incoming ship. A mix of private and semipublic schools offered most white children a rudimentary education, and several daily newspapers championed various political parties. Small private shipyards and workships concentrated mainly along the waterfront, but the only really significant industrial operation remained the federal shipyard at Gosport. In busy periods it employed up to 1,500 workers, mostly whites, such as carpenter Josiah Thomas, but some blacks worked there as well—including caulker George Teamoh.

Not rivals to the industrial center of Richmond, Norfolk and Portsmouth concentrated on trade and commerce. Busy wharves and warehouses lined the waterfront in both cities, and swarms of ferries and small craft darted back and forth across the Elizabeth River as larger, ocean-going vessels came and departed all through the year. Cheap bars and seedy roominghouses catering to sailors clumped in small districts; some shoddy tenements housed poor whites, often Irish immigrants; and other buildings sheltered free blacks, who also struggled on the fringes of the vigorous economy. A large professional and middle class of doctors, lawyers, journalists, businessmen, and skilled artisans dominated the two towns, which were finally beginning to fulfill their promise.[7]

The majority of the white voters in these two little cities were conservative. They remembered how easily hostile warships had penetrated their security in the past, and they realized that their present and future depended on the delicate mechanisms of national and international trade. They rejected the radicalism of Southern fire eaters, and only when the Civil War actually erupted in April 1861 did they join the ranks of the new Confederate nation.[8]

Their tardy but eventual support of the Confederacy is understandable.

Norfolk and Portsmouth had never been in the mainstream of the rural South's land-slaves-crops system, but slavery had still taken deep root along the banks of the Elizabeth River. By 1790 Norfolk's population of 2,959 was more than forty-five percent black, and Portsmouth's population of 1,702 was almost forty percent black. However, over the decades the percentages of blacks declined as the Southern countryside demanded more and more field laborers. By 1850 blacks constituted thirty-six percent of Norfolk's population of 14,326 and just under twenty-eight percent of Portsmouth's population of 8,122; by 1860 Norfolk's population of 14,620 was thirty percent black, while Portsmouth's population of 9,496 was barely more than fifteen percent black.[9]

Accompanying the steady decline in the percentage of slaves in the Norfolk and Portsmouth populations (and the sharp drop in the actual numbers of slaves during the 1850s) was the slow but fairly steady growth in the number of free blacks, especially women. By 1850 Norfolk had 956 free blacks (eighteen percent of its total black population) and Portsmouth 512 (twenty-three percent of its total black population). In 1860 Norfolk's free blacks numbered 1,046 (twenty-four percent of its total black population) and Portsmouth's free blacks numbered 543 (thirty-seven percent of its total black population). Most of these obscure folk labored as stevedores, barkeepers, porters, waiters, laundresses, seamstresses, maids, cooks, and as other unskilled or semiskilled workers. The same kinds of jobs were often taken by talented local slaves—such as Teamoh—who were hired out by their owners. Some blacks, both free and slave, found work as caulkers, carpenters, and firemen at the Gosport Navy Yard, or at one of the small private shipyards along the river run by businessmen such as Nathaniel Nash, who used his own slave laborers. A few free blacks fared better and gained a tenuous position in the lower echelons of the middle class as shoemakers, wagoners, blacksmiths, barbers, fishermen, or as other marginal artisans and entrepreneurs. Nevertheless, most blacks in Norfolk and Portsmouth remained slaves. Among both groups women clearly outnumbered men, and during the late antebellum period whites, including numerous European immigrants, were gradually muscling both skilled and semiskilled blacks out of their jobs.[10]

Even so, most of these urban slaves fared better than did the masses of black bondsmen toiling away on farms and plantations all across the South. City slaves generally lived less restricted lives with more opportunities to develop their innate abilities. Many were hired out by their owners and handled a variety of different jobs and responsibilities over time, and others did their own hiring out and only occasionally reported back to their masters, gaining even more independence. Despite the restrictions of the slave code, some urban slaves learned to read and write. Others mastered some of the technology of the city, and many learned the fine art of coping in the white world around them. Some found refuge in black churches, social clubs, and occasional clandestine study groups. In Norfolk, a respectable white seamstress served a month in jail for running a school for black youngsters in her home. But even greater courage was shown by blacks, such as freeman Isaac Fuller, who ran similar underground schools and risked much more for such defiance of the law.

Gradually these activities led to the emergence of a distinctive urban black culture rooted in black enclaves within virtually every Southern city. By the 1830s a large section of central Norfolk had become a ramshackle black residential area where slaves and free blacks found a little more breathing space and a little more room for independent development. However unimpressive their communities, city slaves generally had the best deal available within the repressive system, and their communities were vital seedbeds that flowered when freedom came. Their country cousins often envied them and did their best to become a part of the more flexible and varied urban environment, sometimes by wangling a "transfer" away from the plantation and sometimes by running away and just blending into the growing black residential areas in the cities. Yet urban blacks, including George Teamoh, were still slaves in essence, and because they had savored a few "fringe benefits" and had witnessed the host of opportunities awaiting free people, they often became the most discontented of all bondsmen.

Discontent on the part of slaves who lived in Norfolk and Portsmouth, and in other Southern seaports as well, was probably also stimulated by the fact that they often gained tantalizing glimpses of the free world across the sea. They demonstrated their discontent by loafing, stealing, ignoring curfews, and by violating the slave codes in various ways. Indeed, if white complaints are any measure, resistance waxed and waned but never ceased. Whites worried about arson and even more about runaways. Free states were not far off by land, and a daring slave might stow away on a departing vessel. Despite security precautions, a steady trickle of disgruntled slaves slipped away, and some, including Teamoh, actually made it to freedom. The trickle increased during the 1850s, as the growing abolition movement influenced restless blacks in cities along the Southern coast.[11]

Discontent never flared into open rebellion among Norfolk and Portsmouth blacks; naval forces at Gosport and the army garrison at Fort Monroe, just across Hampton Roads on the tip of the Peninsula, created a formidable deterrent. But black unrest sometimes rumbled ominously, especially in the wake of nearby insurrection. Only a week after Gabriel Prosser's abortive uprising in Richmond in 1800, a crowd of 150 blacks was dispersed near Norfolk, and two years later another scare led to the mobilization of the local militia and to the hanging of a slave. A generation later a spectacular jailbreak by a black man stirred up trouble in 1829. Then, in the summer of 1831, Nat Turner's revolt cut a bloody swath through Southampton County only fifty miles away, and volunteers and federal forces from the Hampton Roads area marched off to help suppress it while local militia units again patrolled the streets of Norfolk and Portsmouth. In 1835 a mass meeting in Norfolk denounced the rising abolition movement in the North; and a generation later, in the fall of 1859, anger and fear swept through the two cities when abolitionist John Brown and his raiders tried unsuccessfully to seize the federal arsenal in far western Virginia and to incite a slave rebellion. Thus, despite their unique environment, the white citizens of Norfolk and Portsmouth were hopelessly tangled in the complex web of slavery that stretched into almost every corner of the South.[12]

Although slaves and free blacks knew Norfolk and Portsmouth as well as whites, they had no chance to tell their side of the story in the antebellum era, and until recently standard histories presented only the white viewpoint of the South's development. Occasionally an exceptional black broke through the constraints of custom and left a record of the silent, oppressed black minority. Some fugitive slaves—including Frederick Douglass, William Wells Brown, and Henry Bibb—gained notoriety by publishing their reminiscences before or after the Civil War. Eventually, around a hundred fugitive slave narratives (more if one counts those that appeared in abolitionist papers) became available to the reading public. In addition, a few aging former slaves "told it like it was" in private journals or diaries that survived but were never published. Although unsung in their day, these "undiscovered" scribes left a valuable legacy of fact and interpretation for modern Americans.[13]

• • •

Such a black man was George Teamoh, who was born a slave in 1818. A native of Norfolk, he grew up in Portsmouth. His owners, Josiah and Jane Thomas, were decent, humane people who recognized the human dimension of the few black folk they owned. Josiah Thomas was an accomplished carpenter at the Gosport Navy Yard—an artisan and working-class slaveholder. His gentle, kind mistress almost took the place of his deceased mother, for his own parents—slaves named David and Lavinia—died while he was quite young. The Thomases never abused Teamoh—they would have bitterly resented such an accusation—but they did find it necessary to hire the fourteen-year-old youth out to Captain John Thompson's farm and brickyard three miles north of Portsmouth. Here Teamoh got a taste of the regimented, harsh life of most rural slaves, but he soon returned to town and to a series of jobs under different temporary masters.[14]

Much like youthful Frederick Douglass in Baltimore, young Teamoh taught himself "to read, write and cypher" and even began to keep a journal, which he later lost. As a young adult he worked at a variety of jobs: he assisted brickmasons and shipbuilders; he even helped to prepare the corpse of a crusading newspaper editor named Melzar Gardner for burial. Probably through the influence of his master, Josiah Thomas, he learned caulking. At age twenty-one he was working at this craft and also as a manual laborer on federal fortifications, across Hampton Roads at Fort Monroe. Soon he returned to Portsmouth and labored at the Gosport Navy Yard at whatever jobs were available, including, when possible, caulking at $1.62 a day (whites received $2.00 or more for the same task). When a number of black caulkers were laid off, he did carpentry work on the laid-up warship *Constitution* ("Old Iron Sides") for two years.[15]

By 1841, at the age of twenty-three, Teamoh had taken a wife, and he and Sallie had three children—John, Jane, and Josephine—over the years. Quiet and reserved, he continued to work at a variety of jobs—caulking at small private shipyards, operating the presses at John W. Murdaugh's *Clay Banner and Naval Intelligencer,* and often working at day labor when nothing else was available. Although Teamoh perhaps lived better and enjoyed more harmonious relations with whites than most Norfolk and Portsmouth slaves, he did not belong to the local black elite. He was not free, his skills were real but limited and, although he may well have had some white ancestry, he had no blood ties to local whites with power and influence. He lived in a middle echelon of black society in the South, just as his owners lived in the broad middle (or lower-middle) class in the white South, and they could not always protect him.

Sallie and the children had never belonged to the Thomases, and in 1853 an unscrupulous owner decided to sell them. The Thomases could not afford to buy them, so Teamoh's family went to the slave pens of Richmond. There, the two oldest children were quickly sold and shipped away, separated forever from their grieving parents, who had also been separated. Later, after Teamoh fled to the North, Sallie and young Josephine were hired and then purchased by an elderly Jewish merchant in Richmond, who treated them well. After this owner, they came into the possession of a lecherous small-time vendor who eventually forced the still-young Josephine to bear his child.[16]

Introspective and able, helpless to defend his family, Teamoh could stand slavery no longer. His sympathetic mistress understood and made arrangements that indirectly granted him freedom. She and her husband signed him on to serve as a carpenter on the merchant ship *Currituck*, which carried a cargo of tobacco to Bremen, Germany, in the summer of 1853, and after a brief layover brought a load of German immigrants to New York City. Teamoh, who found the German people congenial, waited until the *Currituck* docked at New York City and jumped ship. He lingered there only long enough to contact a lawyer who initiated proceedings that gained his back pay and a declaration of freedom.[17]

Once these matters were dispatched, he traveled north to New England, where he soon learned that, although he had escaped southern slavery, white prejudice against blacks was a fact of life in the North too. For a while during the middle 1850s he lived in New Bedford, Massachusetts, within a sizable black community—almost seven percent of the city's total population of 16,433 in 1850. This industrial center and home base for more than 300 whaling ships offered him the possibility of decent work. In addition, it had a long tradition of Quaker idealism and served as a station on the Underground Railroad that ran fugitive slaves north to complete safety in British North America. Thus, it offered blacks one of the more tolerant, open environments in overwhelmingly white New England.

Still, even in New Bedford blacks faced prejudice, and Teamoh found some shipyards reluctant to hire him as a caulker. Often, especially during the slack winter months, he took the kind of manual labor jobs he had handled back in Virginia in similar lean periods. Another problem was his lack of formal education and his ignorance of polite etiquette. In Norfolk and Portsmouth he had been far more polished and sophisticated than the average slave on the land, but now he was just another Southern black rustic in the urban North. Painfully aware of his deficiencies, he stayed pretty much to himself and held back from most social and intellectual activities. When he finally ventured out to a formal dance, "a beautiful young lady of light brown complexion" let him know in no uncertain terms of his weakness in grammar and pronunciation. In the real world of antebellum America, though, New Bedford was a relatively good deal for blacks. Teamoh soon discovered why Frederick Douglass and many other fugitive slaves found their initial haven there; but, like many of them, he soon moved on, seeking better economic opportunities.[18]

Early in 1855 he quit working as a day laborer and as a caulker in various New Bedford shipyards and moved to Providence, Rhode Island, where in 1860 the black population numbered only 1,537 out of a total of 50,666 people. There he took a job as a servant in the home of recently deceased Thomas Wilson Dorr, who in 1842 had briefly seized control of the state government as the leader of the People's Party.[19] But he soon moved again, joining two half brothers who worked as waiters in Boston.

While not as liberal toward blacks as New Bedford, Boston was a center of the surging abolition movement, and here William Lloyd Garrison's newspaper, the *Liberator*, ceaselessly attacked slavery and defended the rights of black Americans. The average Bostonian was probably only a little less racially prejudiced than the average American. His potential antipathy toward blacks may have been diverted slightly by his rising concern about massive Catholic immigration from Ireland, but he certainly did not welcome blacks with open arms, and Boston's black community remained relatively small, restricted to a few districts, segregated neighborhoods of predominantly poor and working-class folk. The federal census of 1860 indicated that the city's overall population of 177,840 contained only 2,261 blacks—though some resident fugitive slaves probably dodged the census taker and anyone else who might reveal their whereabouts. Black Bostonians differed by class and occupation, with light-skinned Northern-born folk tending to be the most prosperous. But almost a quarter of all black Bostonians, including Teamoh, were Southerners, whose soft accents and awkward manners set them apart, even though they shared the low economic status of most of their black neighbors.[20]

Black Bostonians argued over strategy and tactics, but they all sought equal rights with whites. Spirited, well organized, and aided by white abolitionists such as Garrison, they achieved some major breakthroughs in the struggle for civil rights before the Civil War. While they welcomed all the white support they could get and backed Garrison and the *Liberator*, Boston blacks also produced their own leaders, such as William Cooper Nell. An activist as well as a polished intellectual, Nell was a close ally of Garrison. He also edited Frederick Douglass's newspaper, the *North Star*, in Rochester, New York, for a while, but mainly he emerged as a champion of Boston's black minority. He fought on every front, but his greatest triumph came when, after a long fight, the city finally integrated its public schools in 1855.

Teamoh gained some help in securing his formal education from the kindly Nell, but for the more prosaic task of earning a living in a strange city he turned to another black Bostonian, Coffin Pitts. A working man like both Teamoh and Teamoh's old master in Portsmouth, Pitts was an unassuming and unsung tailor; he was almost as active as Nell in the black cause, but always in the second or third rank rather than in the forefront. He often gave jobs to needy blacks, and he trained Teamoh in the craft of cleaning and repairing clothes, a black specialty in Boston at that time. By 1860 the Boston Directory stopped listing Teamoh as a "caulker and graver" and described him and his half brother John W. Teamoh as "clothes cleaners."[21]

Former southern slave George Teamoh gradually adjusted to life as a free black in the North. He thought that he was safe from the Fugitive Slave Act of 1850, assuming that the Thomases would never try to recover him, but it was a tough federal statute, and it virtually placed the burden of proof on any northern black accused of being a runaway slave. It seemed a real enough threat to runaways such as William and Ellen Craft, who fled from Boston to England when two white Georgians tried to haul them back to Macon, Georgia. Some other runaways left Boston at this time too. Several other prominent fugitive slaves, such as Frederick Douglass and William Wells Brown, had believed it necessary to skip the country for a while even before the stringent law of 1850 went into effect, and sometimes this new law did function dramatically in Boston, where abolitionists were active and where even the average citizen resented the intrusion of slave-hunting southerners. Teamoh doubtless heard of Frederick "Shadrach" Wilkins, who had been arrested as a fugitive slave from Norfolk back in 1851. The property of John Debree, he had then been spirited away to Canada and to freedom by a band of Boston blacks. Even so, that same year Thomas Sims was hauled back to slavery in Savannah, Georgia, despite significant popular opposition in Boston. Later, Teamoh almost certainly heard of the Anthony Burns affair, which occurred in the spring of 1854, about a year before he moved to Boston.

A runaway from Alexandria, Virginia, Burns was working as an apprentice in Coffin Pitts's cleaning store on Brattle Street (several years before Teamoh worked there) when he was arrested and ordered extradited to Virginia. Bostonians protested in mass, and one of the local men who had assisted in his capture was knifed to death, but the unpopular law ran its course. Soon Burns was marched down to the docks for his trip back to slavery in Virginia, but only after a sheriff's posse and federal troops appeared to hold back an angry crowd estimated to be as large as 50,000 people. Teamoh undoubtedly realized that he remained technically a fugitive slave, and he continued to feel the handicaps of his past. Still, despite the long shadow of slavery, he adjusted reasonably well to the Yankee metropolis of Boston; he kept a low profile and worked hard to succeed in his new business career far from his old home in Virginia.[22]

Then suddenly, the beginning of the Civil War in April 1861 reminded Teamoh all too clearly of old Virginia, now a part of the Confederate States of America. Again and again he remembered his black friends in Norfolk and Portsmouth, and also his former mistress Jane Thomas, who had always been kind to him and had practically sent him on his way to freedom back in 1853. He also wondered if his wife Sallie and daughter Josephine might still be in Richmond, now the capital of the Confederacy. But runaways such as Teamoh could only assume that old slave families were lost forever, so finally in the spring of 1863 he married Elizabeth Smith, a thirty-six-year-old black woman originally from Baltimore. But this marriage foundered and ended after only two years. Hence, as the Confederacy and slavery crumbled under the relentless blows of the Union military machine, Teamoh realized that his future as well as past lay in Virginia. After all, he was a southerner; his roots ran as deep into Virginia's soil as the staunchest rebel's, and most of his people were still there. As the war ground to a bloody end during the spring of 1865, he decided that duty as well as opportunity lay to the south, and now at last he really could go home again. So he left forever his home away from home in Boston and headed for Portsmouth, Virginia.[23]

Much had happened during Teamoh's absence. Sectional hostilities had been brewing even before 1853, when he sailed away, but they intensified greatly with John Brown's raid and with Abraham Lincoln's election to the presidency at the end of the decade. Following the Republican victory in 1860, seven Deep South states, led by South Carolina, left the Union. Their representatives then gathered at the state capitol in Montgomery, Alabama, to draft a constitution, form a provisional congress, and select a provisional president and vice president for their new Confederate nation. On 12 April 1861, soon after these tasks were completed, President Lincoln's attempt to provision the Union troops at Fort Sumter, in the harbor at Charleston, South Carolina, was followed by a Confederate bombardment. Consequently, on 15 April, he called for 75,000 volunteers to put down a rebellion; the Civil War, the bloodiest conflict in American history, had begun.[24]

As the Sumter crisis reached its climax, support in the state for the secession of Virginia, one of the eight slave states that still remained in the Union, grew rapidly. The fall of Fort Sumter, President Lincoln's call for volunteers to suppress the rebellion, and the effective propaganda of pro-secessionist spokesmen from the deep South (who visited Richmond regularly during the tension-filled early spring months of 1861) all contributed to this dramatic development. By 17 April, delegates to the state's secession convention opted, in a vote of 88 to 55, to leave the Union; on 23 May, that action was ratified—125,950 to 20,383—by the state's voters. Earlier, on 20 May, members of the provisional Confederate Congress, elated by developments in Virginia, also authorized the moving of their national capital from the lower south to Richmond. These events demonstrated clearly that a large majority of Virginians—with but the notable exception of the unionists who took control of some fifty counties that eventually became the state of West Virginia—now were determined to leave the nation their ancestors had done so much to create.[25]

As Virginia moved toward secession, military leaders in both the North and the South quickly turned their attention to Teamoh's home area, especially to the Gosport Navy Yard, an installation obviously destined to play an important role in the impending struggle. General William B. Taliaferro, the ranking Confederate officer then on the scene, commanded a sizable force—the Portsmouth and Norfolk militia and troops from Richmond and Petersburg—that could have taken the installation easily, but he knew he could not then hold it against the guns on Union ships in the harbor. As Taliaferro considered his best course of action, the yard's commander, Commodore Charles S. McCauley, quickly ordered the scuttling of federal vessels there and the burning of the Gosport yard itself. Explosives were placed at critical points on the grounds. Civilian laborers, sailors, marines, and soldiers then quickly prepared to leave aboard the ships *Pawnee* and *Cumberland*. At 3:20 in the morning of 21 April 1861, they departed as the yard itself and eleven warships were engulfed in a spectacular blaze easily visible throughout the Norfolk-Portsmouth area.[26]

As these two Union ships sailed away, Confederate forces quickly took control of the badly damaged facility and began, by late June 1861, a very important construction project at Gosport. Following approval of Confederate Secretary of the Navy Stephen R. Mallory, John L. Porter started building the ironclad ram *Virginia*. The steam frigate *Merrimac*, one of the eleven vessels left burning during the federal evacuation, was raised, placed in drydock in the yard that Teamoh knew so well, and fitted with heavy woodwork and two layers of iron plate that had been rolled at the Tredegar Iron Works in Richmond. Once fitted with guns, the *Virginia* left the yard on the morning of 8 March 1862 to attack the North Atlantic Blockading Squadron, the Union naval force at Hampton Roads. After sinking two of the five ships in that squadron, the *Virginia* retired, only to return the following day to engage a Union ironclad, the *Monitor*, in the most famous naval engagement of the war. This six-hour action was nonetheless inconclusive; the *Virginia* finally turned back to the Norfolk yard for repairs.[27]

The *Virginia*'s sudden appearance raised panic in the North; its sudden demise shocked the Confederates. Moreover, the Gosport yard itself was soon in great peril. By early May 1862, troops of the Army of the Potomac—a force of some 112,000 men under the command of General George McClellan—disembarked from transport vessels at Fort Monroe to begin the controversial Peninsula campaign envisioned by their commander: the taking of the Confederate capital by moving west up the Peninsula between the James and York rivers to Richmond. As McClellan advanced slowly along the Peninsula on the northern shore of the James, he made no provision for capturing Norfolk, which was flanked by his men. President Lincoln himself noted this on the first of his several visits to McClellan in the field (6-12 May 1862) and devised his own plan for taking the city. After conferring with General John Wool, the seventy-eight-year-old commander of Fort Monroe, about the use of soldiers from his garrison, the president and Secretary of the Treasury Salmon Chase boarded separate tugs and crossed Hampton Roads to locate personally a suitable landing place for their invading force. Before the president's return, however, Wool himself embarked for Norfolk (which had been abandoned by Confederates on 9 May) and took it, the city of Portsmouth, and the Gosport Navy Yard. With the loss of the yard, which was this time burned by retreating Confederates, the heavy *Virginia*, which lay too deep in the water to retreat up the James River, had to be scuttled to prevent its capture by Union forces.[28]

As federal troops under Wool undertook the occupation of the Portsmouth-Norfolk area, good order generally prevailed. Even so, numerous incidents showed clearly the tension between Union soldiers and the civilian population. As a result, civilian government was suspended (22 July 1862), and the region was placed under military rule, with General Egbert L. Viele acting as commander of the newly created Norfolk district. By June 1863, however, civil law was technically restored in the region. At that time, West Virginia became a state, and Francis H. Pierpont moved his government "of Virginia" from there down the Potomac to the Washington, D.C., suburb of Alexandria. In theory, he now had administrative responsibility for the region of Virginia around the national capital and in the area of the state held by Union troops on the coast and the Peninsula. In fact, though, military authorities continued to govern in both Norfolk and Portsmouth and generally refused to recognize the authority of Pierpont's civilian regime. This was especially true after early November 1863, when General Benjamin F. Butler took control of occupied areas of eastern Virginia and North Carolina and became the commander of the Union force known as the Army of the James.[29]

Butler, a longtime resident of Lowell, was a prominent criminal lawyer, a leader in the Democracy of Massachusetts and one of the most controversial personalities of the war. Valid or not, numerous assertions by southerners concerning Butler's alleged unethical conduct while commanding occupation forces in both Virginia and Louisiana have overshadowed a much more important aspect of his role in the war. Once a strong believer in states' rights and one of the relatively few prominent northerners to support southern Democrat John Breckinridge for the presidency in 1860,

Butler changed quite dramatically in several respects as a result of his war-time combat experiences. Most important, perhaps, his racial attitudes, like those of a number of officers in the Union Army, were modified greatly by the impressive performance of black troops in the Union Army. This change, well under way while Butler was in command in southeastern Virginia, was certainly evident in his comments following the battle of New-Market Heights, an engagement of 28 September 1864, which occurred as his Army of the James attempted to move up the Peninsula to Richmond. While surveying the dead bodies of black troops on the field, Butler wrote that he had then taken an oath "that they and their race should be cared for and protected by me to the extent of my power as long as I lived."[30] The missionarylike sense of duty reflected in this comment was apparently one of the major factors that led to his later political career—to his 1866 congressional campaign, to his election that year as a radical to Congress from Massachusetts, and to his subsequent determined efforts to act as a congressional champion of the freedmen throughout the postwar era.

Butler's growing awareness of the problems faced by southern blacks had actually been evidenced as early as 23 May 1861, during his first tour of duty in the Old Dominion, when he was in command at Fort Monroe on the tip of the Peninsula. At that time, three runaways made it to the fort from Sewells Point (across Hampton Roads from Fort Monroe), where they had been at work on Confederate fortifications. The following day, 24 May, Confederate Major John B. Cary appeared before Butler under a flag of truce and asked that these three men be returned (under provisions of the Fugitive Slave Law of 1850) to their rightful owners. Butler quickly and dramatically refused this request, noting that the law in question did not apply in a foreign country (Virginia, of course, claimed to be a part of the Confederacy) and that the blacks in question were instead to be considered contrabands of war. The term *contraband* was picked up immediately by the northern press and by federal officials. Northerners, who hesitated for both political and racial reasons to call blacks free men, accepted this term readily for what it was—an ingenious method of depriving Confederates of the labor of their escaped slaves while buying time for Republicans to achieve a consensus among themselves regarding the degree to which their military effort should be broadened to force a change in the status of the South's bondsmen.[31]

Emancipation, which commenced with the actions of General Butler in Teamoh's home territory, was still to be completed. It was initially a rather slow and tentative process, one that evolved only gradually. Congress took action, in April and June 1862, to end slavery in the national capital with compensation and in western territories without payment. President Lincoln considered at length his various policy options toward military commanders in Missouri and the Sea Islands who had freed slaves without his authorization. He attempted without success to end slavery with compensation to slaveholders in Delaware, and he eventually discussed his final plans with several cabinet members and with a few congressional leaders. Still, after all of this, the preliminary proclamation of emancipation that followed the battle of Antietam in late September 1862 was justified by Lincoln solely on the grounds of military necessity. This position was, in large part, the same one taken back in May 1861 by General Butler. Ironically, he then had been in command of a fort only a few miles from where, in 1619, the first cargo of some nineteen black Africans reached Virginia planters.[32]

Although the emancipation policy of federal authorities in Virginia and in Washington, D.C., was quite tentative, Butler's dramatic action soon became known to slaves throughout the area, who referred to Monroe as the "freedom fort." Most of those who then opted to escape slavery arrived in increasing numbers by water transport—canoes, scows, and oyster boats—on the streams and rivers so abundant in the tidewater region. Others, from areas such as Sewells Point, seized or built boats to get to the ships on the federal blockade, from which they were turned over to authorities at the fort. No matter how they took advantage of the opportunity Butler offered, though, these people understood their stake in the outcome of a conflict that soon became a war to end slavery. One January 1863 was the joyous day on which the Emancipation Proclamation became effective. This fact was evidenced by a parade of some 500 Norfolk and Portsmouth blacks, who celebrated presidential recognition of their freedom by marching down Norfolk's main street to the fairgrounds, by trampling and tearing Confederate flags, and by finally moving on to the city cemetery to burn Jefferson Davis in effigy.[33]

Dramatic demonstrations such as this were sometimes organized by whites (including some of the teachers whom Teamoh admired so greatly following his return to his Virginia home), who had only recently come into the tidewater region. During late 1861 and early 1862, the American Missionary Association established schools for local freedmen at Hampton, Norfolk, and at other locations in southeastern Virginia. Later, these schools, including those in the Portsmouth area, were enlarged, and new ones were established on abandoned plantations in rural areas around the two cities. Other agencies—the National Freedmen's Relief Association, the Boston Education Society, and the Society of Friends—also began their efforts in the black community. In addition, local blacks recruited into the Union Army (they were to see extensive combat in campaigns against Petersburg in 1864 and 1865) received some basic education in newly estab-

lished regimental schools, the most important of which were at Fort
Monroe, Hampton, Norfolk, and Portsmouth. Thus, by 1863, northern
teachers and their schools had already contributed significantly to shaping
the emerging and distinctive culture of the communities of newly freed
men and women in Norfolk and Portsmouth. Their influence spread to
even wider areas of the state after March 1865 with the creation of the
Freedmen's Bureau, a federal agency established to offer educational opportunity and humanitarian assistance to blacks and to loyal whites throughout
the torn South.[34]

Although the contributions these white educators made to postwar black
communities are widely known, it is sometimes forgotten that blacks themselves did the most to form the new settlements of freedmen that appeared
at Fort Monroe and at other key locations in the occupied South. In the
most basic sense, of course, these communities resulted from the determination of thousands of enslaved people, scattered widely about the Confederacy, to cross Union lines and gain freedom. Even in wartime, when
Yankees were often nearby, escape from slavery was often difficult and
risky. As desirable as freedom was, an attempt to secure it involved the possibility of recapture and return to vengeful former owners. In some instances—as had been the case with Teamoh himself back in 1853—it also
required leaving decent owners with whom there existed long-standing and
complex ties, and it almost certainly meant a painful parting with other
members of the slave community. The former slave who became a part of
the new settlement of freedmen at Fort Monroe was therefore a person who
had considered his or her options carefully while evaluating the political
and military situation that made escape possible. Individuals who made
such judgments and escaped slavery successfully would certainly be inclined
(when and if any such opportunity were offered in the future) to demand
some say in forming governmental policies that would shape their postwar
lives.

Still, for the present they were more interested in immediate family
matters than in politics. As was the case with Teamoh, the typical antebellum runaway was a young single man (a bachelor or a family man forced to
leave wife and children behind to better his chances of escape) with the
physical stamina needed to travel rapidly over long distances and reach
safety in a northern state or in British North America. As the Union Army
became an army of liberation, however, slaves did not have to flee nearly so
far to freedom. In ever-increasing numbers, they therefore made the critically important decision to start their new lives in freedom as family
groups. Federal officials across the South noted this phenomenon in numerous written complaints concerning sanitary problems, supply problems, and

other daily difficulties faced in the burgeoning and overcrowded camps. Despite all such valid official concerns, though, a feeling of pride, achievement, and hope remained among these refugees. They were not isolated from family, from relatives, from friends, as Teamoh had been when he escaped to the relatively small black communities in coastal New England a decade earlier. Despite the obvious problems that existed in the camps, their robust new communities surged with vitality: parents looked with pride at children who brought their lessons home from school, women settled newly established households, and men enlisted enthusiastically as soldiers in Mr. Lincoln's army of freedom.[35]

It was this vitality—a vitality born of hope—that brought Teamoh back to Portsmouth from his northern exile at war's end. Upon his arrival, he began immediately to search for his family. He was among the many blacks in the area who deluged government officials with requests for aid in locating relatives lost in the past by sale or separated recently by fortunes of war. He may likewise have been one of the many in his community who kept clergymen busy performing marriages. Husbands and wives who had escaped slavery together—and couples (including the Teamohs) reunited after a period of separation—wished to have their new relationship recognized by a formal wedding ceremony. Whatever the precise nature of his activities during the early weeks following his return to Virginia, however, Teamoh was by and large successful. Most important, he quickly located his wife (Sallie) and a daughter (Josephine). In addition, even though saddened to learn of the recent death of his former mistress, he was pleased that he got a job quickly (at his old profession of caulking) in Virginia's new free-labor economy.[36]

As Teamoh began to reconstruct his life in his native state, the Pierpont government, which had previously moved from West Virginia to Alexandria, was moved again, this time to Richmond, where it was to direct the process of restoring the Old Dominion to the Union. Although Pierpont had been a strong wartime Unionist, he believed that the Confederate defeat had killed both the institution of slavery and the doctrine of secession and that no other major changes were necessary. His major task, he therefore assumed, was simply that of establishing a new government in order to secure Virginia's readmission to the Union. Assuming that this plan could best be accomplished by leniency toward former Confederates, whom he incorrectly believed had accepted the obvious changes brought about by the war, Pierpont worked closely with the state's general assembly—in June 1865—to restore the rights of citizenship to large numbers of former rebels. Such action, he reasoned, was required because very few wartime Unionists remained in Virginia, which had been stripped of its loyalist western counties by the creation of the new state of West Virginia. Former Confederates would therefore be needed to supply a considerable percentage of both the electorate and the officeholders in his new government.

However valid this belief, increasing numbers of people—including wartime Unionists, northern journalists reporting from the state to readers back home, Republican politicians in Washington, northern immigrants recently settled in the state, and politically aware freedmen such as Teamoh—were greatly alarmed by Pierpont's policies. During the fall and winter of 1865–1866, they grew increasingly apprehensive that the state was in danger of being returned to unrepentant rebels, especially after elections that October resulted in the removal of a ban on officeholding by ex-Confederates and placed former military and civil officials of the "lost cause" in many offices. This concern increased when the legislators selected in that election met in December and removed even more native unionists from the few public positions that they still held. The same legislators—worried that emancipation came at a time when the wartime loss of Virginia's largely white western counties meant that blacks were to increase to forty-two percent of the state's population between 1860 and 1870—also quickly passed a black code. It placed the Old Dominion's freedmen in a sort of postemancipation serfdom and showed clearly that the fruits of victory so recently gained were in danger of slipping away from northern Republicans and their potential allies, southern Unionists and the freedmen.[37]

By early 1866 Pierpont, too, realized that he had placed too much faith in the goodwill c former Confederates, and he then tried to realign himself with wartime Unionists in Virginia and with Republicans in Washington, D.C. By this time, though, growing numbers of northerners were greatly disturbed by accounts detailing the return to power of former rebels in Virginia (and throughout the South); they were also dismayed by the growing conflict between President Andrew Johnson and Republicans in both houses of Congress over the proper type of reconstruction to require in the former Confederacy. As this division deepened during the hot summer of 1866, with widely circulated reports of violent race riots in Memphis and New Orleans, northern voters responded in November's critical congressional elections by returning to Congress an overwhelming majority of Republicans. These men were by then determined to overthrow the Reconstruction of Johnson and to replace it with one better designed to protect what had been gained by the Confederate surrender at Appomattox. This determination resulted in a series of Reconstruction Acts, beginning in early March 1867, which divided ten of the former Confederate states into five military districts, each under the authority of military officials. These officers were to register new voters—blacks as well as whites—who were to select delegates (from a pool that was to include white and black candidates) to conventions. These delegates would then frame new constitutions required to return each of these states to the Union. The constitutions were then to be ratified at elections in which candidates (black and white) for various state offices were to be selected. Finally, as each new legislature met and ratified the Fourteenth Amendment to the federal constitution, its state's congressional representation was to be restored.[38]

As the battle between Congress and the president developed over southern policy, Teamoh spent less time as a caulker and more and more time with political matters. He possessed a number of qualities that made him a natural leader: he was literate and could keep up with issues reported in the local press; he was articulate and could speak effectively to these issues at political gatherings; and he had firsthand knowledge of the racial and political attitudes of a northern public that had opted for a more radical Reconstruction. For these reasons, the freedmen in the area turned to him for advice and counsel. Thus, with the organization of Virginia's Republicans in May 1866, with two turbulent party conventions in Richmond in April and August 1867, and with the election of delegates to Virginia's constitutional convention in October 1867, Teamoh became immersed in Republican politics. As an official in the local Union League, he worked tirelessly to organize the black vote in his district, the city of Portsmouth and the county of Norfolk, and his efforts were successful. At the election in mid-October 1867, the convention was endorsed (3,221 to 1,091) in his constituency, and Republicans—among them Teamoh himself—secured all three seats in that body allotted to Norfolk County and Portsmouth.[39]

At the convention (3 December 1867–17 April 1868) Teamoh formed a lasting partnership with fellow Portsmouth delegate James H. Clements, a white machinist from the District of Columbia who was employed as Portsmouth's postmaster for a number of years. Together, they worked closely with Orrin E. Hine, an outside white from Fairfax County, to secure constitutional articles that disfranchised numerous former Confederates and that required newly elected state officers to swear that they had not voluntarily supported the Confederate cause as private citizens. In addition, Teamoh, who feared correctly that the election of court officials by members of the general assembly would lead to Conservative control of the state's legal system, worked unsuccessfully against adoption of constitutional provisions for the legislative selection of judges. Hence, although sometimes unhappy about the lack of black influence among the convention's totally white Republican leadership, and sometimes worried by factional divisions among carpetbag, scalawag, and black delegates within his own party, Teamoh worked diligently on two subcommittees—the Committee on the Executive Department and the Committee on Agricultural and Industrial Interests and Immigration.[40] When the convention finally adjourned, he was justly proud of his role in framing a progressive new state constitution that served Virginia into the early twentieth century.

However, once that work was completed, Teamoh, like most other Republicans, was greatly disappointed to learn that several provisions of the new document alarmed the commander of the Military District of Virginia, General John M. Schofield, who refused to hold the required ratification election unless voters could cast separate ballots on two articles—those written by Orrin Hine that disfranchised numerous former Confederates and required loyalty oaths of new officeholders. Eventually, after months of tense infighting in both Richmond and Washington, Schofield prevailed over the objections of most Virginia Republicans, who opposed separate approval of these articles. The constitution was therefore finally ratified easily on 6 July 1869, but its two provisions voted on individually were defeated soundly (which dismayed Teamoh but delighted Conservative whites). In addition, the Democrats, who were now much better organized than in the 1867 contest for convention delegates, took control of both houses of the general assembly and elected their gubernatorial candidate, Gilbert Walker (a "True Republican" supported by Conservatives and "moderate" Republicans), who defeated the "regular" Republican, Henry H. Wells. Despite this Democratic success, however, some Republicans—mainly those running in tidewater districts with large numbers of blacks—were successful. As such a candidate, Teamoh was one of six blacks sent to the state senate, the highest elected position secured by any freedmen during Virginia's reconstruction.[41]

As a black Republican leader, Teamoh worked hard as a senator (1869–1871) to broaden his political base and to gain more support from whites. To ease racial divisions between blacks in the Union League and whites in the Grand Army of the Republic (led by William H. Lyons, the chief machinist at the yard and a member of Portsmouth's city council), he tried to focus public attention on economic problems common to both races. He thus supported the formation of a biracial labor union that appeared at Gosport in 1869; and in May 1871 he made a well-publicized trip to Washington, D.C., with Philip G. Thomas, a native white Virginian and the mayor of Portsmouth, to confer with Secretary of the Navy George M. Robeson about the problems faced by white and black laborers back home. Using a similar "common front" approach, Teamoh also worked with the larger white community—merchants, businessmen, and laborers throughout the greater Norfolk-Portsmouth area—to try to thwart the creation of the Pennsylvania-Southern Railway, a northern-backed unit that threatened to reduce greatly traffic on the local Seaboard and Roanoke Line.[42]

Despite some impressive initial success—about twenty percent of his votes in the July 1869 senate race came from whites—Teamoh's political base outside the black community eroded rather quickly. Racial factionalism within the Republican coalition had emerged as early as the two organizational meetings in Richmond during April and August 1867. It became even more serious at the party's Petersburg convention in March 1869, when James H. Clements (the choice of Teamoh and most other black delegates) lost the gubernatorial nomination to Henry H. Wells. By 1871 racial tensions within the party were even more divisive. Many local blacks, among them Teamoh, were openly hostile toward their white congressman, carpetbagger James H. Platt, Jr., and antagonism between white members of the local Grand Army of the Republic chapter and blacks in the Union League was so serious that Teamoh failed even to secure renomination for his seat in the state senate. It went instead to Matthew P. Rue (an outside white from New Jersey who was then elected), and Teamoh was forced to seek a seat in the House of Delegates. Even in that contest he was defeated, partly because a second Republican candidate, James W. Brownley (a native Virginia white), divided the radical vote and allowed the election of Samuel Watts, the Conservative candidate.[43]

The victory by Watts also showed clearly that the factionalized Republicans faced yet another serious problem: the bitter hostility of most local whites. Despite Teamoh's best efforts to work with them to resolve common economic problems, Conservatives remained determined to overthrow a government imposed on them locally—despite the repudiation of Republicanism by the state's voters as a whole in 1869—by what they believed to be a corrupt alliance of ignorant and opportunistic black and white radicals. Although the Democrats had failed to thwart the implementation of congressional Reconstruction—their initial organization had been slowed somewhat by the reality of desperate economic hardships, by the lingering shock of military defeat, and by the confusion of mixed signals coming to them initially from the national capital—they were clearly ready to do battle by the time Teamoh actually began his senate career. They had by then developed fully their effective campaign theme, which stressed both the heroic lost cause (a legend with an especially strong appeal in the home state of Robert E. Lee) and their concern that newly enfranchised blacks constituted almost half of Virginia's electorate and clearly threatened continued white control of the Old Dominion. Their use of both the legend and race issue soon reduced white support for Republican candidates considerably from its rather surprising 1869 levels, and their resort to violence (most notably in Norfolk during the elections of 1870 and in Portsmouth during the elections of 1871) reduced black voter turnout.[44] Thus, weakened by internal squabbling and faced with stubborn white opposition, Republicans, who failed to gain control of the state in 1869, found their power diminished further by 1871, even in tidewater communities—such as Portsmouth—that had sizable black populations.

Even though his effort to form an effective black-white reform coalition crumbled with defeat in the legislative elections of 1871, Teamoh remained a black leader at the local level for a decade. In a manner similar to that soon advocated by Virginia-born Booker T. Washington, he worked out a program of self-help for the freedmen of his community, most notably through establishing Portsmouth's first black school, which began classes when Teamoh (and some twenty other local blacks) purchased the Webster Building at the corner of Green and Queen streets in early September 1870. He also continued to speak out against racial policies of white politicians. While a delegate to the constitutional convention, he had already criticized both the disproportionately small number of leadership positions in that body given to blacks by white Republicans and the racial slurs of Conservative delegates and the Conservative press. As a senator, he was disappointed by his party's failure to take a forthright stand favoring racial integration on railroad cars, and as a community leader he helped to organize (in November 1871) an impressive public protest following the shooting death of John Wilson, a black Portsmouth policeman.[45] With each of these actions, Teamoh hoped that he might help secure some elements of the postwar program that his party had first outlined in platforms framed at Richmond during the spring and summer 1867. Unfortunately, it was increasingly clear that the commitment to those goals was weakening, due to the waning interest in Reconstruction by the northern public and to the fact that native whites were restoring "home rule" in Virginia.

Despite the turmoil associated with the bitter struggles between Republicans and Conservatives, however, the economy of the Norfolk-Portsmouth region recovered rather quickly from the devastation and destruction of war. The burning of the navy yard (by retreating Federals in 1861 and again by Confederates who abandoned it in 1862), the Union blockade, and the movement of armies up and down the Peninsula had all combined to disrupt economic life throughout southeastern Virginia. Still, even in the face of such recent hardship and desolation, Norfolk and Portsmouth (as was the case with a number of Virginia's urban areas) soon regained or surpassed their prewar economic standing. The population of Norfolk reached almost 20,000 by 1870; Portsmouth was about half that size—10,492. In Norfolk, a refurbished water system underwent continued expansion throughout the 1870s and 1880s, as did a sewer line started in 1878 and a network of electric streetlights introduced in 1883. A new newspaper, *The Virginian*, began publication in 1865, and even during the early postwar months of that year one observer reported, with perhaps excessive enthusiasm, that Norfolk's houses were beautiful "abodes of wealth and refinement," that the city's streets were "lined with huge trees," and that the gardens surrounding the homes of its citizens were filled "with the rarest, most fragrant, and many colored" flowers.[46]

The surprisingly rapid postwar economic recovery and growth of the region—by 1880 Norfolk's population totaled 21,966 and Portsmouth's 11,390—was tied closely to a boom in railroad construction, a matter often on Teamoh's mind during his years in the state senate. Norfolk and Portsmouth had finally been connected to the interior during the 1850s by the completion of two systems—the Seaboard and Roanoke, and the Norfolk and Petersburg. Traffic on these roads, however, was soon disrupted by the war, and the two badly damaged lines themselves were not restored to even their original carrying capacity until 1866. At that time, though, William Mahone started consolidating local systems and eventually merged three of them—the Norfolk and Petersburg, the South Side, and the Virginia and Tennessee—into a single road, with the impressive name of the Atlantic, Mississippi, and Ohio. Although this creation faced a number of problems (it was threatened by the rival Pennsylvania-Southern System and hurt badly by economic depression during the early 1870s), it was eventually refinanced and organized on a solvent basis in 1881 as the Norfolk and Western. As such, it finally stretched some 400 miles throughout southern Virginia and for the first time gave Norfolk and Portsmouth reliable commercial connections with the states of the Deep South.[47]

This important development coincided with changes in shipbuilding. The new railroads soon could begin carrying ever-increasing quantities of cotton (a crop of very little commercial importance in the region during the prewar years) into the twin cities; the construction of larger ships meant such vessels could no longer easily bypass port facilities on the coast to sail up the James to a fall-line city such as Richmond. This fact revolutionized the economy of both Norfolk and Portsmouth. By the mid-1870s only a few cities, such as New Orleans and Galveston, surpassed Norfolk as exporters of cotton, and businessmen there and in Portsmouth were more successful than they had even dared hope during the antebellum days of frustrating and often unsuccessful competition with rivals in the hinterland for the carrying trade. Now linked securely to cotton supplies further south by miles of railroads and protected from upriver competition by the great size of newly built ships too large to move far inland, citizens of Norfolk County were confident of their economic future. Not only had their area clearly surpassed Richmond as a regional port, but Norfolk and Portsmouth, which now exported more than half of their stockpiled cotton to foreign markets, had finally achieved their twin destiny as one of the most important ports in the entire South.[48]

Teamoh initially shared in the economic recovery of his district. Leaving his profession as a caulker in the mid-1860s, he had been able to save much of his salary—initially as a convention delegate and later as a state senator—to buy a comfortable home in Portsmouth. In addition to that purchase (made in 1871), he had, as noted previously, joined with other local blacks in 1870 to secure the Webster Building, a structure on a lot adjoining the one on which his home was located. Named for its previous owner, Professor Nathan Webster, the building was then used as a school for black children. White teachers conducted the instruction until 1883, when blacks began staffing their own local schools.[49] Thus, Teamoh, who was also active in Portsmouth's Emanuel African Methodist Episcopal Church, was by any measure surely one of the most important leaders in Portsmouth's postwar black community. He had played an important role in the organization of the local Republican party; he helped frame the new state constitution and represented his district in the Virginia senate; he assisted with efforts to unionize white and black laborers in the Navy Yard; and he had conferred personally with cabinet-level officials in Washington about the political and economic problems of his area.

Despite these considerable achievements in which he took justifiable pride, he was increasingly preoccupied by his own problems. By the mid-1870s the local Republican party, weakened by its defeat in 1871 and by continued internal factionalism, had all but disappeared, ending any opportunity to continue with his political career (even at the local level) and forcing a return to his old job as a caulker. Dismayed by poor health and by economic difficulties following the 1873 depression, Teamoh—who defaulted on a loan and lost his home in 1881—was also disheartened by political developments in both the state and the nation. He was troubled by the growing acceptance of segregation (a racial practice he had criticized as a legislator) in his native Virginia. He was also painfully aware that the Republican party largely had abandoned its earlier postwar commitment to building a viable biracial party in the South and had instead allowed the return of the region to the Democrats and to a system of "home rule," which diminished greatly any meaningful political participation by the freedmen. Finally, Teamoh was also unhappy with some of Portsmouth's newer black leaders, including the Reverend Jacob E. Moore of his own church, whom he believed to be more interested in personal economic gain than in the broader problems of his troubled community.[50]

And so the last decade of Teamoh's life reflected clearly a number of the lost opportunities of the postwar era. It is perhaps fitting that he simply vanished from the scene in 1883, the point at which he ended his manuscript. He may have died at that time, but the precise date of his death remains unknown. His obscurity clearly symbolized the status of large numbers of blacks—in Virginia and throughout the "New South"—during the latter years of the nineteenth century. In general, they too faded from center stage, which they had occupied when congressional Reconstruction began in 1867, into a position that allowed them no significant say in shaping their region. Political, economic, and racial issues would still be much debated, especially during the late 1870s and the early 1880s when the means of best funding Virginia's state debt was argued between "redeemers" and "readjusters." However, these matters would be discussed and decided exclusively by southern whites, who in general showed but little concern about the plight of blacks.[51]

Even given all the pressing financial and personal problems he confronted near the time of his death, Teamoh remained hopeful. After all, he had personally witnessed the destruction of chattel slavery, the institution he regarded rightly as the greatest evil in the history of the Republic. Following the Civil War, he had also helped to establish Virginia's new biracial Republican party, a reform coalition that had accomplished much—including the framing of a progressive new constitution and the founding of a biracial system of public education—during the brief years of its existence as a political force. Although sometimes disappointed by what he regarded as the shortsighted opportunism of some whites—such as William H. Lyons and James H. Platt—Teamoh had also been inspired throughout his life by the courage and decency of others, such as Jane Thomas, Melzar Gardner, and James Clements. Even with the hardships and disappointments experienced during his later years, he generally remained firm in his belief that human courage, guided by an uplifting Christian faith, might direct the nation and its citizens—whites, blacks, northerners, and southerners—toward a better and more promising future.

THE AUTOBIOGRAPHY OF THE
AUTOBIOGRAPHY

If, as George Teamoh writes in the opening lines of his autobiography, "it but rarely falls to the lot of one . . . to narrate, in any intelligent form, the history of one's life," rarer still must be the lot of a descendant, some hundred years later, to piece together the story of such an ancestor. Teamoh, my great-great-grandfather, helped to draft the Virginia state constitution during Reconstruction and was elected to the state senate during the 1860s. Yet except for his descendants and assiduous scholars of Reconstruction history, not many know that Teamoh lived, spent a few significant moments on the political stage, and died. As both a descendant and a professional reader of nineteenth-century African-American literature, I face a daunting and twofold task: first, to fill out some of the shadows surrounding a "significant ancestor"; second, to illuminate a recovered text of black American autobiography. For this scholar, the political has quite literally become the personal.[1]

To write about my family almost inevitably leads to a quandary, especially when I reflect that my prose will be read by my university peers. What entertains or fascinates me may be less than interesting to you, the intended reader. After all, the figures in *God Made Man, Man Made the Slave* are long since dead. Will my disquisitions on African-American intertextuality make these players seem more than antiquarian curiosities? Will family tales, bent from passing down and mirroring each individual teller, serve my purposes better than scholarly distance? Can I accommodate family legend and lore within the requirements of scholarship? What matter that George Teamoh has four living namesakes in the New York area?[2] I maintain that family ties invigorate the investigative process. The eldest living George Teamoh, son of Edward and Winnie Bailey Teamoh, had five siblings who grew to adulthood, a fact of more than passing relevance to this undertaking. Two of them—Lethia Teamoh Walker, my grandmother, and Margaret Teamoh Haithcox, my great-aunt—provided me with connections to the past that bring to my work a three-dimensional shape unusual in most academic research.[3]

To begin: during childhood I would listen curiously as my grandmother brandished the standard of our dim forebear, George Teamoh, when my sister and I riotously trespassed against the family dignity. Lethia Walker would advise menacingly, "Remember girls, we're not anyone— we're the Virginia *Teamohs*." Arguing with her was useless, for she believed firmly that children should be seen and not heard. We would hang our heads for a moment in a fair imitation of contrite, well-brought-up young ladies and then race off.

Lethia was bound to be disappointed, for her only child, a jazz musician who'd been drafted out of Julliard, provided no role model whatsoever in the decorum department: Alfred, Jr. (later known as Nooruddin Zafar) found the sidewalk artists of Greenwich Village, the sweet potato pies of the Pink Teacup cafe, and the vistas provided by the Staten Island Ferry pertinent to the education of his daughters. Notwithstanding my father's counterinsurgency, my grandmother continued to hector: "We're not *anyone;* we're the Virginia Teamohs." When asked about this mysterious individual and the lost ancestral home, Daddy would muse how we once owned good property near the waterfront in Portsmouth and had been swindled out of it. Though he many times expressed an interest in recovering our lost domain, previous experiences with southern racism and his losing battle with multiple myeloma kept him from pursuing his fantasy of a return. When he died in 1972 at the age of forty-seven, the recapture of a lost, middle-class southern black life was nothing I could have included among my inheritance.

In 1976 I joined Doubleday and Company as an editorial secretary. The firm had recently published Dorothy Sterling's *The Trouble They Seen: Black People Tell the Story of Reconstruction*. One day at work I found the volume in a stack of complimentary books set out for employees.[4] Paging through the book, I checked to see if Teamoh was indeed the fabled actor my family had said him to be. Half-expecting to find no mention of him, I instead was confronted with his picture. Teamoh existed: not solely for a handful of Harlemites clinging to a glorious and vanished ancestry, but for the rest of the United States as well. Returning the photographer's gaze straight on, Teamoh sports a long, curly beard, white shirt, dark coat and tie. The George Teamoh depicted there resembles me, at least in the shape of his nose. But the picture did not strike me as a duplicate of the one I seemed to remember in my grandmother's possession. (When I later searched for that photograph, human frailty had triumphed over the historian's craving for data.)

By the time I found that public record of family achievement, Lethia Teamoh Walker and I had become friends. Nearing eighty, my grandmother found me, nearing thirty, a sympathetic listener to her pronouncements on modern evils, stories of Harlem days past, and summary judgments on one or another member of our family. Many Sundays I took the train up to Harlem, eyeing the decay on the streets around Hamilton Terrace while noting the fervor with which its inhabitants fought its encroachments. Sometimes my grandmother and I would look out through the tall windows at the back of her apartment, our gaze scanning the tar roofs of the garages on Saint Nicholas Avenue and lingering on the increasingly shabby, once-imposing apartment houses. One day as we looked, she remembered when the view before us was countryside and how she used to sit and stroll among the fields. In response to my surprised exclamation, she laughed and wagged her finger at me, saying that Harlem wasn't always a city—or not all of it. My grandmother could be counted among those few remaining elderly who had seen Harlem from the time the greensward competed with the elevated, through the Jazz Age, and into the decline of the 1950s and 1960s. She was one of many who, with their families, had come north looking for a better life. Had she been able to predict that our talks would in some manner lead me to Harvard University, a doctorate, and my current position, she would not have been entirely surprised. "Remember, you're not anyone; you're a Virginia Teamoh."

Next to a chenille-draped bed in my grandmother's room stood an ancient-looking cedar chest that I imagined had been owned by the family for decades, had even seen days of slavery and abject poverty.[5] In that repository she stored linens, papers, and other items—articles I coveted mostly because they were hidden in the trunk. One of my vaguest recollections is of sitting on the edge of her bed while she rummaged around the inside of this magical storage box: I can still smell the odor of cedar, yellowing sheets, and sachet. On that day she showed me a picture of George Teamoh and some documents relating to his life. This man was my grandfather, she told me, your great-great-grandfather. Undoubtedly she boasted of his service to Virginia after the Civil War, though I don't recall her family history lessons taking place until somewhat later. The photograph, a brown-toned rectangle with crumbling edges, would have conveyed little to a small child: the man pictured was long dead, and the significance of a black senator during the 1860s would not have any meaning for me until many years had passed. Decades later George Teamoh remains for me that indistinct man in the chest, a figure whose outlines have yet to be filled in.

After Lethia Walker's death in 1982, several of the family women went through her things. Some of our discoveries amused us, such as the girdle with rear inserts meant to augment her slim figure, and we were able to stack up piles of things for the Good Will. But pictures, papers, and letters were almost entirely absent. Where were the small paper boxes I had seen tucked into her dresser drawers? Where were the photographs, the letters? The older women sighed, recalling that by the end of her life the past had become taboo for Lethia: she had cast out many of her personal effects. With her marriage fifty or more years dissolved, her only child dead ten years earlier, and her longtime suitor Mr. Clifford passed away shortly before her last illness, physical mementos of the past had been unwanted. We found almost no photographs of her, my father, or her sisters and brothers. The long-ago-seen picture of Teamoh, which I now began to wonder if I had only dreamed about, was nowhere to be found. Dying, she threw away everything that commemorated past lives, history, mortality. Living, I have to reconstruct a past that had become her burden.

I made my debut as a Virginia Teamoh in June 1989. Although I had once spent a week in North Carolina, stepping off a plane onto the tarmac of the Charlottesville airport marked the beginning of my personal confrontation with history. My quest for a lost and fragmented family had become a scholarly enterprise. The initial data I brought with me came not from census records or family Bibles, but from the recollections of my great-aunt, Margaret Teamoh Haithcox. Several years after her sister Lethia's death, Aunt Maggie and I had sat down to record the past before it entirely evaporated. Pen in hand, I had asked her to remember what she could about our family's Virginia life. Those notes on lined yellow paper initiated a process of recovery that continues to this day.

"Your grandmother," Maggie said to me, "was born on Glasgow Street in Portsmouth." (Questions about my grandmother's age were deflected due to practiced sisterly tact.[6]) Their mother's name was Winnie, their maternal grandparents restaurateurs William and Sarah Bailey of South Street. "Sarah was white, you know," Maggie added, repeating a once-surprising detail my grandmother had told me years before. Sarah's maiden name had been either Reed or Geytser; my great-aunt couldn't recall.[7] George Teamoh was Winnie Bailey's father-in-law, as she had married Edward Teamoh. After the younger Teamoh abandoned wife and family in the early twentieth century, the Teamoh clan became rather scattered.[8] Maggie remembers a woman who said she was also a Teamoh appearing at their home; she also recalls how her mother had sent the visitor away. A dismissive Winnie explained that the relationship was impossible—the woman didn't favor any Teamohs she knew. And finally, though Maggie couldn't quite fix on who she was in the family, an individual named Mariah hovered around the edges of her memory.

I have since marveled at the accuracy of Margaret Haithcox's memory. As per her recollection, I found William M. Bailey, eating housekeeper, listed on South Street in the 1905 Portsmouth city directory. Glasgow Street was a nearby thoroughfare. And, according to the United States Census of 1900, the infant "Margarete" Teamoh had an eight-year-old sister named "Mary"—undoubtedly, the missing Mariah. Just by scratching the surface of Virginia records, I confirmed several items of my family's history. However at the very moment I began to congratulate myself on unraveling our snarled family tree, contradictions and red herrings began to multiply. Despite the identification by every living Teamoh of Edward Teamoh as George Teamoh's son, items in the official record confuse, not clarify, my line of descent. In brief, whose child was Edward Teamoh?

In order to flesh out the family account, I went to the Virginia census records of the late nineteenth and early twentieth centuries. Reeling through microfilmed faded and water-stained pages, squinting to decipher the scrawled longhand of the enumerators, I found in the 1900 listings a household containing several of my ancestors. Recorded as living in one household were Winnie and her husband Edward, her parents William and Sarah Bailey, and some of the Teamoh children—Lottie, born in 1891; Mary, born the following year; Edward, born in 1895; and my great-aunt Margaret herself, born 1899. Yet in 1880, enumerators listed two young males in the George Teamoh household on Green Street, neither with the name of Edward.[9] That household included George's wife Sarah, his daughter Josephine, and two grandsons—John, age seventeen, and Samuel, age ten.[10] Where was Edward?

Flummoxed by official records that appeared to deny the parentage of Edward Teamoh—or rather, his parentage in George and Sallie Teamoh— I appealed to some historian colleagues. Both Peter Wallenstein, a fellow summer researcher at the Virginia Center for the Humanities, and Waldo Martin, biographer of Frederick Douglass, emphasized the relative reliability of census data. Your great-grandfather, Peter suggested, might not have been living at home when the enumerator came by, due to such commonplace occurrences as apprenticeship, boarding school, or living with other relatives. Both Peter and Waldo asserted that census counts were sometimes and simply wrong, with misspelled or entirely incorrect names and ages lying in wait for the unwary researcher.[11] Even historians, I discovered, have to make leaps of faith.

Several possibilities presented themselves to me. Clerical error, as noted above, could explain either of two solutions. In the first scenario Edward Teamoh could be accounted for by his being elsewhere—at school, at work, wherever; as had the Teamoh's boarder, young Edward could simply have lived with people other than his parents. A second, equally plausible solution is that Edward's name was taken down incorrectly: the ten-year-old Samuel and Edward, also ten in the year 1880, were one and the same child.[12] Another, less easily proved, explanation for Edward's absence from the 1880 Teamoh household could lie in his being George Teamoh's son by a woman other than Sallie. Though a devout Christian, George Teamoh may have strayed from the marital path.[13] Should I continue with the supposition that Samuel Teamoh was Edward, and that Sallie Teamoh was not his mother (had she been his mother, she would have borne him at around fifty years of age), still another possibility appears. Josephine, youngest child of George and Sallie, is there listed as mother of the two boys. She, however, retains her maiden name. The elder boy, as we know from Teamoh's narrative, is the product of a rape. If the second boy were the result of an affair, might the family at some point have decided to report the younger boy as a son, rather than as George's grandson? Interpretations of the family record cross and countermand one another. The archives call. Conundrums multiply.

Teamoh, Teemer, Teamer, Teimer.[14] As anyone who has listened to regional variations of English knows, Americans from various states pronounce the same word differently. Yard, as any Bostonian knows, has but a lingering remembrance of the letter r; many Southerners might give this one-syllable word a two-syllable rendition. Teamoh, in some mouths, might more closely resemble "Teamuh" or "Teamer." As with common sense, so with the historical record: the Edward known to family and city directory as Teamoh appears in the 1900 census as Edward Teemer. George Teamoh himself, trained as a caulker, appears under that trade in several late-nineteenth-century directories, but so does a George Teemer in 1890–1891.[15] In that year no Teamohs at all were listed in Portsmouth, although across the water in Norfolk there were eight Teemers, a Teamer, and one Teimer. Between the directories of 1875–1876 and 1900, no Teamohs whatsoever were recorded as living in the city of Portsmouth. But at the start of that ellipsis I find George Teamoh, caulker, and at the end of it I find Edward Teamoh, laborer. Where will my search end, if it is to have an end? For the moment, let me withdraw into the security of what is known—Teamoh's autobiography—and bide my time. As Teamoh has waited this long for a national audience, the puzzle of his inheritance can tantalize his heir yet a while.

Let me start again by assuming Teamoh's familiarity with the genre of slave narratives. Numerous structural correspondences, as well as his references to earlier authors and texts, alert us to the existence of influence, of an acknowledged ancestry already present within Afro-American narrative. Even had Teamoh somehow been innocent of the genre, the simple facts of his life and its telling place him within the mainstream of self-liberated African-Americans. Readers with any knowledge of the slave narratives cannot read Teamoh's manuscript without being reminded that those allegedly artless tales were a genre, that the author of the Teamoh manuscript consciously imbeds himself within that tradition. We have only to examine the physical characteristics of the autobiography to be convinced.

Before opening a single one of the many copybooks in which Teamoh inscribed *God Made Man, Man Made the Slave*, we see his debt to the reigning form of black American literature. The outside cover of the second volume, an inexpensive composition book, displays the heading "School Exercises" and features a medallion that is surmounted by a cherub and bears the preprinted motto "written by." Teamoh added in script, "My book written in 1839."[16] On the fronts of six of these copybooks, out of a total of eighteen cardboard-bound volumes constituting the text, Teamoh inscribed the words "written by himself." Overdetermining this motto, he penned "written by himself" across the bottom of the medallion in a firm, dark hand. These three words, innocuous enough when taken out of the context of early black writing, resonate when one considers the preponderance of slave narratives that bear the phrase "written by himself."[17] Teamoh further added "by himself" on the manuscript's first page, as if to overwhelm his readers with this proof of authorship. Given in the front matter as "George Teamoh's *Autobiography*. God Made Man, Man Made the Slave" (51), Teamoh paraphrases his narrative's title as "A brief sketch of the life of Geo. Teamoh," closing his introductory advertisements with the final notation of "by himself" (51).* Had he affixed a photograph of himself in the act of writing, he could not have been more emphatic.

Teamoh's initial sentence follows the format of the classic slave narratives, with its flat announcement of a nearly parentless birth: "I was born in the city of Norfolk, VA. A.D. 1818" (51). For an ex-fugitive to begin with such an announcement, without a simultaneous acknowledgment of one's parents, was a convention designed (among other strategies) to establish one's identity as both human and thing. To state your birth asserts your humanity; to omit your parents from the proposition confirms the improbabil-

---

*All page numbers in parentheses refer to this edition.—ED.

ity of slave family life. Frederick Douglass, writing in 1845, begins much the same way: "I was born in Tuckahoe, near Hillsborough, and about twelve miles from Easton, in Talbot county, Maryland."[18] Although many could not give anything but an approximation of their ages, bondsmen not often being allowed such information, Teamoh did know the year of his birth. To underscore his genealogical isolation[19] and the absence or impotence of slave parents, Teamoh dispassionately relates his earliest movements: "When very young,—possibly not over ten years of age—I was brought to this city—Portsmouth, Va. my owners having made residence here. After remaining in the family until I had arrived at the age of twelve or thirteen years, I was hired to Capt. Jno. [John] Thompson who at the time, and until his death, resided in this city" (52). Whether by dint of not being able to tell their age—an ability Douglass once alleged he had yet to find in a former bondsman,[20] or because they affirm the impossibility of control over their movements— Teamoh and other former slaves tell a common story. Contrary to Tolstoyan wisdom, unhappy slaves were all too alike.

Douglass and Teamoh share more than a birth cohort.[21] In temperament, both were driven by an unslakable thirst for intellectual advancement, a progression that would be equated with freedom. Each man lived under the "milder" form of slavery, and each served time as a field slave whose attempts at individuality were brutally suppressed. Teamoh, like Douglass, escaped to freedom as a sailor. Both men had been employed as shipyard laborers in the upper coastal South. Each fugitive made the requisite pilgrimage to New Bedford and settled for a time in the North. As writers, Teamoh and Douglass advanced the cause of freedom and racial equality: Douglass as the renowned editor of the *North Star* (later *Frederick Douglass's Paper*), Teamoh as a regular newspaper contributor.[22] Moreover, Douglass held patronage positions in the postbellum national government, while Teamoh was a duly elected Virginia state senator. If Douglass's charisma and talent propelled him onto a national stage, the scrappier Teamoh also had his brief, albeit local, time in the spotlight.

Teamoh could not help but be aware of these correspondences. The Virginian remains somewhat reluctant to grant Douglass's influence, however. The second paragraph of Teamoh's autobiography does concede to the Marylander a place of primacy, if strictly a chronological one. "Frederick Douglass, whose towering intellect outstripping all who have preceded him in this country, has been no doubt the most successful of self-made men, and of which he has given full proof, not only in the United States where he was born, but the editorial genius of all Europe has pronounced in his favor" (51). After this encomium, and for whatever reason, Teamoh feels compelled to point somewhat enigmatically to the "scholastic advantages" Douglass and another famed narrator, William Wells Brown, may have had.[23] He then adds a curious evaluation of Douglass's second autobiography *My Bondage and My Freedom*, saying "[T]he *crudity* of [Douglass's] writing however is plain evidence of his never having been schooled, or at least not so by routine" (51, emphasis mine). Rather than praise the genuine mastery of Douglass's narrative, Teamoh gives him a backhanded compliment. He avers that the efforts of such men as Douglass were hampered by their being bondsmen forbidden to read, but asks his readers to excuse him for "waving those considerations." By denigrating the supposedly clumsy efforts of his predecessors, Teamoh invites the audience to substitute his own narrative. To forestall criticism, he explains that "the following [pages are] through the request of many friends" (51). Yet Douglass wrote his first autobiography not to satisfy the proddings of vanity, but to prove wrong the whites who claimed that he had never been a slave—a fact that Teamoh likely knew. Douglass, like Teamoh, wrote on the urgings of others.[24] After Teamoh's initial criticism of *My Bondage and My Freedom*, Douglass receives one additional mention. Is Teamoh simply exhibiting an anxiety of influence, a son's attempt to overcome a literary father?[25] At the time Teamoh composed his manuscript, Douglass's career was still the stuff of the national press; his own, by contrast, was in eclipse. Douglass's stay in the circles of power, however delimited, may have caused Teamoh to contrast his own skills to those of his famous predecessor. Perhaps, like many Americans before and since, Teamoh wanted to reckon himself a self-made man.

Like the ghost of Douglass in Teamoh's autobiography, most slave narratives raise questions that will never be satisfactorily answered. What happened to Henry Bibb's daughter? What became of Benjamin, the near-white uncle of Harriet Jacobs? *God Made Man, Man Made the Slave* is no exception to this rule of an interrupted, discontinuous narrative. As I have long known, Teamoh is quite an unusual surname. George's masters were named Josiah and Jane Thomas; the brickmason to whom he was hired out was John Thompson. Through default, many slaves ended up with their master's name. If they renamed themselves, they were often careful to explain why. Other than stating Teamoh as his surname, the Portsmouth caulker makes no comment. Newbell Niles Puckett's vast compendium of African-American names does not offer any solid match. Yet Teamoh, similar in spelling and sound to some west African names, could as easily announce a Senegambian origin as a European one.[26] In similarly maddening fashion, Teamoh omits his mother's name. He tells us he was an orphan before adolescence, but while writing of his sojourn in Boston, he makes a brief reference to a brother. His father he leaves a question mark; his terse acknowledgment that his progenitor was not his mother's husband by "usages of custom" (56) provokes but does not enlighten.[27] A daguerreotype enclosed with the original manuscript, depicting Teamoh with a long, curly beard, seems to indicate some white lineage. Whether Teamoh attempts a self-portrait of a man risen from limbo or omits details because he has none, the sketchiness of his early life affirms his narrative's literary lineage.

As Robert Stepto has written, the driving force of many African-American writers is the quest for freedom and literacy.[28] Teamoh taught himself to read while still in his teens, although slave education was forbidden. The ingenuity of slaves in learning to read has often been remarked upon. Teamoh's road to literacy winds, starts, and stops. As other narrators had done before him, Teamoh devotes a great amount of space to his efforts to read and write. The relation of his struggles under the subtitle "How I learned to read and write" (58) illustrates its membership in the form of early black narrative. His fortunate—or unfortunate—identity as a thinking young slave is invoked at the beginning: "I early saw the sad and lamentable condition in which a whole race of mankind had been placed" (59). Teamoh visits every spot where information could be gleaned, "churches, political gatherings, theatres, &c." (59). He finds white children in the street his unwitting tutors: "It was while passing to and from the brickyards I had often heard from white children, the alphabet in song; and so frequently had it fallen on my ear that retention proved no task" (60). When the recognition of the characters themselves remained elusive, Teamoh demonstrated the characteristic perspicacity of the slave who would be free:

> Cutting these letters, one after another from a card on which they had been printed, I tasked myself to commit one to memory every night, so as to make the whole perfectly familia[r] with me on distribution, which I accomplished a few days within one month . . . I suspended a cardboard in my quarters with all the alphabets written, or printed on it. . . . I next arranged the letters I had cut as stated, on what musicians term a staff I pasted in every conceivable form of variation and class, the twenty six characters which make up the English language. (60)

Teamoh had located a loophole in the Virginia prohibition on slave literacy: "[I] early discovered that no one had any particular objection to a slave learning written music . . . I was, by such means [as above], amply protected from suspicion" (60). As no one questioned his devotion to practice, Teamoh could continue his lessons without discovery.

Access to knowledge could be blocked by blacks as well. While performing odd jobs in the Norfolk shipyard, Teamoh runs afoul of an older, alcoholic slave's ill temper. When carrying bricks one day, the young boy's primer falls out of his shirt. "Uncle" Peter immediately demands to know how the younger slave acquired it, "at the same time ordering me to leave it at home, and under no considerations must [Teamoh] ever be seen with it" (64). Despite the boy's pleas, Peter is inflexible. Some years later, Teamoh returns to the shipyards as a caulker; there he finds an almost unrecognizable Peter, beaten down by hard usage, overwork, and scanty rations. In an ironical twist not lost on the young man or his readers, old Peter begs the literate Teamoh to write a plea for help. Teamoh "forget[s] and forgiv[es] those discouraging words . . . concerning the 'primer' " (65). In an acute apprehension of the limitations of white mercy vis-à-vis black literacy, he addresses a letter to Peter's owner purporting to come from a white, barely lettered skilled worker: "Mistur capn john tomson i sete miself to write you these fu lines your old man peter is in a grate deegre of sufring . . . he ses you and him was boys togethur . . . i speke to you as a whit man and i beleve he is al rite now excuse my pure spelin for i am a stone mason here by the day . . . respcful yors &c a mason" (65). Teamoh adds that while the letter may have amused Captain Thompson, it had the desired effect of bringing aid. Teamoh, the autobiographer, doesn't offer any clues as to the prowess of Teamoh, the historical character, as amanuensis. At the time of the original letter's composition, the actual distance between Teamoh's skills and those of a semiliterate white may not have been that great. The mature Teamoh, for the purpose of a moral lesson (not to mention human vanity), may have included this fable so that his audience would believe in his superiority, both intellectual and ethical. The re-creation of his letter in the manuscript, a kind of signifying on the white-written "authenticating documents" so frequently surrounding slave narratives, may be viewed as additional evidence that Teamoh appreciated the hallmarks of his genre.[29]

Beyond the appropriation of literary strategies familiar to readers of the antebellum narrative, Teamoh fits his own life neatly into the lines of the prototypical fugitive's story. Like most young adults of the day, by the age of twenty-three Teamoh had married. Also a slave, Sallie Teamoh was believed to be the half-sister of her owner, a Miss Lively of New Market, Virginia. The years immediately following their wedding were about as uneventful as a slave husband and wife could hope. About the only unusual item in their early married life was the performance of the wedding ceremony by a Reverend Eskridge during an era when slave unions were rarely regularized. Sallie and George were soon to have their misfortunes. Following her mistress's marriage, mother and children were sold, then sold again. As the property of other whites, Teamoh could do nothing; their two oldest children, sent "beyond the reach of hearing or recovery," were never to be seen again (79). His mistress eventually suggests an unusual solution, or at least an extraordinary one for a slaveowner to endorse.

Whether out of sympathy for the bereft husband or out of her own maternal compassion, Jane Thomas did more than commiserate. Although in post-Nat Turner insurrection Virginia manumitting one's slaves was not simple, Teamoh and Thomas avoided legal solutions. Teamoh recalls his mistress's thoughts:

> [Mrs. Thomas] having promised my mother that at some time during manhood she would let me go free, found herself, at the time she felt most like doing so unable from the laws of the state to accomplish that very desirable result. She had hinted the matter to me over and often while approaching maturity, stating complications which would inevitably follow should she attempt to do so by legal process. (85)

Jane Thomas encourages Teamoh to ship out as a sailor on a vessel bound for New York City, via Germany, and from there to do as he will. Once on the open seas, a slave became a free man.

In Bremen the black seaman meets a host of friendly whites for the first time. He rejoices that "these hospitable german mechanics [invited me] . . . —through their interpreter—to visit not only their public places of amusements, but their private residences also" (88). His new friends, also caulkers, tell him to go where he pleases without fear of embarrassment. He can hardly believe his ears. To commemorate his visit Teamoh writes a thirty-line poem, the first couplet of which gives the narrative its title: "God made man, man made the slave, / The last degrades him to his grave" (180). Teamoh's sharp social commentary finds an amusing outlet in verse: the Germans, he remarks, welcomed him freely, "not yankee like—automaton"; he is charmed, rather than offended, to find "the children cried the dogs did bark/ To wit mankind was made so dark" (89).[30] Despite the blandishments of European life, Teamoh sails back unhesitatingly to the United States. In New York City the thirty-five-year-old caulker disembarks a free man.

Following the narration of his adventures in the North, including the almost obligatory residence in New Bedford, Teamoh diverges sharply from the parameters of the antebellum fugitive narrative.[31] Rather than ending with freedom in the North, the autobiography closes in to a postemancipation South. Upon returning to his hometown, the literate Teamoh is appealed to by freedmen "to espouse their cause" (104). Sympathetic to their entreaties, he temporarily puts them off to search for his family. After locating Sallie and their youngest child, Teamoh establishes a homestead for

them in Hampton near some friends. And at this point wife and family re-
cede almost completely into obscurity. No more of his memoirs are devoted
to family doings. Instead Teamoh goes on to relate the admittedly fascinat-
ing saga of his brief, heady experience as an elected official. Like Douglass,
Benjamin Franklin, and many early American men, Teamoh looked upon
wives and children as minor, if much loved, characters.

To judge by the space he allots his public life, Teamoh places official-
dom on a par with personal and emotional affairs. Although his career as a
Republican politician spanned but a few years, nearly one third of the
manuscript is devoted to his activities within, and reflections on, Reconstruction-era Virginia politics. That Teamoh sat down years later to record
his impressions is a windfall, for few first-person accounts of the "black and
tan" conventions survive. When Teamoh announces that he was "elected by
the majority of citizens of Portsmouth and Norfolk County" to the Constitutional Convention in 1867, his pride is justifiable (105). He admits his
preparation for the task was minimal:

> Nor was it to be expected that we—colored—could by any possibility, at
> that time have had the most distant knowledge of constitutional reconstruc-
> tion, as many of us could neither read nor write. . . . For my part I went
> there a "graduate" from Capt. John Thompson's brickyard, and finished
> my trade at caulking; hence if there had been anything to perform in that
> particular direction I was on hand to assist in the matter. But in spite of
> their disqualifications, my people seems to have been possessed of a natural
> etching to meet in open debate, every question which came up for discus-
> sion. (107)

Although lacking the expertise of their white colleagues, Teamoh and his fellow black officials "invariably voted right on the proposition from which arguments were drawn," however convoluted the sessions became. Although
Teamoh acknowledges abuse, he notes that "the colored members, for the most
part, bore themselves well, only here and there harassing the opposition" (107).
Historians a century later uphold his confidence in his colleagues.[32]

The freshman state senator found Reconstruction politics murky and
dangerous waters. Black representatives, he writes, "had a turn at the wheel
of fire." Free men of color were misunderstood, taken advantage of, and
harassed: threatening letters from the Ku Klux Klan, as well as open insult
on the floor from white Democrats and Republicans alike, were the norm.
Teamoh sadly comments that Republican principles were "assailed and vilified by the Democracy [southern Democrats] with all that bitter resentment
and revenge characteristic of a once-ruling, but now waning aristocracy"
(108). Despite the discouraging odds (the Democrats held a majority in the

first postbellum Virginia legislatures), Teamoh effected what change he could. He fought to secure equal pay and positions for colored and white workers in the bustling Naval Yard where he himself had worked; he furthermore asserted that local men should obtain the coveted government jobs—not Northern carpetbaggers. "We ask no donation beyond that which, with favoring circumstances, the well muscled arm of the mechanic and laborer can hew out for themselves. But in the absence of these, we shall feel doomed to pass through the ordeal of Reconstruction with no other help or hope than that which leads to despair" (113). As a worker-turned-politician, Teamoh knew how large a part patronage played in job security. But Gilded-Age-style politicking could land more than concessions.

On the night before a critical vote on a state subsidy for the Pennsylvania Railroad, Teamoh hears a knock on the door of his capital rooms. A railway lobbyist offers him a "package of greenback money consisting of Ten Thousand Dollars" (120). Despite the lure of easy money, Teamoh votes with his conscience, ensuring an easy sleep and his future financial insecurity: "My ideas of men are, when they have been called to serve in legislative capacity they should be actuated by motives too high to be reached by any pecuniary or other consideration" (121). While an anonymous admirer sends him money—perhaps cash from his own kickbacks—his honesty does not win widespread allegiance. At the end of his term racial squabbling within the Republican ranks loses him the renomination. Preferring to end this first and longest section with the ring of victory, Teamoh closes with a description of his current activities: the purchase of the Green Street house, the cofounding of a free school for black children.

Teamoh's later years are more or less obscure. His disillusionment, chronicled in appendices to the main narrative, sounds palpably. These last pages tell of the loss of his home, his protemperance sentiments, his dissatisfaction with the outside world. At this point Teamoh disengages from the reader. A cranky, almost petulant tone creeps into the text, evidencing his increasing isolation. When we read the main part of the autobiography, written while Teamoh is in his fifties, a vigorous man still able to laugh at Reconstruction-era foibles rises up from the page; despite his political setbacks, we believe the mature Teamoh will lead an active and confident old age.

But the appendices derail that hope. The aging man, still employed as a manual laborer, finds himself on the outs with the local black church. Teamoh warns church members that their ambiguous stand against racism will produce blacks raised "on the milk of subjugation, cowardice—fear . . . [which] like many other inherited principles takes two or three generations to work off " (140). He then points the finger at whites, thundering "my white brethren, you had done us badly . . . you will be burdening posterity with a debt of your own contracting" (145). The most irrepressible optimist would find the materialism and reneged promises of the Gilded Age hard to accept. A sidelined, fading Teamoh mirrors the dimming of Reconstruction's dreams.

The once-ironic autobiographer ends his story on an almost formulaic note, his formerly lively tone subordinated to nineteenth-century piety: "Never-the-less, I rejoice while recognizing the widespread hand of missionary charity which has been so liberal, so humane and christian in lifting from many of my race the dark clouds of ignorance and superstitions, and can only trust that this good work will be pushed forward with a zeal commensurate with the cause" (149). That melancholic and faintly hopeful strain we hear appears in the black jeremiad from the early nineteenth century forward;[33] in concluding, Teamoh retreats from the specificity of his own experience into generic sameness. Whatever form his personal vagaries of style and commentary took, whatever special turns his personal history made, Teamoh's closing sentences place his narrative firmly within the mainstream of black autobiography. In lightly echoing the last lines of *My Bondage and My Freedom*—"while Heaven lends me ability, to use my voice, my pen, or my vote, to advocate the great and primary work of the universal and unconditional emancipation of my entire race"[34]—Teamoh brings Douglass and his many predecessors strongly to mind.

God Made Man, Man Made the Slave can now take its place in the canon of Afro-American autobiography. In the pages of his narrative, George Teamoh demonstrates a sure touch for the telling detail, a playwright's flair for dramatization, and a sneaky wit that Douglass himself might have envied. Without a near-faultless ear for language, Teamoh cannot be ranked equally with Douglass, especially if we consider the economy and tight framing of the latter's 1845 narrative. But Teamoh saw himself as an actor, not as a literary aesthetician. Propelled onto the stage by an accident of history, Teamoh stepped into a role the majority of Americans said he would never be able to fill. Surpassing such expectations, he learned to read, traveled to Europe, represented Virginians white and black. Taking up intellectual arms against the political enslavement of his people, Teamoh found that he and his colleagues were losing the battle. His cause temporarily fell into the shadows. Resurrected, he now speaks again to the public— poignantly, emphatically, uniquely. As reader and descendant, I take the greatest of pleasure in sharing with you his words and his life. Teamoh, at long last, has found his audience.

Rafia Zafar

A TEAMOH ALBUM

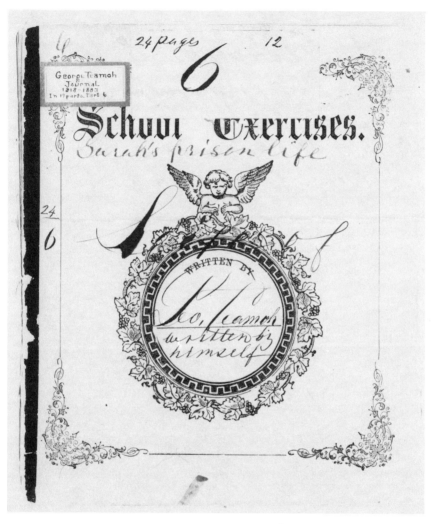

On the fronts of six of the eighteen copybooks that constitute his manuscript, George Teamoh inscribed the words "written by himself." These three words resonate when one considers the preponderance of slave narratives that bear the phrase "written by himself." *(Courtesy of the Library of Congress)*

The manuscript's title page. *(Courtesy of the Library of Congress)*

4

A brief sketch of the life
of Geo. Teamoh, by himself.

I was born in the city of
Norfolk, Va. A.D. 1818.
When very young, – possibly
not over ten years of age –
I was brought to this city–
Portsmouth, Va. my owners
having made residence
here. After remaining in the
family until I had arrived
at the age of twelve or thirteen years, I was hired to
Capt. Jno. Thompson who at the
time, and until his death,
resided in this city. This
gentleman, of whom I shall
necessarily have much to say,
was, besides being a brick
maker, an established contractor in brick masonry;
and, perhaps, none in his day

The opening page of the manuscript. *(Courtesy of the Library of Congress)*

Born a slave in 1818, George Teamoh grew up in the Norfolk-Portsmouth area, escaped to the North in 1853, and returned after the Civil War to play a major role in Radical Reconstruction. This photograph was probably taken in the period when he served as a delegate to the state constitutional convention (1867–1868) and as a state senator (1869–1871). *(Courtesy of the Library of Congress)*

Edward Teamoh—George's son—born in 1870. The recollections of Teamoh family members define Edward's parentage better than the census counts of the time. *(Courtesy of Rafia Zafar)*

The end of Radical Reconstruction in Virginia was symbolized dramatically in April 1870 when the floor of a second-story room at the state capitol collapsed under the weight of hundreds of legislators and spectators gathered to hear a Virginia Court of Appeals decision that would allow conservatives to regain control of Richmond city government. More than sixty people died and hundreds more were injured as rescuers worked frantically to remove debris and bodies from the main floor. *(Courtesy of the Virginia State Library and Archives)*

Following the structural collapse at the state capitol, people rushed from all over downtown Richmond to assist in carrying away the dead and the injured. State Senator George Teamoh and most other Virginia legislators were not in the capitol building at the time, but one senator died and about a dozen other legislators were hurt in this dramatic episode at the end of Radical Reconstruction. *(Courtesy of the Virginia State Library and Archives)*

This panorama shows the Norfolk-Portsmouth area in the early 1850s. The larger city of Norfolk with more than 14,000 inhabitants stands to the left. Smaller Portsmouth with more than 8,000 citizens lies to the right, with the United States Naval Hospital in the foreground. In the background, where several ships are gathered, is the Gosport Navy Yard. Teamoh and many other slaves labored at this federal installation. (*Courtesy of the Virginia State Library and Archives*)

This larger and clearer panorama of the Norfolk-Portsmouth area in the early 1850s shows the predominance of Norfolk on the left. On the Portsmouth side of the Elizabeth River to the right stands the United States Naval Hospital in the foreground, and in the background lies the Gosport Naval Yard with a single large ship anchored just offshore. (*Courtesy of the Mariners' Museum, Newport News, Virginia*)

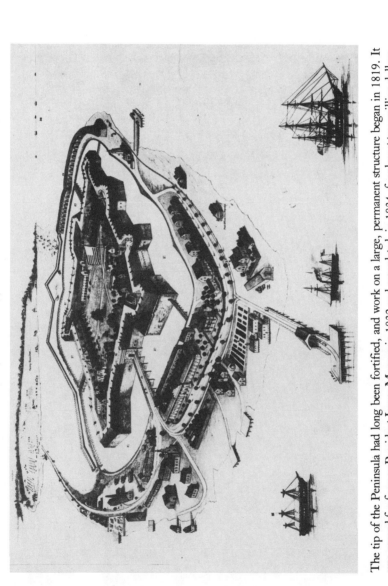

The tip of the Peninsula had long been fortified, and work on a large, permanent structure began in 1819. It was named for former President James Monroe in 1832 and completed, in 1834, for almost two million dollars. George Teamoh and many other Virginia blacks did hard labor there over the years. When the Civil War started, the Union held onto powerful Fort Monroe, which in the spring of 1862 served as a springboard for General McClellan's unsuccessful offensive against Richmond. After the war it served as Jefferson Davis's prison. (*Courtesy of the Virginia State Library and Archives*)

More than a mile out from Fort Monroe in the channel from the Chesapeake Bay into Hampton Roads lay a shoal called Rip-Raps. Here, in 1819, the federal government began constructing an artificial island of stone topped with a small fortress. It was completed in 1827 and named Fort Calhoun in honor of President Monroe's able secretary of war. Additional labor was sporadically needed to keep the fort operational. Slaves, though, dreaded working on this installation, which was only a few feet above waters rushing in and out of Hampton Roads. When the Civil War began, federal authorities hastily changed the name to Fort Wool and, like Fort Monroe, it remained in Union hands. (*Courtesy of the Virginia State Library and Archives*)

The seventy-four-gun *Delaware*, a great warship of its day, was launched at the Gosport Navy Yard in Portsmouth in 1820. In June 1833, it returned to be the first ship berthed at the large, new drydock. The 314 by 100 foot installation had taken six years to build at a cost of almost a million dollars. George Teamoh often worked at the yard, starting as a water boy and common laborer and eventually becoming a caulker. When the Civil War started, Union Navy personnel at Gosport scuttled the *Delaware*, but rebel Virginia troops seized the vital drydock intact. (*Courtesy of the Portsmouth Naval Shipyard Museum, Portsmouth, Virginia*)

This sketch of the Gosport Navy Yard at Portsmouth was done around 1840 and shows some of the federal installation's elaborate facilities. George Teamoh eventually became a skilled caulker here, packing the seams in ships' hulls with oakum or tar. *(From Historical Recollections of Virginia by Henry Howe, p. 401)*

GEO. TEAMOH'S AUTOBIOGRAPHY

"God made man, man made the slave."

It but rarely falls to the lot of one, who was not only a slave of fifty years, but doomed to all the horrors and disadvantages of that institution during that period to narrate, in any intelligent form the history of his life. And it seems almost incredible, when we learn of those who have done so.

Frederick Douglass, whose towering intellect, out stripping all who have preceded him in this country, has been, no doubt, the most successfull of self-made men, and of which he has given full proof, not only in the United States where he was born, but the editorial genius of all Europe has pronounced in his favor.[1] Next we have Wm. Wells Brown, and J. Sella Martin.[2] The first is said to be an able scholar, and great debater; in deed he has written two or three books which are alike specimens of exalted thought great originality, comprehensiveness and scholarship. Of J. S. Martin, more might be said than even for W. W. Brown, although Martin has gone to ruin. Whatever may have been the scholastic advantages of these great men, I have no material from which to inform myself correctly or I would give it [to] my readers. I have seen a book which was written by Mr. Douglass, called "My bondage and my freedom."[3] The crudity of his writings however is plain evidence of his never having been schooled, or at least not so by routine. I could say much, in justice to the literary attainments, untiring labors, oppositions and privations through which these men—together with many others of our race—have passed, to bring our less informed brethren from under that system of oppression which had nearly destroyed the government of these United States; but as I can only give a sketch in brief of my own life, I may be pardoned for waving those considerations.

The following is through the request of many friends.

A brief sketch of the life of Geo. Teamoh, by himself.

I was born in the city of Norfolk, Va. A.D. 1818. When very young,—possibly not over ten years of age—I was brought to this city—Portsmouth, Va. my owners having made residence here. After remaining in the family until I had arrived at the age of twelve or thirteen years, I was hired to Capt. Jno. Thompson who at the time, and until his death, resided in this city. This gentleman, of whom I shall necessarily have much to say, was, besides being a brick maker, an established contractor in brick masonry; and; perhaps, none in his day had a larger patronage in that particular calling. Mr. Thompson was considerably of the aristocratic order of the community, and, if I am not mistaken, both he and his wife belonged to the presbyterian church, certainly she did. He was owner of a number of slaves, and a tract of land about three miles North westerly of the city, known as the "glebe plantations," in Norfolk county.[4] Here, for the first time I was put to test the lash and loneliness of plantation labor. Not knowing the road leading to the farm, I was put in a mule cart with the understanding that "jack" would put me safely through, provided I gave up the reins. He performed his part well, only stopping at old Barrett's on Barrett's road, where his former, or regular driver used to halt for liquor.

Arriving at the main gate, I got down and opened it, when Jack passed orderly through and stood until I again mounted. In a very few moments we appeared before the barn, in which the field hands were employed at the swingle-knife, threshing out wheat—something I had never, until that, to me sad hour seen performed.

Very soon, the overseer, whom I shall shortly describe, came up to the cart and addressed me in the following style. "Whose nigger is you, and what did you come arter?"—In reply, I told him I was sent out there by order of Capt. Thompson to work on the farm. This seemed to please him very much; so much so that he sung out to the barn hands "Stop that thrashing, here is a new nigger,—a city nigger."

When this haggard and torn agricultural committee had surrounded the cart, I instantly alighted, when Silverthorn—the overseer—called by the slaves Silverthorn, crept around me like a cat in a strange garret, and used the following words, "My lord; he is got on tights—where you gwine,—to a ball?"[5] And after pronouncing me to be one of the "spiled" niggers" he ordered the hands return to the barn, stating that he would "tend to my case"; and he did that very thing. Taking my pack from the cart, I followed him until he got to the quarters intended for the farm hands. Here, he invited me in.

These quarters were not very inviting to one fresh from parlor service and the nursery, where I had been up to the time when I was hired to Thompson. The overseer, however, tried, after showing me around to impress me with the belief that I had done well in reaching that plantation, as none others within many miles of the place afforded such ample and comfortable accommodations. These quarters were not dissimilar to others in many parts of the State. It was in the month of February when I went there, that being one of those months when nothing could be done at laying, or making brick—for I was hired for what was then termed a "brick yard, or building boy" which will be shown in another place. But "to quarters." Here there was nothing so promising as to make my "winter of discontent" bear semblance to "glorious summer"—nothing at all. Finding that the burden of the slaves' hyemal song was nothing but one continuous note of sorrow, I felt,—but too sadly—to have been doomed alas; to tread in the paths of my fathers, a life of misery and unrequited toil. It being about night fall, I was put to sweeping out the quarters against the hands got in. While thus engaged I made a hasty survey of my new home which soon revealed the fact that it was in very bad condition, being rent and torn all around, with perforated roof. Just at that moment, the waiter girl brought, and threw down at my feet about 25, or 30 ears of corn, a small junk of meat (fat pork) and a dozen herrings. On asking her who, and what was that for, she replied "it is your week's larrence" The girl was quite dark and of a very pleasant, amusing and Topsy-like disposition, and finding her easy of approach, I asked her where was the bed I should sleep on? Pointing at the smoky joists, and showing me a number of old boards which had been used for stable flooring, said she "dems um". These boards were about five feet long, ten inches wide, and one inch of thickness—nothing to give elevation to the head, but simply a rough board, seasoned with the dirty stench of the stable upon it. Susan—for that was her name—seemed to have manifested a considerable liking for me above any other lads that had been there, so much so that Silverthorn had to keep an eye to his table. She was not at all prepossing in appearance, but certainly a virtuous girl, and like many others of her set possessed those social qualities which always distinguish between the low, vulgar and immoral.[6] Having at once acquainted herself with my case, she would allow no opportunity to pass when she could do me a service. Very young herself, she considered me a youthful capture. She asked me in her style if I had sufficient bed clothing? I answered no, not if I have to sleep in that place. Said she, "Is got a horse blanket you may have ef you don't let Silly know it." I, I shall not let him, or any one else in to any matter of confidence that passes between you and me was my reply. This seems to have increased her admiration of me, and off she went to the great house.

I had been ordered by "Silly" to remain in the quarters until the hands got in, who had been in the forest chopping wood, as also those at threshing.

When the sun was about one hour behind the western hills, the over burdened taskmen came in, resting their axes wedges &c. behind the door. Some of these brought with them heavy burthens of knotted light wood which were thrown in a chimney space whose width was about ten feet with hearth of the naked ground. Other wood was afterward thrown on all of which made a very delightful fire, only that two thirds of the smoke filled the quarters, while the other found its way through the proper channel.

In whatever circumstances of life the slave may have been placed, joys and griefs have not been inseparable to his condition. Yet, far down into his soul the long night of continuous sorrow like the deep diapason of old ocean's solemn beat surges the lashing waves of despair. Such was the case with these my fellow bondsmen. After spending some time at grinding their corn from a mill turning out about one quart to the hour, when driven by a strong arm, they sing and dance a while and then lie down to rest. I took my station at the inner corner of the spacious fire place, but was soon smoked out, when a boy, more used to that kind of "comfort" succeded me. The hour was growing late, big men began to snore, and the youths were locked in the slumbers of rest. Their feet forming an uneven, but compact semicircle around the hearth, I was unable to wedge myself in so as to catch a little warmth from the fire, which, after some time began to burn very low.

Having failed to get my "bed" in, which consisted of the board as described, I was left to calculate on the next best chance, which was very happily conceived by running a straight line directly through the half circle and parallel with the chimney back; and notwithstanding "the greatest good to the greatest number," I thought they had the same "right" to warm through me as I had to do the same through them. It was intensely dark without & cold withall. While pondering over the matter I sallied toward the door opposite the great house, and who, to my surprise should I see but devoted Susan who had been standing there about ten minutes, trying to reach me in an earnest, but subdued whisper. She was in her night clothes, and had thrown about her an old tattered bed quilt. I had very strange thoughts about the other world until I had recognized her. Throwing the old horse blanket at me, said she "here take dat" and off she shot toward the great house.

Having placed my plank on the line discribed, I supposed there would be but little use for the loaned blanket; so I sat it aside for the time being, or until I had tested my new contrivance.

The "bed" being stationed, I laid down upon it with the hope of rest-ing—& warming if not enjoying a little sleep before day-break, at which time our "bed chamber" had to be relieved. But my philosophy would not work, as on several occasions I was kicked from my board into the fire, of which, fortunately for me there was but a small portion remaining. They pushed their feet toward the fire just in proportion as that element dimin-ished, and I arose from that spot covered with ashes and vexed beyond en-durance. It was now past midnight, and what to get as a means of protection from the biting cold until day-break I could not divine. However, Susan's blanket was now in time and served well as I rolled myself in it after get-ting as near the hearth as possible, and thus I spent my first night of planta-tion life.

As I promised to give my readers a discription of Silverthorn, I know of no better place, or time for the insertion than just here, and now.

It is said that the nigher man assimilates to the beast in external appear-ances, just in that degree does he partake of their nature. And this is a fact put beyond question by scientific investigations conducted by professional ethologists, phrenologists and others. In thinking now of Silverthorn and making, what seems to me the necessary comparison between him and a well known quadruped, I am forced to the conclusion that these professors were right; and this without any further teaching than that of visiting the menagerie, where, from the cooing dove to the stately lion I have observed certain traits of character, externally and internally in those animals which more than confirms me in this belief. The hyena, or tager-wolf, bears many, very many strong marks as depicted in the physiognomy of man's make up. But I hope my readers will not suppose for a moment that it is from any motive of malice or spite I have selected this carnivorous and fe-rocious animal as a proper type with which to judge of man's propensities &c. I only follow in the channel made by professional skill. Old Uncle Joshua,[7] who was one of Thompson's slaves on the plantation, was very fre-quently heard to say, what we all knew, that "when old Silly laughs very lustily, holding his head downward, grating his teeth and refusing to see the light, you may look out for a storm." With my limited knowledge of human nature, even, as also with that of the above quadruped, and my ac-quaintance with S.'s disposition, this, to me, at least, was a very significant expression, coming as it did from a pious old gentleman who had known Mr. S. for many long years. The above is my discription of the man, mul-tum in parvo [in brief]. He was a hard task-master, always holding in mental reservation that deep hatred toward the slave, which he supposed he was employed to cherish, and which, but too often, for Capt. Thompson's endurance, he had manifested toward the plantation hands, as on several occasions I have known him to be checkmated by Mr. Thompson while administering the lash to the slaves. On this plantation and the brick yard—the latter situated near the city—I served two years. However cruel Silverthorn may have been previous to, or during my stay on the farm, from some cause I managed to escape those terrible punishments which, on so many occasions I had seen inflicted on others. Nor do I make this statement to show that obedience is the common heritage of the African race more than others, for where the lash has been the rule and mercy the exception, judgment must be at fault in deciding this question affirmatively. That we have, during the last 250 years drawn the very milk of submission may be traced even, to many of the most enlightened of our times. I do not read books, but if any credit may be attached to recognized scientific historians who lecture us from the rostrum, the denial may be given to the assertion that any race was ever pre-ordained to a state of vassilage. Feeling as I do that my ancestors were forced to this depth of degradation by the low cunning of a race having in every respect superior advantages I could not, with my apprehensions of Deity as the Author of man's existance, charge Him with any such folly or unfairness. And I regard it as a reflection on heavenly justice to make such shameful misrepresentations of God's revelations to man, as those characterizing the clergy of my native section, and I may say throughout the United States of America.

But all this has passed into history,—and there is nothing new. Time—the great developer of all things,—will, in the future, roll up to the surface, in fixed view to the unwilling gaze of falsely inspired man, wringing from him the reluctant recognition that Jehovah, [demanded] equal justice shewed to all.

Being obliged to quote from memory all the material facts connected with my narrations, my readers will allow me some margin in recalling much that may have been forgotten in the out set, as well as a great deal which I may yet over look and which can not be systematized in the absence of defective memory or any real data.

Proof of the facts to which I have alluded, and all that may follow, must be left with those whose lives have run parallel with my own in this city and vicinity.

For the sake of brevity I shall be under the necessity of omitting a considerable portion of my experience in junior years, contenting the reader—if may be—with a brief sketch of such reminiscences aided by retrospection, as I may be able to gather. And these seem to cluster around me in one confused mass, so much so, that memory shiftings seems to find no attractive magnet save it is one round life of fruitless toil.

My mother—whom I well remember—bore the common name "Winnie." She died when I was quite small. My father, who was not her husband by the usages of custom died some time after.[8] She was the mother of three or four children, whether all by the same man, I am not prepared to say; but what I do know is, she was a kind, and an affectionate Mother, one true to her offspring. She was raised with my old Mistress to whom we both belonged; and of whom I take the liberty to say, I do not believe that, the ligh of God's son ever looked upon a more generous, virtuous and fair minded christian lady than Mistress Jane Thomas, who came of the Needham family on Back-river near Hampton Virginia.[9] After the death of her first husband—Mr. Jordan Winslow, she was then married to Mr. Josiah Thomas, by both of whom she had four or five children, each.[10] Those by the first, are all dead but one, & those by her second husband are all living, to this July 1871. These children, whose nurse I was, (I mean those by her last husband, Mr. Josiah Thomas, who is yet living) seem to, and indeed do bear, both morally and religiously, the true impress, or strongly partake of all the characteristics known to their loving parents; for the father of these latter, has been, since a young man, like his deceased lady, a communicant of the Methodist Episcopal Church. In infancy I drew from her breast; at the same stage of life, her first children, nestled in my mother's arms, pressed their tiny fingers to her breasts, and drew therefrom that milk, whose transmission becomes a part of our being. This must be so, or else ethnology is at fault.

I shall refer to a few prominent acts of her life which throws her character out in bold relief, showing at once that those rare virtues which she possessed, inhered in infancy, grew with her growth and strengthened with her strength.

Though having a nice family residence on Bogg's Point, Norfolk, with five, or six head of slves—mostly children—at the death of her first husband, she was far from being relieved from that state of dependence with which poverty's willing grasp but too frequently drives us to the walls of despair. Her connections were rich,—some at least,—her sister and nephew. But she did not belong to their chirch, and consequently found but little favor with them, more especially after her second marriage. "Slow rises merit by poverty depressed." O that I could for ever obliterate from memory her silent sobbings as they fell upon my youthful ears. On being asked by her sister "why she did not sell some of her little negroes?" she replied, with all the modesty of a saint, that "such a thing she had never done, and so help me God I never shall! She kept her word until she fell into the arms of Him unto Whom it was given.

And the cases are numerous to which I might refer, all bearing the strongest testimony to her christian qualities, and one more of which I can not refrain from calling attention to. Many years before her death, and while her children were yet young, an old lady who was near being sold, ran off from her owners, and a reward was offered for her apprehension. In dead of night she came to my old mistress to befriend her by some means. The former had no money, and she could not therefore buy the old lady "running"—as that was the object—but told her to go up stairs and accommodate herself to the garret, and that all that could be done would be done by her family to make her comfortable, whether her stay be long or short. Be it ever said, to the honor of that good lady, and her entire family—large and small, white as well as colored—that she "harbored and gave comfort to" this hunted down fugitive for the space of fifteen months. Free persons (col) when pressed by persecution and want, she has proven to them the "friend that" was "ever nigh." She was known by the name of "good old Miss Jane" In 1832, when persecutions thick and fast, fell upon the colored inhabitants, or slaves of this state, many of whom were said to be Nathaniel Turner's associates, who was supposed to be the ring-leader, and when ministers of the gospel had affirmed the belief, that there was not a negro child in the state over eight years of age but knew in advance—from instinct I suppse—that all who were slaves were to "rise" on that notable day and assert their right to freedom by slashing their way through human flesh. She rose to a dignity and humanity which would put to blush many of the pretentions of present day patriotism, for on being interrogated by the family physician on the subject, she was fair to state, that, "while in Southam[p]ton County, Virginia, a few poor ignorant colored people, inspired by a superstitious leader, one whose nocturnal visits were among grave yards and holding dark communion with familiar spirits, could, possibly be persuaded to believe anything that looked as though it ought to be so, encouraged by religious incentives, she was far from believing that the colored people in Portsmouth and vicinity knew anything at all about what had transpired in the section referred to, nor did she credit the story that such as were here, whether young or old, had meditated any violence upon this community, or any individual within its confines."[11] I do not pretend to know her pedigree beyond what has been stated; but if she was not an offspring of Plymouth Rock, she was, to say the least, firmly planted on the "Rock of Ages." No historic mention having been made of this great woman, as she moved in humble life, and while oppressed by the tidal wave of proscription, I have dared to dedicate these few lines to her memory, only regretting my inability to do so in a more perfect style.

How I learned to read and write.

Perhaps one of the greatest puzzles I have ever had to master in looking back upon a life of fifty two years, is, how I learned to read, write and cypher. It might be said that under kind owners my "freedom" was, or must have been far superior to that of other slaves. In this particular instance however, it was not so by any means. The same law which forbade educating the slave, equally applied to all who were in that condition; and the rigidity with which this most unchristian measure was enforced, left no doubt as to what must have been the certain fate of those—Master or Slave, rich or poor—who violated it.[12] More given to meditation, deep and serious thought than most of the colored youth of my day, I early saw the sad and lamentable condition in which a whole race of mankind had been placed by a power then beyond the reach of their control (slave power). Not being able to weigh this matter intelligently, I took every opportunity to visit churches, political gatherings, theatres &c. with the hope that something might "leak out" or some revelation made as to the existance of an institution which had already been condemned by the moral sentiment of the world. The further however I pushed investigation into this matter, the more I witnessed, or the more evident it became to my mind that no slave was to take share in any literal instruction; or in other words all who bore in any degree marks of having descended from the African race were not to be taught, or allowed to read God's holy word. One of the most striking as well as the most shameful instances of its injustice occurred to a young girl who was seeking to learn the Episcopalian form of worship.—Though a slave, she was clairly white, her mother, in all her physiognomic developments corresponding to the blue eyed Saxon.—Her father was a white man. From a knowledge of her mother's servile condition, this girl was known to be "tinged", as that is the word in general use when speaking of the degrees of admixtures. Such a one offered to take the holy Sacrament at a church, which it is only necessary to say is in this place. Information of the fact was at once conveyed to the Officiating Priest, when this humble Christian girl was refused the sacred rite. But to return. As stated I was hired to Thompson for brick-yard and building purposes. The memorable summer of 1832 found me quite a raw boy, 14 years of age at which time I entered the brick-yard, and such were the representations made to me of its character, that I despaired of ever rising above the level of those intemperate and wicked youths who followed the same occupation. Having early learned that there was a God, One who was the Author of all things that could be seen by mortal eye, as well as the invisible, and that His aid, and assistance would be given to any one, whether a nation or an individual on condition of obedience to His laws, I lost but little time in finding out the relationship which man bore to his Maker. After many long years of investigating the subject, mean time rendering such obedience as I thought to be in consonance with the Old Book and the gospels, I came to the conclusion, that youthful petitions were answerable at the throne of heaven, and that whosoever walketh uprightly, the same is accepted of God. At this period, I did not know one of the twenty six letters which make up the English alphabet. Yet, such the confidence I had in the Supreme Being, I considered nothing too difficult for His wisdom to Master. And, not withstanding the persecutions of 1832, when colored people of this State were slaughtered as sheep for the shambles, had brought me into serious doubt as to the existance of an omnipresent, as well as an all creating Being, still with a lingering hope mingled with despair, and a mind, floating as it were into empty space, I hoped on, in the midst of hopelessness. It was while passing to and from the brick-yards I had often heard from white children, the alphabet in song; and so frequently had it fallen on my ear that retention proved no task; yet to look at these on paper, they appeared to me as so many Chinese hieroglyphics. Cutting these letters, one after another, from a card on which they had been printed, I tasked myself to commit one to memory every night, so as to make the whole perfectly familia[r] with me on distribution, which I accomplished a few days within one month, getting large and small letters, of Roman, Italic and Script. That is, I got one each of the whole six different forms of letters, in the time designated. How did I know they were mastered? This was done in a manner which is very difficult to explain here: Suffice it to say however, to be brief, that I suspended a cardboard in my quarters with all the alphabets written, or printed on it.—Struck the key note of "A" and with the air, following the line, found I was all right so far as singing was concerned. This not working as well as I had anticipated, being in full possession of the air, I next arranged the letters which I had cut as stated, on what musicians term a staff, and on this staff I pasted, in every conceivable form of variation and close, the twenty six characters which make up the English language. The very same rule I applied to numerals also. As a matter of recreation, and being remarkably fond of music, more espicially the guitar,—on whose richly softened shell I have often played my alpha beta,—I made that instrument accompany each letter while I sang them. Having early discovered, that no one had any particular objection to a slave learning written music, provided he confined himself within given limits, I was, by such means, amply protected from suspician of learning my letters. Truly, we have been often arrested, and frequently striped, on being assembled over five in number, for the purpose of instruction in sacred music; but this was no bar to the discouragement of musical talent with those who belonged to the more wealthy classes, be the number of learners small or great, the only conditions being in such cases, that they were to be on their ow[n]er's premises, and at no time to be found with educational apparatus, not even a primer; yet in many cabins have I seen some of the latest editions of sacred music, and piles of other professional works, such as Blackstone, Jeffreys, Shakspeare, Milton, John Knox and others, all lying on smoked shelves and covered with grease from rude candlesticks, appearing as though the inmates had learned their contents and thrown them aside.[13] In most cases, however, these books were the refuse of their Master's gilded libraries, donated as holiday and task presents, which together with all letters, or other matter however private were subject at any time to examination by the Master, or his appointee. But to return.

I could spell (orally) long before I had mastered the alphabet. This was obtained also, from a frequency of hearing the children go over their lessons, but not by the singing process. Strict attention to the language used by public speakers, had enabled me to pronounce some of the most difficult words known to our tongue. Such words as "constitutionality", "individuality" incomprehensibility &c. &c., were among the first of polysylables I had learned (orally) some two, or three years before I knew the alphabet. This may appear strange to those who have been taught by routine but not more strange than true.

After learning the alphabet, I next turned to the vowels, or elementary sounds, as from observation I found that their key would greatly facilitate the task in hand. I was however, not much of a proficient in that direction, and it was not until I had advanced in reading and spelling sufficient to comprehend the rule laid down for their government did I obtain any reliable knowledge of them.—It was an up hill work. However far from consiseness, simplicity and clearness being the objects then in view, as well as being thorough in what I was learning, I purchased what was called a "New York Primer"; and another primary work styled "grammar made simple", neither of which however rendered me any service. It was, I think in 1829, or 1830, while sporting with youth on high Street near old Mr. Nicholson's stationery[14] I chanced to pick up from the ground the remains of Walker's Critical Pronouncing Dictionary, which, on examination I found to contain very many wards with which I had previously made myself familiar, excepting their definitions.[15] In that lexicon however, these, as well as the pure sound of each word, were simplified in a manner which touched, and gave spirit to my loftiest aspirations in literature. I very soon bought me a new one. And it is with great pleasure, mingled with oceans of trouble and sorrow attendant on my career, do I throw back in the distant past, and thank heaven that such an ingenious writer ever lived to discover a scheme, the principle of which comes within reach of the humblest, and so well adapted to English pronounciation. And yet how small the effort when compared with the Herculean labors of the Websters and the Worcesters.[16] I am more indebeted to Walker, so far as authors are concerned than to any other standard writer.

My reader will have perceived ere this that my method of learning, while there may be nothing in it very original, must be commended where, and when nothing better could be had. Those who have lived in obscurity, such as our writers of antiquity whose chances to improve a single talent by way of mental, or educational improvement were poor to those of mine, could understandingly appreciate the amount of labor necessary to see their star in the ascendant. In deed, there are those, perhaps, now living who have had a similar experience. It has been very wisely stated that "colleges does not always make men".—It is no mystery however, from freshman to sophomore, allowing, even, that they may have had as Teachers the most talented and purest culture of the country. After his creation, man makes, or unmakes himself. From youth, I have grown gray over the mid-night torch, at trying to "learn how to learn"—have given more time possibly to erroneous study, or that which added nothing to the object sought—than many a collegian has devoted to his entire course. To narrate all the various means employed as auxiliaries to my literary improvement would not only render the reader impatient, but incredulity would supersede whatever of forbearace might remain.

Never being very talkative while young—nor even conversational since grown up—soon after I had familiarized myself with spelling, I formed a resolution not to speak a single word at any time, if possible, unless I could spell the same, which I found to be an important lever in my orthographic exercises. Nothing that bore letters on it of any considerable size, escaped my critical examination. Having known the parties names, I have learned much from sign-boards, handbills, posters, &c. &c. I have always been a dear admirer of Shakesperian plays, only when, by inexperienced actors the language has not been over strained, nor raised to its full volume.—Of course, I was not to be judge, but nature teaches some things, and I had a little margin for the imperfect. Since man-hood, however that admiration has greatly increased, and I now regard the Theatre—with the exception of its vanities—as being one of the greatest educators of the nineteenth century. Next to this, comes the Established Church of England—at least so far as I have been benefitted by them. Following the Episcopal form of worship, one who cannot read learns, verbatim,—even in spite of himself—all that is laid down in the Book of Common Prayer, and can recite—after some years attention—any passages it may contain. If all other denominations could, or would adopt a system of religion similarly adapted to the growth of intelligence and education as well as spirituality, our Superintendent of Public Instruction would, in the next decade furnish us with a more favorable report as to the education—at least—of adult age; for where one's religion is thus systematised, and he has to read, or be governed by what is written for its enjoyment, if he is devoted to his church, more especially, the presumption is, or ought to be, that he would become a proficient in intellectual worth of some sort. Nothing has ever surprised me more, perhaps, than when making a casual visit, a few years ago to an old lady's residence who had known me from child-hood.—She was of the Romish persuasion. Our subject turned on church matters. She took from the mantle her book and "beeds"; and although having no knowledge of letters, by some means she recited the latin mass; and, after handing me the volume, anglicized that portion of the service with an aptitude which would do credit to professional translators, showing that by the aid of reading, she might have excelled in scholar-ship. I have now in my possession a journal of events which I recorded as they transpired in this City and Vicinity in 1839.[17] In that whole year, I carried to record every hour of sun-shine, rain, cloud and thunder storm; marriages, births and deaths; distinguished visitors; ministers of the Gospel, where they hailed from; and, following them up, what their first and second lessons, hymns and what their texts. This portion of the journal, takes note, more particularly of the Methodist denomination in this city—Portsmouth. Indeed I put every thing that ear could hear eye could see, or hand might reach, under contribution to serve my ends. In those days when cannon loud proclaimed its notes of triumphant Vanbure[n]ism,[18] though often driven from political meetings, I would as often shoulder my broom or be seen, bearing a pitcher of water some where in among the crowd near the stand, as their "most humble servant"—"at large." On going to Norfolk to attend one of these meetings, I neglected to take with me a "pass". A very fine speech had been delivered from the varanda of French's hotel by one Mr. Carrington.[19] His first words were, "auspicious omens greet."—I was five years in trying to find out what he meant by the enclosed sentence. But I found out. On returning from the meeting, I was arrested by Capehart—a noted night watch & cunstable in that city.[20] He asked for my "pass"—[I] told him I lost it; "then" said he, "you must go to jail." In reply, I said, "it was a very poor place for one to stay who was afflicted with small-pox like myself." He had nothing else to say in return, but, as though struck with a new idea, he instantly sidled to an opposite corner, bellowing to the top of his voice "stop that nigger, hes got the small-pox." A party within hearing responded, "go to h- -l and take him with you". I had no further trouble—went down to the foot boat, and found my way home. But for this "small" dodge, on the next morning I should have "hugged the widow" very severely; such being the language employed in whipping-post parlance.—But to go back a little.—I have said the primer rendered me no service. Before leaving it, however, to fare its day I would state this: Capt. Jno. Thompson, to whom I have formally alluded, among others, owned a capital brick-mason This man was very cruel toward every boy which his old Master put with him as brick-bearer (hod-boy) The old gentleman, at times, would drink very freely; so much so as to often loose his momentum. When carrying brick for him while building what is termed a stack-chimney, he chanced to see my primer as it accidently fell from my bosom while dumping brick from the board. He at once inquired of me how came I by it, at the same time ordering me to leave it at home, and under no considerations must I ever be seen with it about my person. I told him I meant no harm beyond that of learning my a-b-c s, and having neither mother or father, I was trying to be a good boy and learn some sense; and further besought him not to prevent me from doing so. But this appeal from his decision only served to damage my prospects by increasing his vigilance, as he questioned me on several occasions after, as to the book and my disposition of it. I gave up the primer, or the study of it during the space of three years from that time. Pending this period I was again hired to one Wm. Collins, as brick and mortar bearer. Mr. C. was a small contractor, at that time in brick masonry, though grown quite popular since as an architect.[21] Unlike Thompson, he was careful of those he hired, having regard for their individual comfort. Brick-moulders, such as T. were very severe in their dealings with hired boys, as I purpose on showing in another place.

I again turn to our "stack-chimney" man, "uncle" Peter, for that was his name.[22] During the lapse of ten, or twelve years, uncle P. had so indulged in his potations, or intemperate habits, as to render it necessary that T. should confine him within certain restricted limits, which was not done until liquor had reduced the old man to a mere skeleton. T.'s patience having been exhausted, he sent him to Fortress Monroe, under a hiring agent there, whose title was Capt. Laughton, the very mention of whose name has brought terror and alarm to the "home" of many of Virginia's bondsmen; aye, upon the sand banks where they have been thrown near that guilty garrison, in God's sunlight, bleaches, in all their torturous deformity the bones of many of our loving fathers.[23] Hither the old sire was sent, as stated. By this time I was of age—21—and had learned a branch of mechanics known as (cauking-ship work) He had been there about ten months when I took a "job" of caulking at the same place on one of the government flats. After finishing a day's work I retired to my quarters within the garrison, and just before tattoo, or drum beat, when all should be in their quarters, the old hero of the trowel entered the door. On first sight I failed to recognize him, such being his haggard and tatter-ragged appearance. On knowing who it was however, I was quite driven to tears. He asked me "if I could do anything for him?" "What shall it be" said I. The request was that I would write to his old Master in regard to his (Peter's) then present condition. After causing him to be seated on a trunnion—as within these casemates, pieces of experimented cannon which were freely laying around had to serve as seats—I attentively listened to all he had to say. In common with other laborers, he had been sent to the "Rip-Raps" to help on the works of that mud stationed Monitor.[24] Here the inexorable Lau[g]hton with his hostile cue dangling behind seems to have been in the extacies of delight when torturing these unfortunates.—Like the Devil in brim-stone glory— "when human victims feed the flames, then shines my altars brightest." After truckling massive blocks of stone, as necessary labor on this sea girt Fortification which is in mid ocean between the Fortress and Sewell's Point, being three miles from the former—he would turn to rest him from his day of toil.[25] "Sure bind sure find" is an old adage. Here where the slave in ceaseless labor has worne bright his chains; here, where the deep diapason of a mighty surging sea as it parts to sweep down its course; here was the granite bed of this poor old man.

Quite forgetting and forgiving those discouraging words addressed to me by him concerning the "primer" I at once went to work and wrote his Master the following crude letter.

"Mistur capn john Tomson
i sete miself to write you these fu lines your old man peter is in a grate deegre of sufring he aint got no shoos and no close nor hat and the wether is very inclemence and cold and rany and he ses you and him was boys togethur he ses ef yu wil giv him sum close and things and take him home agin he wil do bettur and i speke to you as a whit man and i beleve he is al rite now excuse my pure spelin for i am a stone mason here by the day to capn john tomson of the city of portsmouth the brick laer respcful yors &c
A Mason"

However amusing such a communication may have been in Thompson's estimation, it claims the merit of having caused the old man Peter, within one week after it was writtten, to receive from his master all that was necessary to clad, and shod him for that winter, beside being recalled to his home at Portsmouth in early spring.

The deep moral to be learned from this sad experience is, that every safe gard and protection should be thrown around aspiring youth, and that no one should be guilty of arresting its onward march to the temple of intelligence. When forbidding my use of the "primer" he was not aware of the great injustice he was doing himself, for had he have known, or foreseen his future troubles as above stated, the presumption is that he would have assisted rather than retarded my progress. But the old gentleman has gone to his long home, and over his grave I drop the sympathetic tear and leave him to rest.

Having served Collins two years, I was hired to first one and then another of our citizens for various purposes. Indeed, while I am now cogitating in retracing the past, I regret that I cannot do myself that justice which a proper regard for the subject requires. Much that is needed therefore to make this volume the history of one's self must be omitted from causes which naturally suggest themselves to any impartial reader. As in primary study, my peculiar style was not to follow in the traces of others, so now I take indirection to find direction out.—In a word, I have to "progress backwards."

Under the circumstances, and to be relieved from writing lengthy articles under their several heads, I shall give a summary in brief of many sketches which should be dwelt upon some-what, as in this day when everything seems (to me) to be accomplished by lightning speed, it appears to be at war with what God intended man to be, to see one with the intellectual wealth of ages piled upon him, sitting down to write a book in the old ordinary style of English. If such men as Benj. Franklin had lived till this day, they would telegraph you—no dout—without the wires, and in less time at that.

I have but few dates to give. My recollection carries me back to the time when a monument was erected on Briggs Point, Norfolk, to the memory of a distinguished Roman Catholic by the name of Riley.[26] Also, I well remember when nearly, if not all the buildings on the Northern side of Fenchurch Street in said city, were destroyed by fire. Such a conflagration, in the same locality, I am informed had never occurred before, certainly not since. I am reminded of the monument from its association with the pompous display in funeral, over the remains of Riley while being interred. This monument (which time has demolished) was the first gothic architecture I had ever seen. About that period, a colored Sabbath School was taught in the same neighborhood by Isaac Fuller, a well known free man.[27] This I remember with great accuracy as I have often cried while standing in my linen, because, from my condition as a slave I could not be admitted to the School. The launching of the Del[aware] Seventy Four gun ship from the Norfolk Navy Yard is among those reminiscences unaccounted for from date.[28] When hired in the domestic service of one Saml. Bingham who resided in Gosport, I have, as a reminder the commencement of the Norfolk Dry Dock, this gentleman being a machinist and employed by the U.S. Government having taken me as assistant fireman for the first engine that ever lifted water from that Dock by steam power.[29] An incident. Not understanding the theory of this mechanical movement, one morning about four oclock—for we had to raise steam very early in order to relieve the Dock of water that the hands might go to work—when I had put on the necessary supply of water and got on a good head of steam, and kept it at the usual guage. Having so often noticed the Engineer and his Assistant while starting and stopping the concern, it some how worked in my brain that I could do the same thing. With this notion I proceeded in the regular way—went to the fly-wheel—which was about twenty feet in diameter, and put the old "scrub" on a "hair." I then ascended the platform in front of the starting bars which latter was similar to two pump brakes. Every thing now being in readiness, I seized the levers, pump-handle fashion. The cylinder being a perpendicular, with beam of the old sea-horse style, by the time I had lifted the supply valve, down fell the piston rod with burst of thunder carrying away, or demolishing the cylinder cap, and beside over flowing the boiler and fire room by a cistern cock which in my eagerness to have some "fun" I had neglected to shut off, disarranged, and materially injured the whole machinery. I had never seen things on this wise before. While in this dreadful plight I used, of course, every exertion to extricate myself, but all in vain. I pumped and she stuck and stewed out music like a ten horse power calliope. More scared and tired than vexed, I remained silent for a moment when an awful lumbering was heard in the pump room, one of the main pump rods with box attached—having slipped its key and fallen to the lower box. It was now nearing sun-rise, and as I could see no one at the time to whom I might refer my case excepting one of the Dock watch men, I approached him in the following manner. "Mr. Manning, do you know anything about steam engines?"[30]—"No was his reply, I know nothing about them." "What's the matter, I heard something sound like a cannon just now, is the boiler busted?" continued he. I went on to tell him that "in getting up steam the engine ran away" &c. In reply, he said "that was very bad, and that I ought to go and look after her." I returned, tormented with all the horrors of a culprit awaiting the tilt of his scaffold. The second Engineer, Thos. Symington, by name, whose severe temper and haughty ambition reached its climax by murdering a colored man at one time, in the same Dock, was the first one to make his appearance in the Engine & fire rooms as witness of the "ruin I had rought."[31] S. was by no means to be numbered with the sociable and agreeable, but on the contrary he possessed one of the most boisterous and hateful dispositions that could possibly characterize any fallen creature. His external make up was of an unfortunate mould though a true index to his morals. He was very large in stature, clumsily built, rough featured, red hair and face, feet a slue, and moved with head erect and a quick limp, as though afflicted in one limb. In fact he was the very embodiment of cruil revenge and all its accompanyments. This man, who was the most obnoxious of humanity, though filling only a secondary position (for he was a boiler maker) had, for a long while been watching his chances to bring me into trouble of some sort. He had now presented him the fairest opportunity to slake his thirst for the lash and bask in the blood of his victim. Before he was aware of what had happened to the engine, only looking at the flooded condition of the fire room, he at once, and without asking any questions, began to put up his "prayers." He looked and swore double,—looked again and swore thribble, and then he turned and looked, when english billingsgate failed him. He said I had "ruined the U.S. government, and the Dry-Dock in particular," and that no one could, or ought to live who had been so neglectful of their duty and that I should look about myself with serious reflections, as he would surely have to discharge his duty.

Prepa[rations?] for death

Knowing that such was his threats concerning the damage done in the fire room, how, thought I must it be when he sees the destruction done the machinery? I knew well too, that he had, on several occasions, previously, whipped me unmercifully for the merest fault, such as being late at work, not making steam within the same time out of wet sappy wood as of dry heart &c. &c. After thus admonishing me, he went up on the platform, and looking at the demolished cylinder cap, he commenced with a long drawn "O-yes! O-yes!—I see! ah ah ah ah!—every thing is gone to h--l." Here he renewed his vocabulary of swearing and "rose to a sublimer height" in filling the air with imprecations loud and blasting. Then, turning to the pump-room, one might have thought that pandemonium had lost all its fury in the man. While he was thus going the rounds like a raving maniac, I thought it high time that I should be doing something to meet the emergency. The gates being guarded by watchmen heavily armed, to escape by flight was entirely out of the question, as this was the only accep[t]able avenue to which I could look for escape. As seen, Symington had already announced his intentions of punishing me when speaking of a "discharge of his duty."

On one of the upper tool shelves, for a long while had been lying an old flint-lock brass pistol, (army size) left there, for some purpose, by one of the watchmen. I examined it, found it loaded and primed.—Secreted myself near the cock turning water from the boiler, and with a wrench renewed the friction edge of the pistol flint. I was then prepared as I thought with concealed weapon to dispatch Symington at once, and then destry myself by drowning. Such a fatality I had meditated on long before my last trouble arose. It was now getting late, and on returning from behid the boiler I found in the fire room Mr. Jaellett, the regular fireman.[32] J. was a good man, and in every way opposed to Symington's over-bearing austerity. His first words to me were, "well George, we are in bad luck boy" "Whats the matter, did the old thing get away with you?" I told him "it did." "Well" said he "I met Tom just now—he was in great haste going toward the gate, and swearing vengeance on all hands of us, but me in particular. He says I am to be reported and then discharged". I asked him "for what purpose?" "absence from duty" was the reply. By this time Symington had met Bingham,—chief Engineer,—coming on duty. S. who never dared to rule in wrath when B. was present, here received a palpable check to the bloody carnival which he had thought to hold. B. was also a swearing man, but not "gifted" like S.—I believe all engineers (machinists) swear some; if they do not, they ought—not. The above affair was one which would have vex[ed] the patience of an anchorite. S. who had returned with B. was now in deep and earnest conversation with the latter, while standing in the pump-room, during which time, Jaellett and myself were shovelling and baling water from the fire room at a tremendious rate. J, though a good old gentleman, was not as sober that morning as I had known him to be at other times; hence while throwing water with the shovel, his foot slipped and down he fell, receiving quite a warm bath, which also brought the "best" of his swearing out. B. had retired to his office which was on the same floor with the pump-room, while S. was yet in the latter. B. gives a succession of fierce raps on the floor; these were answerable, either by J. or myself, but J. being "water logged," I hurried up stairs and went to the office door. On confronting B. said he "where is J?" "down in the fire-room sir" said I. "Tell him to come here, and you get out of this office, and go to h--l as quick as you can." Said I "Yes sir." I was not very far from it either, because for me to be near S. was to be not very far from that place, as he seemed to live in its atmosphere. J. did not go to the office, for the reason that him and S. were having a "brilliant" time at swearing.

You will now find me resting on my shovel while B. [,] S. and J. are in conference in the wheel house, or pump room, and from all I could learn, and what was afterward shown, I was left entirely out of the question

S. changes base

During the quarrel—for B. and S. had one—it was shown that both of them had adopted the habit of being late on duty, which forced J. to say that he did not care to make steam so long before the old machine was put in motion, as on several occasions he had to lock the fly-wheel to keep her on the centre. In this statement, S. and B. both acquiesced, the former saying that he thought the boy had been fooling with the Engine. B. also said that for some time he had been warning the second Engineer as to the danger to be apprehended when steam was up and no one present to work it off.—Of course, any of us could turn it off. But like an old gun, she would some times go it half cocked, which B. very well knew; and after charging S. with the injury done the machine, he turned upon J. concerning the over flowed boiler. Poor J. was not in a condition to stand very severe questioning of which B. was aware, and therefore reprimanded him pretty sharply and finished by saying that the whole concern for a long while had needed repairs. And thus the matter ended by being smothered.—The Steamer was repaired, but not until B. and S. had had one of the biggest kind of quarrels—all to themselves—in which "the boy's" name was freely mentioned as "not being responsible" &c. I was not touched, and the Engine discharged its duties better after being repaired.

But this whole affair confirms in my mind a familiar proverb—"when two thieves fall out, stollen goods find their way home." They had all been filching time from the United States government, and I felt to be perfectly at home when they were at war. Never did S. trouble me after this occurrence.

A few days after, and when things had resumed their accustomed routine, I reexamined my weapon—that old relic of 76—and found that had I have pulled trigger I would have been a "dead cock in the pit," while the object of my aim would not have been touched.—It shattered every where but at the muzzle, breaking a window light in the work-shop.

I was, for some time, water bearer in the above Dock while it was in building.—Helped dock the first ship that berthed there (Delaware Seventy Four gun ship).[33] I have worked in every Department in the Navy Yard and Dry-Dock, as laborer, and this during very many long years of unrequited toil, and the same might be said of vast numbers, reaching to thousands of slaves who have been worked, lashed and bruised by the United States government like the horned ox; and which matter of injustice done an already injured race was not only practiced on us here, but Fortress Monroe and the Rip-Raps—places to which I have formally alluded—comes in the same category, or were found in the same predicament. And, for shame, as a sad reflection on a Republican government, to this day, the lingering relic is there, in the form of inferior wages paid colored men who perform the same labor, in point of quality and quantity, as those of the opposite race. It is nothing strange, therefore, nor should it be wondered at, that all the applied science in topography, such as relate to civil engineering,—constructing Fortresses &c. rendering them permanent, and impervious to shot and shell,—should be in sad mockery of the genious, time, labor and treasure spent upon them, the one crumbling to earth, and the other sinking beneath the depths of the ocean. Justice and time points with significant finger to the first stratum of imbedded rock there deposited by the unrewarded labor of the slave. I have wrought upon these "works" in common with my fellow bondsmen, receiving the same scanty ration as dealt out by the commissary. Before leaving this subject, I will here take occasion to make mention of two colored men now employed by the government and at work on the above Fortress, who were there fifty years ago. Their names are Joseph Gorham and John Robinson.[34] Until the termination of our great Civil War, I had not seen these two during a space of twenty years. Soon after the Proclamation of Emancipation by Abraham Lincoln, all three of us met at the above old battle ground of Slavery. These are known throughout Elizabeth City and County as being christians "indeed and in truth," and that for very many long years. They are moral standards for their church and the community among whom they were born and raised. We met, as stated, and in rehearsal of our past experience on the spot where we stood, Robinson, moved by the deep flowings of a holy pathos, after "stifling back the mournful sigh," addressed himself to speech, and with streaming eyes said he, "George, I am yet striving for the kingdom; it is all we and our poor brethren— many of whom have gone along since I saw you last—can hope for." The meeting was a short one, we having no time to argue, and there being many thousand soldiers at the Fort and the block-ade being yet on, while I was attempting to get a permit from the Provost to go up to Norfolk—Robinson, who was waiting on the Officers, had no time to converse. I shall dispose of this subject at present, taking occasion to refer to it again before having completed my writings.

When approaching man-hood I had but little time to learn anything about letters, and having taken a wife at mature age, my chances were doubly reduced for anything like literal exercise. Having learned the caulking branch of ship-carpentry under Mr. Wm. H. Hunter of Norfolk,[35] I was—after passing most of the junior portion of my years in the Dry-Dock and Navy Yard as water bearer and common laborer— again returned by my old Master to work in the same Yard as a Mechanic. In the Constructor's Department I was thus employed for a number of years under the Master Caulker, Peter Teabeault wages ranging from one Dollar and fifty cents to one Dollar and sixty two cents per day for colored men and two Dollars or more for white work men, being drawn, or paid in silver and gold.[36] There being a discharge among the colored caulkers, I was again hired by the U.S. Government to work in its ordinary service.—was there some two years or more on board U.S. Ship Constitution lying in ordinary

off Norfolk Navy Yard, and commanded by Capt. Piercy.[37] Have known
all the principal Officers to be off duty when a draft of two hundred, or
three hundred men (sailors) were on board, and on return of the boats,
loaded with whiskey-skins, have seen the whole ship's crew, pettit Officers
included, in the wildest state of intoxication. Some who had retired to their
hammocks were thrown there from by the netlings being cut, the galley was
attacked, and all its furniture strewn from one end of the ship to the other.
Rum ruled until the Marines at the yard were sent for on the arrival of the
officers, who had gone that night to a ball, given at French's Hotel in Norfolk. At sun rise they had not sobered down, and quite a large number of
them, for swearing, and resisting the officers, were gagged to fife rails
ring-bolts &c. &c. After being court martialed, thirteen—two colored—
received one dozen each, well applied with cat-o-nine tails. This happened
some time about 1844, or 1845. The government had patronized, and
given encouragement to Slavery to a far greater extent than the great majority of the country has been aware. It had in its service at the time mentioned
above hundreds, if not thousands of slaves employed on the government
works, possibly within a circle of eighteen or twenty miles here abouts. I
have in my possession two cirtificates of discharge from the U.S. Ship Constitution, or "old iron sides," at the time lying in ordinary.[38] And it was on
this vessel the drunken frolic occurred which I have briefly noticed. These
cirtificates bear on the vignette with which they are decorated, "E pluribus
unum" with eagle pirched shield, and the whole finds its base in a bed of
roses. Now for the discharge, of which there are two.

"E pluribus unum. No. 30.
This is to certify, that George Teamor O. Seaman is regularly dis-
charged from the United States Ship C. in Ordny N. Yd Norfolk, and
from the sea service of the United States, Sept. 10th 45
Appd _____ Saml Forrest
B.W. Hunter, purser"[39]

The other cirtificate, No. 79 is done up in the same hand writing, and
in every way an exact copy of the former excepting the date (Dec. 6th
1845) and one name, which is Benj. W. Palmer, acting for Saml Forrest,
purser.[40] It is no marvel that the respective dates of these papers should be
so close together, when it is remembered that that branch of the U.S. service, so far as hierlings were concerned, was but little different from letting
one out to a building contractor, varying only in point of punishment—
whipping-post and cow hide—gang-way and the cat-o-nine tails. Lawfully,
these now constitute no part of American institutions, the first having been
whipped, the last, shamed out of existance. And thus by the Democratic

government of the United States have we been firmly held for two and half centuries beneath the burning hatchways of Oppression, guarded, mean time, by the most approved arms of Modern warfare. Well may the country congratulate itself on its riddance from an evil, than which, no greater ever blackened the face of the sun. In its mighty sweep, all but the ruling classes (wealthy and refined) had to do obeisance to it. The poor mechanic and laborer, through the deep cunning and educated craft of the influential and designing have been made to violate their own honest convictions of the right in support of opinions put forth, and wrought in to law by the governing classes. Without means to defend themselves, they could only regard their grievances as tantamount to slavery itself, with but few exceptions. And I am here reminded of a circumstance which occurred in this place some time I think it was in 1842 or 1843. It is known that from time immemorial the poorer classes—whites—have had to suffer these wrongs. And while I never did believe they would ever resort to any very effective measures to have these wrongs redressed, still an effort was made, and though well planned, only demonstrated the fact, in keeping with the "bravery" of a certain general who "marched up the hill and then marched down again."

The Editorial labors and genious of Melzar Gardner are well known to most of the older citizens of Portsmouth and vicinity. From all I could learn by my peculiar way of getting in to their meetings, Gardner had been sent for by certain persons, representing the great majority of whites then at work in our Navy Yard, for the purpose of conducting a journal devoted to the interests of free men, or tax payer's claims to the patronage of the general government. Its columns, therefore, were opened to all communications bearing on that subject, and all others looking to a reformation in the morals of Society. My memory may be at fault in some particulars relative to G.'s operations at that time, and having no material at hand as a guide, my recollection must be some what vague in point of any thing I may attempt to show which resulted in his death as a faithful martyr to the poor white man's cause; and I think on a fair showing, by those who were best acquainted with him as a journalist, that, however hidden to those employing him, it was an initiatory step either to free the slave where he stood, or to so circumscribe the limits of that institution within the Common Wealth as to render, or bring labor of all sorts entirely within the control of those who had secured his services. Slavery was so interwoven at that time in the very ligaments of the government that to assail it from any quarter was not only a herculean task, but one requiring great consideration caution and comprehensiveness. Gardner, therefore, in manoevring to attack it so as to meet the approval of the opposition, succeeded in getting a card in the Her-

ald,—I believe it was, (a Norfolk paper) it may have been anonymously
written for all I am aware—showing how shamefully those alluded to had
been cheated of their rights. The Herald not only gave it publicity, but followed with a favorable comment. Of course this was just what G. wanted as
a basis for action; but when the scheme was discovered as against the slave
interest, and other papers began with showing it up as such, the Herald
"caved", not darring lik[e] Peter, to return to its former faith. Mean time
G. was plying his pen to the tune of three or four columns of solid editorial. (daily) G. could think and write with astonishing rapidity and with all
the precision of a scribe. He met (editorially) and refuted every point raised
by the other side, until those bitter personalities followed resulting in his
being shot through the heart by Mordacai Cook in a rencounter on the
ferry dock, or wharf at Norfolk. On learning this, the great swell of popular indignation knew no bounds. His supporters called meetings and after
passing resolutions, expressive of their deep abhorance of the murdurous
act and the actor, further resolved to make a public demonstration by pa-
rading the streets of Portsmouth and Norfolk, thus giving their opposers to
see as well as feel, the force and weight of majorities. I was in that mass of
dense humanity following the procession, and with all that carelessness that
attaches to an irresponsible slave during such calamities "when swarms the
populace, a countless throng; youth and hoar age tumultuous pour along",
it could not be expected that I should have felt any interest in this whole affair; yet when taking such comprehensive view as I could arrive at with the
light afforded me at the time, I was clearly in sympathy with Gardner, for
the reason that he had been accused and hunted down as an abolitionist by
those from whose hands he received the fatal shot which ended his mortal
existance. While Cook was suspended in effigy from the old sycamore trees
near our Court House, the aggrieved procession was moving throug[h]
Norfolk—passing the streets of hoarded wealth—inspired as by the sign
"bread or blood". I noticed carefully the more gaudy and stylish mansions
as the body moved on. They were all closed as against the bolts of thunder
during a storm. But the poor man's doors were open, as an acceptance of
anything for a change not excepting even the slave's emancipation, provided
their—the white's [—] condition could be improved thereby, which, of
course had been foreshadowed by their martyred chief, first by removing
all slave labor from the government, and secondly, by causing all who were
in bonds, practicing the use of edged tools to relinquish them and go to
other fields of labor. At that time I was, occasionally at work in the Navy
Yard, and with the hundreds of others in my condition felt to remain there
rather than being worse situated, or sold. One has a dear liking for one's
self, however circumstanced. I never did believe Gardner very favorably

disposed to ward the colored race, or if so he had a very poor way of showing it. And yet he may not have loved us less, but his own race more. Whether it may have been credited or otherwise, my opinion at the time was that a practical solution of his theory would not only have resulted in the slave's emancipation in the State of Virginia, but where ever the foot of the bondsman desecrated God's soil on this continent, there would the shaft [of] abolition have found its way. I said I was some what observant as the procession moved on. I was quite so when passing the residences of the more retired and refined, from reasons which led me to believe that they must have felt considerably alarmed, knowing as they had a right to know, that this indignant demonstration was the legitimate fruits of their own actions, which gave momentary check to their ambition, without, in the least bringing them to grief, for if I am to believe such as came under my immediate observation and confirmed by their own domestics, they were only terror stricken at thought of retaliation. The old sire, pale, and with trembling lips could be seen within closed blinds nervously adjusting his specks, while the young, as though the main prop had lost its standing, were rather given to mourning and despair, as they knew well, that that threatning croud of hardy mechanics and laborers, could have successfully disputed its way, not only through Norfolk, taking with them the poor and middling classes, but in their prowess could have swept over the State and challenged the decision of the country upon their cause, or the justice of it. Thus the poor white men had been kept in a state of vassalage, but very little different from that of the African bondsman, their only appeal being from "Cesar to Cesar," or from State Democracy to a Democratic Congress, into whose support the eagle eyed politician with his "ebon-shin, bandy-shank" and amalgamation batoon had driven & kept them spell bound, and in great doubt as to their freedom under a Republican form of government. Before closing this article, I will here state that no small number of the wealthy and enterprizing citizens of Norfolk and surroundings, denounced Cook in the most scathing terms for the perpetration of this broad daylight, and heaven-darring deed, and one also which put all of that class under suspician.[41]

I have thus spoken of Mr. Gardner, for the reason that I believe he was true to the poor of his Race, and fell while in the full discharge of his duties for their deliverance from the many deceptions practiced upon them. My family were living in the basement of Mr. Gardner's boarding house on County St. at the time of the sad occurrence, performing the duties of a servant, and being called upon to assist in arranging the corpse, I did so, and saw and felt the open orifice while cleansing his remains for their transportation to Massachusetts.

Having married in 1841, there was now no time left me to further pursue the work of self improvement as troubles accumulated "thick and fast". Being discharged from the Navy Yard where I had been usually at work—caulking—I next found employment in the Shipyards of Messrs. John G. Colley, Wm. H. Hunter (the latter with whom I served "my time".[42] Wm. A. Graves was also apprenticed to the same gentleman while I was in service there.)[43] Nathaniel Nash, Wm. A. Graves and a Mr. Miles, the latter at Ferry Point.[44] When not in their service, I was found at the common labor of carrying grain, lading and unlading ships freighting Rail Road iron, and, perhaps there is no species of labor, such as may be reckoned in the catalogue of Norfolk's history but I have been engaged at. I was at work in the press room of John W. Murdaugh, Esq. while that gentleman was editing a paper devoted to the principles of whigory. It was called—I think—the "Clay Banner and Naval and Commercial Intelligencer"[45] It was an able paper and conducted with great ability, and was assiduous in it[s] efforts in trying to make the great Henry Clay, president of the United States, but not being rough shod like its Democratic cotemporaries through out the country, this advocate of the great man, here as else where, failed in seating him on the presidential cushion. With both of these great national parties, there was a oneness on the question of human slavery, only that Mr. Clay "thought" (and some body heard him "think") that the institution might give the nation some trouble in after days unless provision should be then made to meet the anticipated difficulties. This was quite too much for Democracy, and it "went down" for him. Indeed, any one who aspired to leadership in either party, had, first of all to "renounce the Devil" (Republicanism) "and all his works" by an unmistakable deffinition of his position as being filial to the "old cause". Should he dare think and speak other wise, he would not only be subjected to a severe investigation, but our locals would hunt him down by criticism, and even by characature.

My wife lived with, and belonged to the wife of Olice Amidon and was said to be half sister to her Mistress, (and I learn this from her own lips, as also from the testimony of those who were her youthful associates—the likeness is "striking".) In regular order, from time to time she gave birth to three children, John, Jane and Josephine.[46] Having been married in Portsmouth by Rev. Vernon Eskridge, until her and our first child was sold she remained in the family of her Mistress, then residing at the extreme Eastern end of high street where her Master, Mr. Amidon was then doing business as a finisher in cabinet work.[47] Being unsuccessful, he soon became insolvent, which, being followed by a distress warrant resulted in the sale of Sallie (for such is her name) and her child. The state of the case having been known to John Lindsay—then living and acting Master carpenter at Fortress Monroe, after passing the "necessary" examination as to S.'s physical condition, bought her and child, for the purpose, as stated by L.'s wife, of going to Richmond and setting a house in order for his family preparatory to their removal thither.[48]

He kept her in his family at the Fort until she had become the mother of her third child when the contemplated Richmond "ruse" was carried out. At this time the slave market in Richmond being at its maximum, S. and her children were forwarded to the Capital. But before going further I wish to say, that Sallie was raised by the Liveley's at New Market near Hampton, Va. and the marriage of her young Mistress brought her to Portsmouth. With the exception of schooling, Sallie was raised, having all that care bestowed upon her which favored the Liveley family, and when in riper years she had been called to experience those heavy troubles which makes the human heart sicken to contemplate, none felt in sorrow more keenly her unfortunate circumstances than the family alluded to. She was a virtuous country girl, unpretending and very plain in manners and style, and one, who lamb like, would be led to the slaughter with nothing in her heart but forgiveness to her enemies. Children she has always considered as being the perfection of human nature or angels on Earth. Indeed, all that might be said of a good affectionate nurse may be well applied to her, and there is no one in whose service she has ever been but has endeavored to have her with them again. Either that, or call and see them often.

Before being shipped for Richmond such was Sallie's confiding nature that she could not be induced to believe that her new Mistress, Mrs. Lindsay would have dared sell her and the children under any circumstances whatever, and I labored to otherwise impress her, but all in vain—told her that in my opinion the sale of herself and children had been already made, and on the grounds of such conviction addressed a letter to the keeper of the jail, Geo. Cooper, a youthful associate of mine, who was sold from this place.[49] I put the letter in the bottom of her carpet bag, with the instructions, if she should see George to hand him the communication, which she promised to do, and did as will be shown; and I have often thought how singular it was, that of the many slave pens then in Richmond, I should have pointed out the very jail of which my family became inmates. But it was a kind of a faith in what I really believed which had increased to a passionate intuition. And it must be remembered that the sold were always placed as far beyond the aid and influence of their friends from without as iron barred double apartments could divide between; for had it have come to the master turnkey's ears that Cooper, who was the trader's slave driver, was at all friendly to myself or family, she would at once have been removed to other quarters. Being sold on Saturday night, with all dispatch S. was hurried off on the following Monday morning, taking with her the three children named, the youngest being three years of age. These and the valise containing their clothing made up the freight.—No, she shamed them out of her large feather bed which they had expected to retain until she had "returned" from the chief city of auction blocks. On the arrival of the Steamer "John Sylvester", like other valuable freight they were hastily, but with "great care" put on board, watched by—to them—an unseen eye, and "labelled", "Sol. Davis' jail, Locust Alley, Richmond, Va."[50] Low cunning and concealment had done its best to render this whole transaction a profound secret, not only to me (for I could not, and dared not speak or think of the matter) but to those from whom she had been purchased, as the latter, it would seem had sold Lindsay a bad right [of ownership]. On her arrival at Richmond there were parties in waiting who conducted her and children to Sol's iron den, where she was put under my old friend Cooper, the whipping master. Poor woman!—She then realized for a second time the "situation". In frantic despair she had for the time being, qu[i]te forgotten my letter, and only recalled it to mind a few days after, when in her calmer moments she saw from her place of confinement, the friendly George as he passed among the slaves on the jail yard. Though knowing her well, he dared not say so. She importuned him for a hearing, but being well versed in prison discipline, he could do no other at the time than treat her as a stranger, which he did until his duty called him to her cell. Here, the interview was anything else but pleasant, as Cooper had for several years been sold from his wife, children and friends,—Sallie from her husband, relatives and others whom she counted most dear. In bitter tears each attempted to reveal the other's woes, but all in vain, for the vigilant Davis and his keeper were not to be baffled with in this style, so Cooper left and attended to his business in routine, not forgetting to see her when most convenient. While in these jails were congrigated, from time to time, as subjects for the auction-block some of the most devoted christians, there were also others quite to the reverse, and it was among the latter Sallie with her children had been thrown. Here, the striking resemblance between the prison house and its occupants—while it might be subject of remark, there should be no room left for surprise. It was in the midst of summer when S. was sent to Richmond, and such the condition of the jails at that place, that the sickening stench arising from their walls saturated with filth,—and equally so in her room—feavored both her and the children. Herded with the vulgar, and surrounded by whipping-posts, stocks and cages, from one stage of suffering to another, she soon took to pining, in which state, Cooper, on his second visit found her when she handed him my letter, and after having it read he told her its contents, and very soon returned me an answer, which reads as follows.

"Richmond, Va. Aug.   1853
    My Dear old friend George, I seat myself to write you a few lines about your dear wife and children. I don't know how you could tell that she would come to my jail; but her and the three children did come and are here now, and well except a little cold they took on the boat and sleeping from home. You know how it is with me here, how I am watched and how little I can do to help her and your children. I am sorry for poor Sallie, yourself and the children, as they will all be sent off in a drove next week unless she & children can be bought to remain in Richmond, which I hope will be the case. You didn't say anything about my wife and children, but I recon you forgot it or didn't know Sallie was coming here. Please don't write any letters here to me, but if your Master will allow you, you had better come right up, and say nothing but keep your pass and lay around until you see me. Your wife sends her love to you and says you told her the truth. She says come up very quickly
        I am Your Old Friend
        Geo. Cooper"

I instantly applied to my Old Mistress to know what relief I could find, but she not having the means where with to mak[e] the purchase, nothing could be done in S. behalf. And fearing some trouble might follow between myself and the trader, she would not—without repeated overtures,—give her consent that I should go to Richmond, which I did after writing my own pass.

Pending the time of receiving the letter and my arrival at Richmond, a resident jew named Henry H. Rosenfeld, then doing business as a dry goods Merchant on broad Street No. 175, having visited the jails in quest of a servant for general house work, made choice of Sallie and the youngest child, but only as a hierling on trial.[51] But, in order to glut a long cherished revenge upon this innocent woman, as also to dodge a legal investigation as to their (the Lindsay's) right of property in her, she was again remanded back to Old Point [Comfort, Fort Monroe], but not until they had kidnapped her two eldest children in open day on broad Street, and sold them beyond the reach of hearing or recovery. The more she raved about her children being taken away without her notice, the more intense grew the ire of her mistress, who even then declared that she "would sell Sallie and her babe as far as wind and water could carry them". "Hell has no fury like a woman's revenge". Thus far the programme of Virginia's slave breeding market had been carried out, and it was for me and Sallie in this case to stand as the objectives.

I now leave S. at Fortress Monroe, where, on the most trifling pretense she is clubbed to the earth by her young Master, then only about thirteen years of age. His father however, chastised him for thus maiming a valuable piece of "property". Even the neighbors who knew S. well, declared the act to be one of the most inhuman that had ever been perpetrated at that place.

I said I went to Richmond. I did so, and found Sallie at the number stated. My presence only served to increase her sorrows however, for so soon as I entered the kitchen, with a wild shriek of despair she embraced me about the neck, and while the big tear[s] fell heavy and fast, with momentary chokings and sobbings, in vain did she try to express her weight of woes. She swooned and fell to the floor, but soon revived; and rising to a stooping posture, with clenched hands she exclaimed in a voice of pitiful undertone, and hesitating accent—"My children!—they are gone—gone—gone!!—God have pity on them—have mercy on me!!" On recovering and rising from her place, she said, in staggering speech, "George, your children are gone for ever, poor little Jonnie's hat and jacket, which I had thought to keep as in memory of my child, were stolen by the jail thieves, and Jane—and Ja." Here again she fell to the floor, not being able from mental incapacity to articulate, or repeat the name. On telling her that I was there to seek employment, and would likely remain a few weeks, provided if within that time she was not sold, she felt some what renewed in spirit—arose, and with heavy heart went forward in the discharge of her domestic duties. I soon informed her that I was well aware of what had taken place, and though powerless to effect any good on her behalf, I would remain there and await further results. I sought, and found employment during a few days. It was at what is familiarly styled the "Basin," near which Messrs. Howell and Messer were then running a Dock Yard, and it was with these I wrought about one week at $1.25 cts per diem from which my perquisite was very small indeed.[52]—I was pennyless when I arrived in Richmond, but through the indulgence of my owners I was allowed to appropriate to my own use any monies that I might earn when absolute necessity would justify the expenditure. It is just that I should make this statement of them here, as this act was in keeping with their conduct toward me from infancy to manhood.

After giving Sallie three dollars, I used the remainder in defraying my expenses home. As shown, the object was to get rid of a legal investigation as to the right of property in the woman if not in the children, as the latter were now sold. After returning to F[ort] Monroe with her young child, and there remaining twelve months, Lindsay sought out a more private way to effect the sale of S. and her infant, which was shrewdly accomplished by way of secret plottings known only to dealers in human flesh. This time she was to be taken through Richmond to Petersburg, with the understanding that she was to be sent as far down South "as wind and water," or rail roads feet and Steam boats "could carry her." Instead of going to Petersburg, however, she was, on landing of the Richmond boat put in jail at Rockets, not very far from the boat landing. In this jail was a young man named Henry Banks whose mother, Sallie very much resembled in every other respect as well as features. He was the jail wagoner, and had considerably to do by way of keeping the slaves orderly &c. His duties were similar to those of Cooper's. Banks, like Cooper did what ever he could to relieve the distressed, and was highly esteemed by those who know him best.[53] And while it is true that the majority of these colored men, who were stationed as Cooper and Banks, would far exceed their masters in punishing the slaves, these two may be regarded as exceptions; at least in S.'s case. Grief for her children, the cruel tre[a]tment of the Lindsay's added to the prison life she was then under going had now reduced her to a mere frame of human bones. Patrons of the auction block swore it to be shameful, that one, so like themselves—complexionally—should even be allowed to stand the usual examination to which females were put in these prison houses of despair. In deed such was her debilitated condition that she could do but little else than that of looking after her child. While in this feeble and emaciated condition, the inexorable jailor ordered her, on pain of being lashed, to rise, and like a gymnast, play the part of active health if she had it not. On her [k]nees she besought him to excuse her from being mustered out in common with others at muscular exercise. She informed him of her sufferings, past and present, with which he said he had nothing to do. The friendly Banks now interposes, and through his influence she is released from the shameful exposure. I shall not attempt to discribe the character, or manner of these examinations and exposures; humanity revolts, the soul sickens, and indeed the whole moral sense of our nature seems to loose its proper channel on contemplating the demon dens where respectable ladies were stripped to be put on exhibition for the speculators in the trafic. I will however go so far as to say, that the majority of the younger females who were subjected to these scrutinizing examinations, if proven to be in good condition, having fair proportions &c. were generally bought up, either as wives for the buyer, his child, or children, or else to be traded off further South at the best market, and for the same purpose, or purposes. It is, or would be very amusing to vulgar eyes to see some letters forwarded from Georgia, La. and other places south to Agents in Richmond. And it is only that I can not break faith with my old friend Cooper, who, on showing me certain letters the names of whose authors he requested me never to mention, that I do not give their names as they stand in their communications. But these letters are "funny" and "Frenchy", and some of them written by those not over conversant with our idiom. As an illustration of their character, I give the following, which were written with the evident intention, that, should it be lost the finder would be none the wiser though he read it again and again.

["]Dare frendes, me write you as i shed. i say hear me i will pay you one thosan what i shed for one like i tole you bout of for my sun one good young tender beef i tolds you what sort it was not in last drove from Atlanta i wates for it wid great anxiety for my sun is great for nothen beef i tels him Mr. _____will send me some what is sound and good ef i will pay him for his trubles he dont want what is bin to work in Richmond and round but som from the country—young and good breth and hare and feet i tolds you what colur will be best and size."

There were some few words in this epistle written in French which I could not understand

An other

"Mobile, Ala.
July 16th 1853

—Dr. Sir:—

Your telegraphic dispatch has been rec'v'd.—Drove not in yet—the cause was an accident on the road;—See the news papers. I learn that you have, after all, agreed to sell Kate's sister. You are well aware that I made you a handsome offer for that girl, and you had partly agreed to let me have her. I did not care so much about her in consequence of her being Kate's sister, but I really thought you would have thrown her in at what I said, knowing how I suffered in the purchase of lot No 27. See my note for $3000-00 on lot No. 19. Fan—(copper)—Mulish lady, would not surrender—died on my hands—loss—$900-00 on her. Send me a good sprightly mulatto boy (not white) one who is honest—can keep bar, tend in a salloon &c. &c. I hold a copy of your prices, marked No. 32 to me. I will see the consignees. The negro—"Casey" of lot 27 marked to me, was ruptured; though I fixed him up and sold him at a small loss. Cotton, not brisk—markets down. Watch the Office.
Very Res'y
Yours _____ "

Comment is unnecessary if to show the horrors of the auction-blocks as they existed in our Southern States, taking Virginia as the great Mogul.

While thus undergoing the combined punishments of incarceration, mental and physical infirmities, having also a helpless child to care for, Sallie was again called upon to make a show of good health. In deed, this time she was given the sum of Ten Dollars as an encouragement to the performance of sound health and mind. While the object sought by the Lindsays, as stated, was to send her to the "ends of wind and water," that of the speculator was to sell her any where at the greatest profit.

Finding herself, as it were, in the merciless trough of an unbounded sea while the Phariohs, from pride of place were launching down upon her barbed arrows from well sprung bows—and I use this language, because it seems the best I can find to represent her hopeless condition at the time— she no longer, or rather failed to look for relief from any source. In the midst of her anguish, both mental and physical, her old employer, Rosenfeld made his appearance at the jail, he having previous knowledge of her being again exposed for sale. By their way of doing business under cover of secrecicy, this time, instead of hiring, she was sold to R. by what is termed private sale. And I am forced to say, and take pleasure in doing so, that this german family, on seeing the sad circumstances in which Sallie had been thrown through bitter hate and revenge, waved all considerations as to money and purchased this sick woman and her child at an almost fabulous price. Mr. R. knew well her character and the value of her services with the blessing of good health. His wife was of the aristocratic order of the race and "fared sumptuously every day", and being one of extra ordinary beauty, she cared but little to have her children with her—and she had three, or four—on the promenade and else where, hence she could find no better domestic guardian than Sallie. Like Pharioh by Joseph, they two, soon forgot the care of their children and house hold affairs, such being their confiding trust in the newly purchased servant. Mr. and Mrs. R. paid every possible attention to Sallie until restored to perfect health, giving her full control in the family circle and both him and her always respecting Sallie as one of their own relatives. Indeed there was no article in Rosenfeld's large dry goods furnishing store to which her and daughter was not made welcome. Mrs. R. besides learning the latter the science of millinery and dress making, tought her the german language to some considerable extent, and never objected to her learning on the piano forte. When Lindsay, for his wife, had learned that S. had been thus disposed of, inspite of all their efforts to send her and child, as it were into banishment, it is easy to learn how they must have received the tidings. But, alas; she is again doomed to disappointment, for she could not look on with indifferance and see the confidence of her late Master betrayed in his wife. O, no!—R. had done too much for Sallie and daughter for her to see his honor and integrity assailed by a faithless clerk who was, at the time employed by R. and who had grown to such familiarity in R.'s family, that he not only assumed to be dictator, but in obedience to her behest had used the lash on S.'s daughter, in consideration of which, she (S.) at once and very promptly informed too, that she could "not serve two Masters". Mr. R. was an elder gentleman while his wife was quite young, and like her wooer remarkably fond of the sports, gay festivities and high life in general. Rosenfeld loved his wife too well to distrust her in the least though ocular demonstration furnished the proofs. Josephine, Sallie's daughter, had been punished on several occasions by the would be Master, and for no other reasons than those of entering the parlor while the two were wrapt in love's sweet embraces. The girl did not go there however without being with in the line of her duty.

After this discovery—and it was a palpable hit—there was no more peace for S. and her daughter. She—Mrs. R.—controlled her husband in every thing. Thinking, and acting in co' 'opperation, these two caused the unsuspicious R. to part with Sallie and her daughter. They were sold, not out of Richmond however, but to one Henry Smith a low liquor dealer.[54] This man, for some years had been watching his chances to bring both mother and daughter within the control of his morally depraved appetite. To succeed in his nefarious purpose he kept his out posts ever on the alert with bribes and inducements of various kind to win them to his charms. He bought them at last, and long ere blooming youth had a peep at its own horizon, long before infancy had arrived to the years of accountability, compelled the daughter into his fiendful service and thus accomplished his diabolical purpose upon the inocent daughter of a hunted down mother. To the former he professed love in a thousand forms; nor did one have to make a pilgrimage to Salt Lake City to learn how well another could enjoy the unholy embraces of a plurality of wives, for of all that Richmond held of Brigham Youngs, Smith bore off the palm. After figuring for some time under the Utah license, and when he had abandoned his legitimate wife and by some means got rid of his property, he left Richmond followed by the tearful thanks and deep sympathies of its high bidders for virtuous girls, or what the above letter terms "good tender beef."

Being obliged to push on with my own narrative, or that which more particularly concerns me individually, I shall not be able to show what disposition Smith made of Sallie and daughter until I have traced my history from 1853 to 1871 inclusive.

To go back to the time (1853) when Sallie was first sold, I would say I was at the time employed at my trade in Norfolk, along with many other slaves caulking a merchant ship, or bark, named the Currituck. She was built in Portsmouth, Va. and partly owned by the Messrs. Hardies in Norfolk and parties in New York.[55] We had been at work on her several weeks and when nearly completed, the Captain (Mr. Seth Foster of Matthews County) sent on to New York for sailors to man her.[56] She was to take a cargo of tobacco from City Point to Bremen in Germany. The Capt. being in want of a Ship's carpenter for the cruise, on inquiring among the caulkers then at work on his Ship, he was informed that I could be hired for that purpose, and accordingly he came to Portsmouth—made a bargain with my old Mistress, she telling him, among other things that having raised me from an infant, she hoped he would pay every attention to me while on the voige, which he certainly did as a gentleman, as I hope to show in another place. It was some time in June of 1853 when this Ship was towed to City Point for the purpose named.—I was on board while the bark was being worked to the point. At this place we laid nearly two months awaiting the arrival of her cargo. It came very slowly in, so that it was not until about the first of August when she was freighted for her journey across the vasty deep.[57]

In speaking of going to sea in this Ship I would here record, as a matter of justice to the deceased, that my old Mistress having promised my mother that at some time during manhood she would let me go free, found herself, at the time she felt most like doing so, unable from the laws of the State to accomplish that very desirable result.[58] She had hinted the matter to me over and often while approaching maturity, stating the complications which would inevitably follow should she attempt to do so by legal process. Hence she claimed the right to hire me in the mercantile service on the grounds that I held two honorable discharges from the United States home Service. She was always opposed to sending me to the far off and wild shores of Africa, and equally so to my going north to be hunted down by the great Daniel Webster's blood hound and rifle.[59] She was also well aware that the ship, on her return to the U.S. would land its cargo some where north of "Mason and Dixon's line". Of course she said nothing to the Captain on this wise because she knew him to be owner of many slaves on a large plantation in Matthews Co[unty], only asking his protection of me while on the voige, which as I have stated was amply given. Her plan, therefore, was admirably adapted, not only to my staying in this country, but also to my relief from the terrible operations of the "Fugitive Slave Bill", as that national, and inhuman monstrosity was then the law of the land. To be carried on the "high seas" even was also tantamount to giving the slave his freedom. It was now left for me to choose whether I would accept this favorable opportunity or allow my freedom to go by default. That I had been unjustly and meanly deprived of my family, my owner knew as well as myself, and the whole family, when aware of my going interposed no objection. I was sure that my services had come to an end—at least for the time being—with my afflicted family.

While at the Point coopering tobacco tierce, just one day before our departure a colored man from Richmond approached me asking if I had heard from my wife. I told him I had not since I last saw her, and that if he had anything to say whether good or evil I would much rather he should keep it to himself, and help the woman if in his power to do so. He said nothing further, and I have not seen the man since.

The ship having now been freighted, she was taken in tow and anchored in Hampton Roads where, after a few days riding at halser, she received her crew, and the pilot when the Capt. set sail, bound to Germany.

In vain had I tried to forget all I left behind of family dear, of kindred and friends But For the moment this would pass away only to return with added troubles, for it was about then when I heard the captain state that on his return with a load of emigrants they were to be landed at New Orleans, and this news had gained credence among the whole Ship's company until we arrived at our destination. Taking this to be a fact, I soon concluded to quit the Ship in Germany and find my way to our free north by a different mode. I well remembered an old adage which I had learned in early youth, and which I put well to memory—"where there is a will there is a way."—The "will" was not lacking—the "way" was before me. Thus with the horrid memories of wife and children crowding around me my cup of sorrows was full, even to over flowing.

When the sails were set and we had fairly laid our course, I viewed the western shores of the Chesapeake and bade them a lasting farewell; and as Cape Henry receded from view, I stood in sad contemplation gazing as upon vacancy, while The deep briny ocean began to show its frightful heavings as landscapes faded from view. At last my profound and spell-bound silence broke into extemporaneous song which I accompanied on my sorrow soothing guitar. It was now growing dark when I was sitting on the hatch combing of my tool-room, and in very slow time sung and played until I fell into tears and weeping. And I found the lines of Byron with slight alteration well adapted to my then present condition. They were his last "good night" or final adue to his native shores; and another which runs thus:

"Hear me my mother earth, behold it heaven,
Have I not had to struggle with my—lot
Have I not suffered things to be forgiven" &c. &c.

The Ship was on a "taught bows line," or "close hauled"—as the mariner says—when the starboard watch turned in. Being Ship's carpenter, my business was of a general character, hence not being in any watch, I was content to occupy my leisure moments in listening at the sweet music of the waters. These for a while greatly contributed to the relevancy of my troubles, when I was seized by that most pleaguesome visitant—sea-sickness, whose terrible scourgings during thirty eight days I was doomed to endure. I retired at a very late hour. On rising the next morning I found us fairly on the lashing ocean with every sail strained to its utmost tension. The pilot, before leaving, said he would take letters home for those who felt to send any; accordingly I sat or knelt near the main hatch taking that for a desk, in which posture I was found when all at once Diggs, the second mate began to throw at me the most provoking slurs which, finding I did not notice again commenced with bitter slang, such as "nigger writ'n letters, Sambo's guine to glory, take me back to Old Virginny" &c Diggs was also of Mathews County, yet I could not believe that Capt. Foster would have allowed it had he have been sensible of the occurrence, which soon proved to be a fact, for D was arreigned on several subsequent occasions for his abuse of the sailors.[60] In deed when we had reached our port of destination he was affraid to trust himself ashore as the crew had sworn to "thrash" him. At one time he let fall from the main top a marline-spike which in its descent stuck on end in the deck near the spot where I stood. It was about the prettiest instrument of the kind I had ever seen,—to day it moulders in the English Channel, and [I] would have driven it through the wretch at the moment but for his being aloft. He could neither read or write. He was a very stout bull dog head, red hair and face, and etchy kind of a man. He was to be pittied more for his ignorance than any one thing else. The sailors termed him "a canal-boat Captain. He made a dread-ado about the marline-spike, but no one seems to have known its "where-abouts." We were some three, or four days out when, as the day was breaking a sail was espied under close haul off our starboard quarter, working to the wind-ward. This craft was a very suspicious looking concern being very long, narrow and black, and submurged to all appearance nearly to her gunwale. The glasses were again and again brought to bear but nothing very deffinite had been arrived at, yet all believed it to be something like a pirate. This soon reached the Capt.'s ears, and seizing the spy-glass he bent it on her, and without venturing an opinion at the time, called his brother Shepperd Foster—first mate—requesting him to look and give his opinion which he did on this wise—"I believe" said he "it is an African slave trader driven off her coast."[61] The Capt. who was of some what an excitable temperament bade him look again and then tell all he thought of it. He did so, and after a more careful observation arrived at the same conclusion as at first. Having so stated it to the Capt. the skipper raved terribly saying Shepperd didn't understand his business &c. We were then fairly in the "trade" and

driven by an increasing stiff breeze, making about ten knots, or that many
English statute miles to the hour. An order from the Capt. at once brought
the ship up when studding-sails and every "rag" that she could float under
was raised. Mean time the faithful barometer indicated a rising storm and
of which the first mate informed his brother, the Capt. The sea, sweet
breezes beneath Italian skies which but a few short moments before had
heightened our hopes of an uninterrupted voige, fast began to assume a
dark and thunderous aspect. To me,—until that inauspicious hour, all that
poet ever sung of silvery bedecked clouds, "rocked in the cradle of the
deep", "like a bird of heavenly plumage fair" &c. I could very highly appreciate, but when these began to open the exhibition I was greatly concerned about some work I had to do down in the ship's hold, and there I
went and there I stayed until I had heard a deep dirgeful sound like an organ vast pouring its rough music through a private passage leading to the
cargo, while the latter was laboring and screeching like fifty toy fiddles
playing second to a steam calliope. The rising storm, the rolling sea and
rocking ship, with a supposed to be pirate in the distance were poetry
enough for the sanctum of the landed muse of verse, but quite too much of
the practical for an inexperienced sea sick adventurer. By the time I ascended from the hold the Capt. had brought out the "jug" and a decent supply of the article prepared the crew for any emergency whether going to the
bottom by sea roving thieves or that of thunder storms. Amid this howling
storm the Ship was again put down heading for her course, and while the
first mate was prevailing on the Capt. to shorten canvas, his reply was,—
"no! run her to h--l and let her come up on the other side—better than to be
captured by that d--n pirate". So onward she pressed through the combined
and maddened fury of the distructive elements which had met as in deadly
conflict. The rain fell in torrents accompanied by hail and sheet-lightnings.
A fouling of the jib halyards having caused that sail to part such was the report amidst the confusion of the moment that I mistook the sound as being
the first gun from the pirate ship. But Foster was a seaman worthy of his
sails, and knew exactly what he was doing and where he was going, though
hundreds of miles from the nighest shore. We out rode the gale after a few
hours, when we were again on the lazily rolling and smooth surface of the
ocean. The suspicious craft was again seen at times when our ship was lifted
on a breaker. She had in this way been keeping off and on for about fourteen days, at which time we espied a very large English man-of-war, said to
be protecting—I think—the Eastindia trade—She was far off our leeward,
and by us signalized as to the position, or course of the dangerous looking
vessel; we were answered back and for the first time, during many days we
breathed easier. Our Capt. was mistaken for once at least in his life, as the

Ship which brought on our fears, over took us, and proved to be a merchant man destined for the same port that we were. After encountering the usual storms &c. at sea, we arrived in Bremen, where, unlading and lading we remained fifteen days, during which time the Ship under went some temporary repairs (caulking) by German mechanics assisted by myself. From these hospitable german mechanics, I had, received a number of invitations—through their interpreter—to visit, not only their public places of amusements, but their private residences also, requesting mean time that I should not feel myself in the least embarrassed where ever I might choose to go. Fresh from slavery, with its effluvium resting upon me, such a tender was only entertained on my knowledge of their ignorance of my ever having been in that condition.—

> God made man, man made the slave,
> The last degrades him to his grave.
> I viewed before and cast behind
> A glance betrayed the german mind
> When finding I was of their craft,
> In staggering accents how they laughed!
> But when detailing of my land,
> They wept and gave the pittying hand.
> A stranger; far from clan and kin,
> They vowed their will to take me in.
> Thus hand in hand I was led on—
> Not yankee like—automaton
> And though my manhood was unnerved
> What'er they had to me was served
> Not grudgingly, or want of will,
> But shared their bounty without bill.
> And after feasting at their board
> We took the agricultural road
> —Saw their fields in waving grain
> Late freshened by the falling rain
> The kind of plough I used at home
> E'en to me with pains was shown
> In many places which were theirs
> They'd seen no blacks for scores of years
> The children cried the dogs did bark
> To wit mankind was made so dark
> They crowded round from place to place
> And with their fingers tried my—face
> It was as "fixed" as nature's laws
> Nor need of asking for the cause

After filling the invitation, I returned to the Ship, accompanied by the same parties who gave it. Taken in his own home, the german possesses a kindness of heart truly in sympathetic beat with the oppressions of mankind the world over; not narrow minded, but of that broad patriotic liberality which should commend itself to a world of hypocritical pretenders to mortal sufferings

The movements of this people at their daily avocation are not such as may be observed among the laboring classes in the more northern sections of the United States. They seem to be perfectly satisfied after having performed a fair, or reasonable day's work, which when done they recreate themselves by readings, lectures, social gathering, dances, theatres &c. &c. There also the wealthy seems to associate with, and respect the lower classes of society more so than in this country. As a general thing, the anglo Americans make too great a sacrifice of pleasure for business. German philosophers, or many of the ancient and modern classics of that land so economised life that proper attention seems to have been paid to all those requirements necessary to one's happiness on earth. That young America, however, out strips the world in most improvements in the arts and sciences of the nineteenth century none can doubt, the trouble being—in my estimation—that the living age seem to forget that they, as well as posterity should be the beneficiaries of what has been the life long study of their ancestors, and being so, to enjoy it with all that simplicity and peace of mind so remarkable in german society. After being in Bremen fifteen days we took on board two hundred and eighteen emigrants and set sail for the port of New York. We had been but a few days out when, one after an other, sea sickness made its attack on the passengers until all became its victims. Thirty Eight days after lifting anchor, we arrived in New York harbor, where, after due inspection we were admitted to the wharf (Peck Slip)[62] The sailors were paid off and discharged, and the passengers turned over to their consignees or agents, myself alone being detained by the Captain, of whom I inquired in to the cause, when he answered me by saying that he had "put himself under certain obligations to my owners to take me back to them". I informed him, however, even admitting that, it was highly necessary that I should not only go a shore, but that he ought to give me a little "change" with which to clad myself ere I returned to Virginia—He gave me Five Dollars—allowed me to go a shore along with an apprentice—a relative of his—by the name of John. The Capt. had on a former occasion, expressed some doubt as to my willingness to return home; indeed he had some months previously told his brother Shepperd that I was too well informed to ever think of again crossing "Mason and Dixon's line."—Seth was right—but how he came in possession of such information was more than I could well understand.—Got my Five Dollars, and John went ashore with me as "corporal" in charge of a suspected sailor on liberty. Destitute of low cunning, Capt. Foster was very high minded and direct in all his ways and was rather bold in announcing his intentions of having me arrested should I attempt to escape, but I doubt very much whether he made any effort to prevent it beyond that of sending the boy along with me, or if so I at least beat him on the "manoeuvre". After having stopped at a number of clothing stores in the neighbor hood of Peck Slip, I pushed my way yet further and further up the street occasionally making a zig-zag line by crossing and then wheeling around some corner, and so continued until I had gotten some two miles from the Ship when John asked me "how much further did I expect to go?" I told him I intended to keep travelling until I could buy a whole suit,—hat, boots and a watch for Five Dollars. Told him I had the money—showed it to him ($5-00). The little scoundrel was trying to run away himself, but like the boy who seeing others crossing a ditch ran up to its margin and vaulting around said "I want for to go but fraid for to venter." John however, now becomes very much exercised about my return to the Ship, and just at the time when I had discovered a furnishing store opening on two streets.—This store had its full complement of every article in the furnishing line; from a twenty five cents swallow tail (coat) to a handsome frock costing as many dollars. I told John, as we entered the shop the kind of goods I needed, and what I knew was impossible to be had with the money I held. I left John at our entrance end of the store after asking him to inquire the price of a pair of "self-adjusting—double action back-spring—cross at will—and ease me down", suspenders. The store was nearly filled with purchasers. I went to the opposite end placing myself as near the door as surrounding circumstances would seem to justify. I looked behind and ascertained John's exact position, as having his back toward me while drawing a pair of suspenders across his hand.—I walked out that door, nor have I seen John since. With all my troubles I certainly enjoy a good laugh when thinking of the boy and the kind of suspenders I asked him to price. On inquiry, I got me a boarding house—I think it was on Thompson Street or some other in that neighbor-hood—it was kept by a black man having a white wife (Irish)[63] I rather suspected this inn on account of its nudity and unaccommodating appearance, but being without money I was compelled to remain there until I could take my "reckoning". The landlord and his wife, I found, had reduced quarrelling and fighting to a system, for they were wrangling all day when ever he was at home, and no night found them without a fight. I never knew them to agree but upon two things, one was in drinking each other's health, and the other to get the boarder's money in advance, otherwise after he fell asleep. My appearance was well adapted to the surroundings having on, as I did a pair of hard worked overalls and tied round the middle with a piece of spun yarn—half sailor rigged. At this place I remained about three weeks. Finding myself perfectly secure from arrest, I brought suit against the Capt. for the recovery of my wages. The case, on application to Judge Culver—since that time however has been honored with the judicial ermine—then practicing law on West Broad way, I think it was, referred it to what was named to me as being the "Court of Kings Bench" At the time, this court must have been in vacation as the business was conducted by my counsellor, it seems alone by private interview when many interrogatories like the following were put and answered.[64] What is your name? Ans. Geo. Teamoh Where were you born? in Norfolk, Va. Ever a slave? My mother was born in that condition and I have been so up to about three months ago when I was hired by Capt. Seth Foster to cross the high seas as ship's carpenter. Who did the Capt. hire you from? Mr. Josiah Thomas.[65] Did you belong to J. T.? I did sir. When did he (Foster) hire you, and when did you go on the ship? I think it was near the middle of July, or it may have been about the first. Then you don't know exactly? No sir; but you can learn from the ship's journal, I think when I was put on duty—Yes, yes—I see, I see. George, what wages did the Capt. promise to give you? Not any at all. Then what did he say he would give Thomas for your services as carpenter?—I heard nothing beyond what my old Mistress told me.—Well, what did she tell you? She told me that she had charged the Capt. Fifteen Dollars per month for me; eh; eh;—In places of your employment in Virginia, what wages did your Master receive for your services?—For that branch of ship-carpentry termed "caulking", I have worked for from one dollar to one dollar and sixty two cents per day. Then you are not a practical carpenter—are you? When the master apprentices his slave, it is with the understanding that he is to learn what ever business is performed at a Shipyard. Where were you at work when your Master received a dollar and Sixty two cents for your services? That was in the Norfolk Navy Yard, but when hired as ordinary seaman he got for my services Eighteen Dollars per month. only. On board of what Ship, and when did you serve as ordinary seaman? It was on board the U.S. Frigate Constitution in 1845-46 then lying in ordinary off the Norfolk Navy Yard. How long did you serve there, I mean on the Constitution?—I think it was about two years in all, I served there sir. Who was in command of the Con. at that time?—One Capt. Piercy and Lieutenat Murphy, often called "Pat. Murphy".[66] You said you had worked in the Navy Yard at one dollar and Sixty two cents per day; were there any white men employed there at the same business and for the same. wages which was given your Master for your work?—There were some five, or six white men so employed getting two dollars per day.—How many colored were in the department as caulkers?—The average number was about fifteen colored as well as I can remember. Were they all being paid at the rates named when you left the State of Virginia?—They were. Did you perform your work satisfactorily to the Captain while on the voige?—I believe I did; that is I have never heard him speak other wise. You and the Capt. were on pretty good terms all the while were you?—Yes sir, he seems to have been more careful of me than of any person on the Ship.—In deed I regard the Capt. as being a gentleman. That will do at present,—call at my Office tomorrow morning at 9 O'clock, very good Sir, I shall not fail in doing so. Having made my appearance at the time agreed upon, it was decided in the first place that I was a free man from the very moment when I was taken on the high seas. And secondly being free and so circumstanced that a bargain could not be made between myself and the Capt. I was empowered to bring suit against the owners of the Ship for the recovery of an amount of wages not exceeding that paid to ship's carpenters employed in the marine service out of the port of New York. The Ship's journal was consulted, and it was found that I had been free three months employed at the rates then paid which were Forty five Dollars per month being equal to one hundred and Thirty five Dollars to sue for. Having signed the necessary papers, I left the collection of the debt in the hands of my attorney. I would know whether I could return to the Ship and demand my carpentering tools, bedding and some articles of wear? I was informed that I could do so, but that it would be safe while doing it to be accompanied by a couple of policemen, who would be furnished if desired. The protection was given, and on the third day after leaving the Ship I returned for my "pack." Of course, I had been apprehensive of some difficulty arising between myself and the Capt. growing out of my "sudden taking off" but fortunately for me—I presume—the Capt was called off on other business, and the mate, finding I held the vantage ground, interposed no objections, although he as well as his brother was of the opinion that I could have been arrested under the operation of what was known as the "fugitive Slave bill" whose terms however I had carefully examined as affecting my own particular case.—I knew I could not be arrested under its provisions. My fears consisted rather in being spirited away until a convenient opportunity might offer to take me back, than any thing else. But so far as I am aware no attempt had been made at reclaiming my person, nor had I any trouble while taking my things from the ship. The judgment of the court, after declaring me free, awarded me the sum of money for which I sued, & the bill for which being presented to the Capt. by the proper officer, the former refused paying it on grounds above stated. An attachment was about to be served when the

Capt. hastily tellegraphed for instructions to Messrs. Hardy and brothers in Norfolk (part owners of the Ship) and lost no time in seeing other parties in New York for the same purpose; and from all I could learn he was ordered to pay the money and let the ship go free. I continued my visits to the office from time to time to wit what action had been taken. Counsel delivered in my hands the sum of one hundred and fifteen dollars, I think it was, Capt. Foster refusing to pay any more. Of this money I paid the lawyer Twenty Dollars, that being the sum which he deducted on turning the remainder over. He thought it advisable that I should be content with what had been given; consequently I became satisfied at the result. And thus the matter ended after some three weeks remaining in the City of New York. My boarding master, on being acquainted with my case in the off set, made great pretensions in his considerations toward me as a philanthropist, but when finding I had gained the suit and recovered the money, it was found that he had but few cares other than those of trying to secure the majority of it for himself. I foiled however, his attempted unfairness. After having passed the above ordeal I took passage to the City of New Bedford Massachusetts, New York having reduced my hundred and fifteen Dollars to about Thirty four Dollars. The cold weather was now fast putting in on the New England coast or State and I anticipated having a very uncomfortable time of it at least during my first winter there. In New Bedford I passed under the appellation of "fugitive" which at once commanded the sympathy of that patriotic and generous people, and of whom it would seem useless that I should mention a single word after saying what, perhaps most readers know,—that this locality has always been considered the fugitive's Gibraltar—a truth which puts poetry and fiction to blush; as I had been there but a short while when, acting as without the intervention of reason or deliberation its good citizens gathered around me with charitable offerings and a protest of eternal hatred to slavery and all its alliances.[67] How like their great prototype, (Wm. Lloyd Garrison) the distinguished author of emancipation in these United States, who, while criticising the American pulpit,

Called the church, and bid
it stand its _____ground;
He argued not, but
Knocked it instant down.

And so with that loyal people, they had no argument for slavery but that of instant death to the institution. But notwithstanding their repeated manifestations of kindness, I was doomed to share a hard lot in that wealthy city. Once there you were "free indeed," and then thrown on your own resources after a few weeks of indulgence. Why I have always held that municipality in highest adoration is, what I have ever loved most, they, with a zeal which knew no bounds, had long long years ago, laid down as a principle and nailed to the mast-head of their little bark that had crossed so many rugged waters,—the full and untrammelled possession of one's ownership of himself, and then striking out for success with his own independent arm, exhibit to the world that nothing but oppression alone degrades an individual or a race when the colored man's misfortunes have been viewed from a complexional stand point.

Being in the midst of a refinedly educated people—if I may except the many who fled there as from the talons of the American eagle—I feared making any pretensions to letters, or even the usual formalities of American etiquette though repeated overtures were made to have me visit their lecture rooms, sewing circles, exhibition halls and other social gatherings of industrial enterprise and mental improvement. Not even could I be indeed [induced?] to go to their Evening Schools where the best Teachers were in attendance and education given without money or price; these opportunities I have since that time sorrowfully regretted, although there was no Teacher for my established method, in which case, or had I have went as requested, it would have been necessary for me to retrace the alphabet and all that I had gone over up to that time. In deed routine Teachers but rarely succeed with such cases, as I had witnessed sad failures of the kind in many who could spell, read and write tolerably well from self teaching while in Virginia, but having availed themselves of the advantages of these Schools which kept them tied down to prescribed rules, the learner's progress was not what it would have been had normal Schools prepared a Teacher for the case. There is something, to be sure, in classifying a School which such a method would forbid but then to meet this very great and just demand of advanced age is not beyond reach of the science of our times, for if one, by dint of perseverance against the heaviest odds known to the lettered world, could irregularly master two thirds of the English language proper before reaching the age of forty years, with mind still progressive, the argument seems clear, that under proper tuition such a genious, long before mental weakness or constitutional infirmaties—which are smoe [some] times the results of hard study—assailed him, and should his days be protracted to old age, he might ere that time have acquired a thorough knowledge of the English language. I regret that for lack of the very kind of teaching of which I have spoken, I must utterly fail in making myself as intelligible on this subject as in my opinion its character demands: The moderately intelligent reader, however may very readily see what I have endeavored to show in this connection, as well as in other passages of these writings. It will be a long while before our world can say "I have no need of such Teachers" Before parting with this subject, I here make mention of a circumstance which occurred between myself and one of the classical scholars of New Bedford, and this too, long after I had published a short article in the New Bedford Standard, defending the colored caulkers of that city from the unjust proscription under which they had been placed by the hand of associated corruptionists, or banded villany. And I will say here that said article had the desired effect, as we were all given employment the next day after its publication. There are those now living in that city who know the facts in the case.[68]

But to our heroine. Near about the time when Anthony Burns was returned to Virginia, a splendid and unusual entertainment was given at concert hall in that city.[69] I was served with a ticket (of course for the money—one dollar I believe it was) This hall, situated I think on Purchase Street, was splendidly decorated, being festooned with ever greens while within the ample folds of the American flag sat the goddess of liberty with hand firmly grasped on the hilt of the sword of justice and pointing heaven wards.[70] In addition to these, many other attractions, such as tables loaded with viands, pyramidal cakes, and every luxury that could satisfy the most fastidious appetite were there. The company had all nearly met when the floor of this spacious hall was cleared for a grand promenade, which consisted in a circular walk around the floor of the hall by a gentleman taking under escort one, or two ladies. The gathering had thus formed themselves, and on the "tramp" when I was viewing the liberty goddess and considering with what artistic skill it was executed. Indeed I had brought, or drawn it out as it were, into conversational relief,—if I may use that term.—Its well traced facial delineations were strongly marked as to firmness, resolution and execution, while its feet triumphantly rested on the riven chains of the slave. It was made to me of greater interest from the company's singing hymns, patriotic songs &c. &c. While thus enjoying a mental feast on viewing this beautiful picture, I was suddenly interrupted by a beautiful young lady of light brown complexion tall and of slender proportions. She was attired in all the style and fashions of the belles of 1854—and she was a scholar beyond all question, however disappointed I may have been in her at first as such. New England girls, whether white or colored are very "fast," and on such occasions as the above, are apt to make a lazy southerner fly round nolens volens, (willing or not willing) This beautiful fair approched me by saying "Sir, I perceive you are a stranger.—you have never been here before sir, have you"? With a long drawn "no mame" in reply said I "I have not, being late from Vigina". Said she "I have always, some how, had a dear liking for those who come to us from Virginia. I have an aunt now living in Cannada who was born in that State." "Was she ever a slave"? I inquired. "O yes," said she "hence her going to Cannada while young". By the time she had ended this sentence she hastily seized me by the arm, and skipping off with time to the singing, said "on with the promenarde a world of pleasures before us". I thought I would at once cut loose dull cares and enter in to the spirit of the meeting; and I began with saying, O bees-wax! that aint the way to call that word. She at once jumped behind her grammatic battery and riddled me. Taking the word from its root, she piled its original construction upon me in English, greek and latin; and I never heard a woman—and you know they have tongues—talk so fast, and yet so precise in pronounciation, in all the days of my life. Having finished mauling me with "promenarde", she next paid her respects to "bees-wax" saying "she was little surprised at hearing me call her by that name, a title she had never borne before that moment". In an instant I disclaimed "using the term in any such sense."—Here she gave me another most awful pounding with the contents of the grammar book. When she had finished speaking, I replied, "well Miss Having Delivered Yourself, I am none the better informed as to the correct pronounciation of the term in question". Without thinking I was using these adjective pronouns—if I may so call them—as a title, she let me off with an admonition, stating that "it would be utterly impossible for me to comprehend the rule which she had endeav-ored to teach, or point out to me without some scholastic experience on my part," all of which I very readily admitted, of course I did, and after she had advanced to a considerable extent into another subject, I informed her in very plain words, that "bad, and out of place as the term "bees-wax" may have been, I certainly did not employ it in any sense as applied to her as an individual, and that if the English language was self-supporting I had com-mitted a very grave error, in her estimation by addressing her as "Miss having delivered yourself," and continuing the connection." This was quite enough. She then struck out after the authors, and punched each of them in turn from Murray down to Bullions, and stated that there were but few rules in any edition acceptable to the last author, saving those of Mur-ray's.[71] In closing she said I "might—in all possibility be a good writer, or soon become so, but that I certainly did not know much about grammar." I thanked her for the complement, and after spending an agreeable Evening together, we parted in peace. I have only referred to this case in order to show how necessary it is for one to be acquainted with the language he pre-tends to speak or write. The condition I found myself in, as compared with the young lady in question was a most pitiable one. Then I reassert, that it will be a long while before our world can say "I have no need of such Teachers".

I have said I was doomed to share a hard lot in the wealthy city of New

Bedford. Not more so however than those who had preceded me from various parts of the South, Via of the "Under Ground Rail Road". About that time, the good people of N.B. had a very large number of fugitives to provide for besides others (freed and free borns) who preferred going there to make residence rather than remaining in the South to be reduced to a condition far worse than that of the Slave, by being hunted down under the slightest suspicion of a devotion to human liberty. Yes, rather than be sold for taxes, shipped of[f] to Africa, Hayti, South America, or any where else on God's green Earth. N.B. was our magnet of attraction. My pecuniary circumstances became such after being there a few weeks without employment that I was clearly forced to seek shelter under the roof of some friend who was able to protect me from the blighting and relentless fury of a New England winter then fast approaching My scanty means, which I thought would have lasted until I had gotten employment, had now quite deserted me. Having learned that snow shovelling was a paying business, I accordingly made me an implement for the purpose and went to work but with very little success, owing, in many cases to such work being put out by the season while much of it were performed by experts. Here thought I was another beautiful picture for the muse of verse—the ice-bound and snow covered city with clouds along the skies like mountains of flint, while piercing winds from frozen oceans, left no nook unsearched by their chilling blasts. Rain, hail, slush and then sleet were the common companions of that—to me—severe latitude. While seeking employ, I have often shifted f[ro]m side to side of ware houses groaning under the weight of life's luxuries, in order to catch some warmth from the sun. Very little business, such as give employment to the laboring classes is done there during mid-winter; in deed the spring is far advanced before work revives. Thus I lingered along, some times doing chores at others shovelling snow, &c. I had finally spent my last penny with which I bought me a biscuit. Feeling that stubborn independence which will not even yield to the laws of necessity, I could not, and did not play beggar. Some supposed I had money, others that I had good common sense which was regarded as its equivalent. Having always been remarkable for concealment, hiding the intent and purpose until realizing success or a dead failure, I did not reveal my condition to but one of the generous people of that city who but about two years previous had made his escape from Portsmouth, Virginia. After being there he assumed the name of James Pritlow. He was a grand son of the old man, Rev. Jeffery Tatem, who for many years led the colored pulpit here.[72] Pritlow was of refined taste and qualities and possessed a heart truly in sympathetic beat with the fugitive sufferers where ever known. And he was one of the few who by application had learned himself to read and write. He deserves honorable mention here. It was on a very cold morning in December as I stood near Waterman's auction store when Pritlow—riding in a small chaise owned by his employer—saw me, and at once weighed the burden of all my troubles before I had made them known to him.[73] After a few moments consultation he referred me to Deacon William Bush, than whom no better Patriot[—] none who could enter more fully in to the feelings and measure the depths of human woes—ever trod the soil of New England. It was about noon of the same day I saw Pritlow, when I applied to Deacon Bush as a boarder without having money and not knowing when I should be able to settle any bill I might make with him, as there appeared to be nothing doing, as shown, to justify shuch a hope. Having made this statement to the Deacon, he had no questions to ask but at once invited me to his residence—then on First Street—to bed and board. Mr. Bush kept a very respectable boarding house principally for the accommodation of mariners from off whaling voyages. He had a very large family to provide for, there being not less than eight or nine children alone; three, or four of these were married, however, which reduced his expences to that extent. But quite a large number of fugitives for a time stayed at his house and received the same hospitalities as did his regular boarders, notwithstanding the former were not able to pay their way. If any reliance may be placed in the statement of many of the older citizens of N.B. Deacon Bush,—now deceased,—has been one of the most zealous, hard working and liberal friends the fugitive ever found. Over such, I have often seen him weep in bitterness of soul while rendering all the aid and comfort within his power. In this respect he did what he believed constituted one of the most essential principles of his profession as a christian, "love thy neighbor as thyself." Mr. Bush has sacrificed much in delivering numbers of our people from the many deep distresses consequent upon human oppressions. No one has been more rejoiced at the several measures adopted by the general government, before or since the rebellion of 1862, for the amelioration of our condition than Wm. Bush, who, with his family was originally from the City of Washington, D.C. Mrs. Bush, indeed the whole family were not less humane in their devotions to mortal sufferers. The "family altar" was erected in this house, and regularly did they do sacrifice upon it unto the Lord of hosts which may they continue to do until called away by that common messenger who whispers at every breath we draw, "you must die, and can not live"![74]

Besides being a boarding Master, Mr. Bush would engage at any common laboring occupation of an honorable character, and on many a wintry day such as discribed above, him and myself might be found occupied as follows: lading, or unlading coal vessels; with pick-axe and spade digging through the rocky and frosted soil of the city for foundations upon which to erect edifices and other buildings; rolling staves—cording wood &c. &c. As mentioned else where, I had been, in Virginia well accostomed to that kind of labor, only that in my new home I was not sufficiently clad to endure for a very long while the rigors of winter, which Mr. B. well knew, and would often catch up some sailor's jacket which had been lying around and lend me as additional warmth. Seeing this great display of generosity on the part of Mr. B., I entered upon my new duties with a cheerfulness which follows on that of a settled board bill, and continued hopeful until he could find no paying employment, still I was secure during that winter, having been respected as one of the family. In spite of all the work I had performed, at the beginning of Spring I found my board bill had run upon me to an alarming degree. When Spring had fairly set in business commenced at the Ship Yards and on application to the Stowell Brothers—caulking contractors—I was taken in at the usual wages—Three Dollars per day.[75] I was not, at this, very steadily engaged, but could make as much time as others there employed—have often worked six days in the week. I did endeaver to get work at the Ship Yard of one Mr. Cannon, but soon found out that he did not give work to colored men. There was at one time a colored man at work for Cannon by the name of _____ Brown, who, with his family, in consequence of dull times in N.B. went to Canada.[76] The old gentleman—father to the Stowells—like his boys, always seems to have been touched with the feelings of human sympathy, as they have steadily given the fugitive something to do for a lively-hood. Such christian hearted people being the soul of a city, it gives me great pleasure to put these gentlemen's names to record here. My land lord, desiring to see me enjoy the fruits of my labor would but seldom receive of me over one third of my money, made out side of such employment as he would, at times give me. By this time I had again and again retraced my history from childhood and found that a despair, exceeding that which exiled pilgrim braved hovered around me as to again being in the presence of my wife and children, for in such rapid succession had one trouble trod upon another's heels, all hope, like the flickering light had vanished and all the mental forces such as affectional emotions &c left to roam as in blank void. Having written to Providence R.I. to a good old fugitive friend there he soon secured me employment as butler in the family of the famous governor Dorr. The governor, however, had deceased several weeks before I went there, though I was the first to enter his office after his death; indeed the removal of his library to [an]other part of the building was among the first labor I performed there. This was a very wealthy family, but did not negle[c]t a liberal bestowment of its charities upon the poor. Mrs. Dorr, Mother to deceased, always had her servants called in every morning to prayer and thanksgiving.[77] Acting in the capacity of a servant, I doubt whether I would have been better cared for in any other family in that city, not withstanding my wages were very small, being only Fifteen Dollars per month.

But not liking that kind of house work, I remained there during the three hardest months of winter only, and when the Spring opened I again returned to New Bedford; and having struggled on a few weeks there, I wrote to a brother of mine then and now residing in Boston, stating my circumstances. Receiving from him a favorable answer, I immediately packed off to that City.[78] Here I soon found employment at office keeping—and I might be better understood by saying office sweeping—under one Mr. Tisdale, said to be a millionier, who was then doing broker's business on, or near the north west corner of merchants Row and State Street. This gentleman, though doing a cash business of from one hundred to five or six hundred dollars per day, was a very parsimonious old gentleman after all. I have known a three penny piece to fall from the desk and elude his vigilence, but which, in his eagerness to find he has torn up the well secured mattings of his office floor. He was one of the Directors of the New England Bank of Boston, and read as his bible the "Boston Post,"—"Courier" and commercial publications generally.[79] He did not possess one spark of that patriotic fire which brought Old Massachusetts to the Holy Cross where, with uplifted hands before Almighty God, she renewed her devotion to suffering humanity—no,—not a spark of it. By being in that greatest of cities in this country, however, I soon found other work of a similar character, and it was not very long before I engaged in business at remunerating wages,—it was that of cleaning and repairing gentlemen's clothing, for which purposes I have rented shops in the immediate vicinity of the city hall and else where within suburban Boston proper. This seems to be an old institution in that city, and like "doing chores" is, or was at that time, conducted principally by colored people. By care, and a proper attention to business, many of these have risen to considerable wealth and popularity. Their principle mart, or place of trade is on Brattle Street where, on one side there well regulated stores are continuous from the corner of Court Street along way toward Quincy Market. They are, at present, scattered over the city. It was here I learned their branch of business, under Deacon Coffin Pitts, of whom it may be said, truly "no better tactician at that particular calling lived in the City, excepting, perhaps some two, or three others.[80] In Boston, as well as in New Bedford I might have availed myself of the many superior advantages of Day and Evening Schools, only from causes which I have already here considered. William C. Nell, Esq. of Boston,— whom all knowing ones must acknowledge to be the great historical writer of the colored Race, or at least one of the writers of our history,—seems to have a better knowledge of the kind of teaching I required and require, than any with whom I have conversed on that subject. Having become a member of his Lyceum, "Union Progressive Association," I was open for such improvements as he and his associates could make.[81] Without paying any regard to what he might have supposed to be a superficial covering, Nell took me at once from the raw, undevelop[ed] material, and like a skillful doctor sounding his patient found out the seat of my disease. There was not, however, a prescription in his vast library which could reach the case. After citing a number of authors who had been similarly circumstanced with myself, he went to work first by seeing what was healthy, and secondly by creating animation in the unhealthy parts. In all, Mr. Nell's manner of tre[a]tment,—though, perhaps nothing patent—seems to have over come an opinion I had long entertained, which was that similar cases could not be successfully dealt with by the routine Teacher unless the latter had been tought as above shown, or alluded to. The pressure of the times, however, not justifying my attention to letters, I did not receive that instruction from Mr. Nell which under more favorable circumstances I might have obtained.

A word for Mr. Nell before parting with this connection.

This gentleman was from his youth identified with the old original uncompromising abolitionists, having been raised as it were at the very feet of our great distinguished author of emancipation— Wm Lloyd Garrison, the very name of whom "tyrants dread to hear". For the many, and arduous labors both mental and physical which Mr. N. have rendered the hunted down fugitive he will never be rewarded in this world, nor does he expect it.—His whole life—as attested by those who have known him longest, has been one eternal round of devotion to the slave. Mr. Frederick Douglass, on a certain occasion while speaking of the many who from time to time he had in his employ as Clerks, writers, &c. after calling them over severally by name, said he, "then there is Nell, the only one I have ever known who was willing to work without any pay"[82]

Mr. N. has labored for our Race until that labor had even become burden some to our own pulpits in that they would but sel[d]om allow his notices of anti-slavery meetings to be read from the Desk, and it is yet ripe in my own recollection when I received of him a notice of the fact that our unmatched antislavery lion—Wendell Phillips, Esq. was to deliver his famous lecture on "Tousaint Loveature [L'Ouverture], the unmixed negro general" that on handing it in for publicity in one of our fashionable churches, I was careful to ask that it would receive a hearing.[83]—The paper was not read, and on asking the reason why, I was met by the objector who said its reading would have left some vacant pews in his church. I instantly informed him however, that, if he represented that Body in the particular named, his church was not only very weak but very wicked. Mr. P. did lecture as proposed in Joy St. Church, but to a very slim audiance, Mr.

Nell offering an apology that the public were not duly notified. He has been unremitting in his efforts in bringing to our assistance the best culture of the age at public halls and lyceum rooms. To the galleries of art and science, public library &c. &c. Mr. Nell has presented many of us tickets of admission free, thus showing that so far as his duty, and the great duty of man were concerned, ignorance and superstition should give way and be driven before the whirl winds of superior intelligence. His programme of the American revolution of 1776[–]1812 in which the colored soldier fighting foremost fell, is a yearly celebration in the City of Boston, and often attended with heavy expences. And I would say here that while the Old Colored gentleman, Deacon Foster's concerts[,] which seems to have had no earthly, or other significance[,] could be largely patronized by the citizens of Boston,—white as well as colored, Mr. Nell's representations of solid historical facts, could not—in most cases be made to pay for their getting up so small was the attendance on such occasions. Nothing discouraged however Mr. N. continued to show by lectures, publications and exhibitions that the black man had achieved many, very many darring deeds for which the world had not only failed to give him credit, but was in combined labor to blot him and all his works for ever from the book of memory. Our historian has brought forward much to our credit that might have been entirely lost.[84]

As an "Underground Rail Road" Agent, Mr. Nell had no equal, in the City of Boston, at least. During the most inclement weather and in the mid night hours I have known this good man to be plodding his weary way through slush and mire while conducting his fellow man beyond the reach of whips and chains. Such his tenderness of soul, I have known him refuse take the life even of a fly, when that insect was annoying him, considering that everything had rights, and that we should not destroy life whose pleagues we might endure but animation never restore. Were it a matter possible I should take much pleasure in giving here a biographical sketch of Wm. C. Nell, Esq. and let his memory live close beside my own, so that should the latter ever come before the public in printed form it would show, at least that one of the many formally oppressed Sons of the South, had not forgotten to make honorable mention of a patriot, whose life has been devoted to the freedom of his Race. But abler hands and more skillful brains will not,—it is to be hoped—fail in carrying to record the genious and mighty labors of this great, as well as good man.

I remained in Boston until about three years after the commencement of our civil war, consequent upon the slave holding states going out of the Union, and having then, left that city I entered upon my journey, "bound in the Spirit" once more to reach the land of all my former sufferings. An unhappy marriage of twenty four months during a twelve year's absence, served only to augment the desire to see, not only devoted friends living in Portsmouth and surroundings, but to learn, if possible what ever I could of wife and children, beside being near the remains of a loving mother.[85] Having heard that the old lady to whom I had formally belonged, and to whom I was indebted for my escape, was at the time lying very low, I made several unsuccessful attempts to reach the place—Portsmouth—previous to her departure to the heavenly land. The block-ade, being the cause of my delay, was not yet raised. By a permit from the Provost stationed at Fortress Monroe, I came to Portsmouth, but the remains of the lady referred to had been entoombed for several weeks. I visited the graves of her and my Mother, and called on all her surviving relatives, one of whom, Mrs. Mary Ann Grant, with whom I was raised, eldest, and only one living of the old family, met me as I entered the door, saying, in the deepest agony of soul, "George, Ma is gone".[86] And here she burst forth into a flood of tears with occasional suppressions of further details of her Ma's death, upon which, after addressing herslf to speech, she had much to say as well as of other family affairs. This lady has all the characteristics of her Mother, and I rejoice to record that I was received by her with no less of a humane, christian spirit than that, which on so many occasions I have experienced in her Mother. Indeed, we met as it were—all of us—around the family altar, and retraced, in sorrowful strains the history of our lives. It was a gloomy picture, enlivened alone by the hope that our future reward would be such as to place us with her so well beloved by us all. I had been at home but a few weeks when called upon by the freed men to espouse their cause by my assistance in giving shape to a political sentiment which would most likely accord with the administration and the Constitution of the United States. However willing I may have been to render them aid to the extent of my abilities, in the particular named, I deemed it my first duty to go in search of my long lost family whom I had left exposed to the patrons of the auction block at Richmond when I was shipped to go on the german ocean. As soon as convenient I went to Richmond, and there found my family living in what had been a horse stable. She was bed-ridden, emaciated, pale and al-most speechless. The child I left with her had now grown to the age of a young woman, and made a mother per force of slavery by her licentious master, and the master of all diabolism, Henry Smith a Richmond rum sel-ler.[87] He it was who was the last purchaser of mother and daughter, but by some means during the occupancy of that city by the Federal troops, they (mother and daughter) again fell into the hands of the Lindsays, who know-ing that this strong hold of the Rebellion would soon be obliged to release its grasp upon these chattles, began at a new point of persecutions just at a moment when they were compelled, by military authority to relinquish their claims in them.[88] They had been, however, several months given up when I found them and I here take occasion to speak of Rev. Chas. Bowe in grateful praise and thankful terms that gentleman having given my distressed family bed and board after being hunted down as they had been by those who owned them; and it is with no reflections upon Mr. Bowe what ever when I mention "horse stable"; for he had fitted it up as well as he could to be tenanted.[89] His family moreover, be[i]ng very large, this was the only accommodation accessable to the strangers. Returning home as pennyless as when I first left the Capes of Virginia, I was of course, in no condition to render my circustances any better, but only begging that no one lay hands on me while working out my destiny. We were in Richmond but a few weeks after my arrival there, when I sent mother and daughter to Hampton, Va. near their better acquaintances, until I could make suitable provission for their comfort and be present with them. Coming to Portsmouth, my old home, I here tendered my services to the loyal people in what ever form I could accomplish the greatest good for the struggling patriots in a moral warfare to reconstruct the State on a basis of perfect equality before the law, for all men.[90] In obedience to instructions from the general government, acting through a Military Commander—Governor Pierpoint[91]—I believe it was—each county in this, as in other states which had seceded from the Union, were required to hold delegated conventions to choose members to be voted for by the people, for the purpose of meeting at Richmond in 1867 in general convention to form a constitution—Republican in form— for the State of Virginia.[92] Having entered the canvass in favor of such convention, I was duly elected by the majority of the citizens of Portsmouth and Norfolk County a member of that distinguished body, the labors of which having been watched with so much interest and published accordingly, throughout the country, makes it unnecessary that I should comment thereon even were I capable of so doing.[93] I would say, however, that out of the great number of those who costited [constituted] its member-ship, but few, (if I may except the conservative element) who were very good expounders of constitutional law; these, cradled in the science, could only be put down by the weight of the majority, while it must be confessed that argument met argument with a force and purpose which none but a critic of keen penetration could distinguish between.[94] Never was this more manifest than near the first days of the sittings of the convention when the first shot was thrown from the conservative side by one Mr. J.C. Gibson,[95] as to the intellectual and educational complexion of that Body. Rising in his place, and addressing the Chair, Said he "Sir, I would like very much to inquire of those best prepared to give the desired information, what is the intent of this vast Body of people from every section of the State meeting here? Is it a convention to make a constitution for the State of Virginia?—certainly this can not be. What are the ulterior aims and objects you would accomplish by this unusual conglumeration of odd commixture?—Now gentlemen, to look stern facts in the face ought you not to feel ashamed of yourselves?—and I speak it in all seriousness. Not content with subjugating our people by one of the most unprecedented sacrifices of life and property that the world ever read of; not content with the honorable surrender of gen. Robt. E. Lee than whom no greater soldier ever crossed steels with a superior enemy! I say not content with these, but by reason of your unsystematized military dictation you have insinuated yourselves in to our back yards and kitchens, begging our negroes—poor ignorant creatures—to vote you to this—so called—convention, and that you would tack their names to the ticket—good for seven, or eight dollars per diem—yes, you have scraped our farm yards and dragged our plantations by the rule of bayonets, in order to complete a system of persecutions upon these poor deceived people, as well as your infamous endeavors to make them our masters and then work up a double deception to bring this proud old Commonwealth under your own control. Who I ask have you brought in here to make your constitution? I learn that Dr. Thos. Bayne[96] is about the ablest man you have on that side of the house—best scholar, acquainted with parliamentary law &c. And I would say that the Doctor has made some very good points if his language has been understood—certainly it was beyond my comprehension, for the most part." It was a source of regret to some of us that the Doctor should have swallowed this bait so readily, as was shown on a subsequent occasion, when, to create a little merriment, the brother to J.C.G.[97] who had relieved the president, yielded the Chair to the Rev. Doctor, who accepted as he had a right to do, though amidst roars of laughter. In the above, I have merely given the substance of Mr. G.'s remarks, showing the animus characterizing the more spirited and out spoken members on the Democratic side of the hall. The vilest epithets were applied by the opposition to those who constituted its loyal membership, as, even Congress itself had been called an infamous Body. Fresh, from the boiling caldron of war, however, with their disappointments and losses passing before them as in panoramic view, little else could have been expected than that of the most virulent givings out. True it is that many of their prophetic expressions referring to the colored race have already found a solution in the process of reconstruction, however erroneous we may have considered them at the time! Yet we were well aware that much was said in that way to cover themselves with appearances, such as would justify them in believing that they could, by these repeated surges at the very centre of radicalism, take off its "wire edge" if not reduce its numbers. But this was a failure in either case, and only served to add fuel to the flames, as the radicals from that circumstance carried their temper up to white heat, often resulting in the most bitter personalities. Indeed we have known angry debate to culminate to a point so provoking as to end in physical strife between the parties to it.—But the colored members of the convention, aye the weakest of them—if I may except one of the number—displayed remarkable good sense in not allowing themselves to be wrought upon and captured by these sophisticated arguments, founded as they were upon prejudice the most hateful. In this convention, we did not have a colored member who could off set a speech of any great length coming from the other side but we have invariably voted right on the proposition from which the arguments were drawn, independent of the many stages of amendments &c through which it may have had to pass. Nor was it to be expected that we—colored,—could by any possibility, at that time have had the most distant knowledge of constitutional reconstruction, as many of us could neither read or write, having gone there as shown by Gibson "from the farm yards" &c.[98] For my part I went there a "graduate" from Capt. John Thompson's brick yard, and finished my trade at caulking; hence if there had been anything to perform in that particular direction I was on hand to assist in the matter. But in spite of their disqualifications, my people seems to have been possessed of a natural etching to meet, in open debate, every question which came up for discussion; So much so, that the previous question was often made operative against members from either side who had prepared written speeches of some length to deliver. On all questions of great importance, debate was restricted within certain limits, such for instance as the "Test Oath" and "Disfranchisements," allowing for these, from an hour to an hour and a half's to each member.[99] Under all the circumstances, the colored members, for the most part, bore themselves well, only here and there harassing the opposition as chance would offer,—in their style. For our self, we had a turn at the wheel of fire, and in about forty minutes it burnt all the education out of us which we had gathered within that number of (40) years. Agricultural degrees and brick yard diplomas I found passed for but very little. After delivering our speech we had but very little to say during the entire session, beyond that of voting, and rising to questions of privilege &c. I was either misunderstood at one time, or advantage taken by the greedy reporters, in regard to explaining my vote. I was opposed to allowing any member an hour and a half to speak on any question because I thought it not only injurious to the reputation of the convention but a shameful and uncalled for sacrifice of time.—It was on the question of disfranchisement, when the ayes and nays were called. The Clerk having reached my name, I arose in my place and said:—"Mr. President: Sir, in explaining the vote which I shall cast on this occasion, I desire to say that, after having witnessed such a shameful consumption of time which has been occupied by this body from its first sitting to the present moment, and sir, because I am not disposed to be a "bane" to the Convention, I vote nay". This created quite a titter on both sides of the House, as Dr. Bayne had been remarkable for his frequency of rising and holding his position, until shown whether he was in order or otherwise. From this circustance, the Dr. was placarded at once as being the "bane of the convention." None figured more successfully in making this an exposure than that well known Democratic Journal— the "Southern Opinion,"[100] which paper had already rendered itself obnoxious to the loyal members by its transformed and transferred photographic publications of the convention, which was, I believe, published weekly. Besides this, it would be well to say here, that free circulation was given to whatever would intimidate, or retard the progress of radicalism. Pictorial representations of murders, skull and cross bones, and many other frightful exhibitions, all intended—no doubt—as boding the sound of the funeral bell to those in the convention who had assumed a position antagonistic to the Democracy of the land, were scattered around as freely as a salesman's card. These scare crows, however, far from impeding its progress only had a tendency to stimulate the Republican side, often causing them to originate vexatious measures as an off set. The initials of the Ku Klux Klan were here also blazoned forth with appropriate arguments—in disguise—to give that organization the deepest significance where ever it existed. And while by the Radicals a decent respect was paid to the public opinions of such men as Henry Clay, John C. Calhoun, Daniel Webster and others, the principles of the Republican party were here assailed and vilified by the Democracy with all that bitter resentment and revenge so characteristic of a once ruling but now waning aristocracy. As shown, not one of the colored members was sufficiently qualified to enter up on the brod field of constitutional debate, which we regret to say, being one of that class. But as with others, the fault was not ours. Yet there were some two, or three of the colored delegates who, if they did not then distinguish themselves as scholars, being young and progressive, they will—it is to be hoped—yet live to show mankind that though born, and fastened in the anaconda folds of slavery,—the curse of God's fair image,—they will, at no distant day bring out from the rough block the polished stature; and although the cold shoulder of a reluctant recognition may be given, still the workman-ship will stand the test, and invite the keenest criticism.—"Slow rises merit by poverty depressed" is an adage from Ben. Johnson,[101] and perhaps never more true than in our case. The Representatives from our

District (Norfolk County and the City of Portsmouth) were the honorables Jms. H. Clements, Luther Lee Jr. and my humble self, as already shown. Aside from voting, there were but few men who did the work of that convention,[102] as quite a number of the colored delegates could score well with the majority of white men—on the Republican side—who made up its numerical strength.

Mr. Clements was an active hard working, member of the convention and could place the making of a constitution for the State of Virginia upon no other grounds than those of the highest statesman-ship. Recognizing the position of the Democracy, he gave them no time to glory over the glove, but when they threw it down he at once snatched it up, and pursued them as with Roman sword, from the first, until the sine-die adjournment of that Body. His consistancy and manly bearing gained him many friends among those who at the out set were his opponents. Mr. C. originated many measures in our constitution which if not now realized with a just appreciation, will within a few years meet the approving consideration of all who love equal laws for the government of a community of races.[103] Mr. C. has—pursuing on the adjournment of the convention—followed up our victories with no less zeal than that which distinguishes every great leader in a patriotic cause. Since those days this gentleman has given his entire support to the loyal masses in our District, and else where, while engaged in the desperate struggle to maintain republican ascendency; principally confining his efforts to that of purifying the party, or that portion of it which was always etching to "bolt" on account of the presence of the negro. The people of Virginia having a high admiration for manly courage and consistancy, have so conducted themselves towards him during, and since the exciting days of the Convention, that he has rather gained on their esteem than lost their confidence. Perhaps I could not give a more convincing proof of his republicanism than that which occurred in the campaign of 1871 when the candidates from either side (republican and democratic) were running as representatives for the Lower House of our State Legislature This spirited canvass having caught the republican ranks divided, the democrats gained their man;[104] and it was on the event of celebrating their triumph when a colored policeman of this city by the name of Jno. Wilson was assinated by the bloody hand of democracy on the Evening of the 11th of November 1871. He was stealthily fired upon and shot through the head. Such an amiable young man as Wilson, beloved by all in the community, being so murderously dealt with was more than the friends of humanity could well endure. Indeed the deepest regrets were expressed by our opponents as to the foulness of this most atrocious act—whose character receives additional blackness when it is remembered that the offender could not be brought to tryal. As an off set to the bl[o]ody tragedy, Mr. Clements, therefore, as in vindication of his principles, had Mr. Wilson's grave opened, and his remains interred in the white people's cemetery, close beside his (C.) own deceased relatives. Nor was this all; himself and other distinguished white gentlemen acted in common with their less favored brethren as bearers of the pall on this very sad occasion. [105] This was regarded as an unprecedented act in the annals of our State, certainly so in this section of it, and many were the whisperings as to the "whys and wherefores" &c. some vowing to unearth the sleeping dead, while others declared it a base reflection upon the character of our white community that such an outrage should be tolerated for a single moment. While this unprovoked murder reluctantly found editorial regrets, the same democratic journals did not fail in their censurable criticisms of those who were party to obtaining the lot in which this colored man's remains were buried. To save our city from riot and blood-shed consequent upon the assassination of the lamented Wilson much is due to the advice of Mr. C. and other leading republicans who early saw that the colored element had been driven to exasperation. And being without warrant that the decision of our courts would have given us any redress, admitting the assassin had been arrested, seems to have kept alive the fire of revenge among the whole republican party; for although disunited but a short while previous to this sad calamity, they were at least agreed in sentiment, that the perpetrator of the deed, if not found, his friends, aiders and abettors should be summarily dealt with. The concentrated strength of the republican party being no mean power, in this District, where, as in opposition to the democracy, force would have opposed force, created an uneasiness among the friends of law and order much in proportion to that recorded of Melzar Gardner. [106] And while I may say that that gentleman— Mr. C.—is no particular friend of mine, I must ascribe to him a power, and force of character in bringing peace out of confusion which is remarkable in a man of humble birth. When freedom for the negro was about to be launched into being, and the dark and thunderous clouds of persecution were breaking around us, beyond the influence of Hon. Jms. H. Clements and a few others, none dared to "curb its fierce lightnings and hold the trembling fire". Therefore in noticing that gentleman's career during many years, and observing his devotion to the poor and needy of all classes, I felt it my duty to speak of him as I have.—More I might have said, but certainly not less. Our opinion is, that had, even one third of those republicans who made up the constitutional convention, have acted up to their convictions, and in accordance with the will and wishes of their constituents after the adjournment of that body & in the same conciliatory and determined spirit which has again and again shown itself in Mr. C., the sterile and barren fields of Virginia, aye all her vast commercial and other interests, might now be in an advanced state of prosperity far exceeding that which her proscriptive legislation is now strangling in the middle passage. But by their greed of office we lost the Legislature, and that settles the matter.

On the adjournment of the convention I came home and assisted in general to make the constitution which we had formed a living reality. Having made myself perfectly familiar with the situation of affairs, I entered the contest with a full determination to follow up the victory so recently achieved by the friends of impartial freedom. To accomplish any thing very desirable in this way required almost a super human effort as we were now, for the first time brought into juxtaposition, with hither to distant associations. Anticipating this state of things however, previous to the assembling of the convention, there had been a preliminary meeting called, consisting of about Twenty five or Thirty citizens, for the purpose of laying down a platform or principles upon which republicans generally could unite. This meeting assembled in one of the class rooms of the North Street methodist church, and was represented by equal numbers of white and colored. Being appointed as chairman of Committee on resolutions, I wrote, and brought in, at a subsequent meeting, held, at the same place, a series of resolutions which was received and adopted over several other platforms which were presented, the arguments showing that they were more in consonance with the Federal Constitution and the promulgated laws of reconstruction by Congress than those which had been offered by our white friends. After being critically examined by sections, they were then unanimously passed as a whole, and for some time after the ratification meeting, it was known as the "Teamoh Platform". And although the measure was published in one of our supposed to be republican papers," [part of page is missing] I was given no credit [part of page is missing] I do not pretend to say however, that this oversight,—if I may so call it—was at all attributable to the Editor, as there were two or three colored men who regretted my prominence as father to the measure.[107] These were on the committee, but failed to advance a single idea, or write a word as contained in the platform, and when interrogated in consequence, the lame excuse was, that they "had supposed I could—unassisted—furnish a document sufficient to meet the emergency," which—as shown—I had to do.

While my efforts have been untiring in other directions in support of the party, never have I labored with more determined zeal in any particular field of its calling than that of establishing an equalization of labor and pay in the Norfolk Navy Yard among all classes of its operatives.[108] The various plans employed for this purpose it is not necessary here to mention, however successful I may have been in the performance. The principles of the Chicago platform gave ample margin for my theatre of action, and keeping which steadily in view, I claimed every inch of ground covered by its provisions. And just in proportion as congressional legislation favored our cause by amendment after amendment to the Federal Constitution, just in that proportion have I fallen behind those measures, urging our claims while within safe distance of their constitutionality.[109] My advantage—or at least one of them—was, that not less than two thirds of our laboring classes of whites were in a large degree dependent on government patronage for support, and that those people had a right to expect it—and has now—from the day of gen. Robt. E. Lee's surrender until the rebellious states had been fully restored. And although much has occurred since that day, causing the government to hesitate in its favorable considerations towards our people, in its attempted discriminations between the good and the bad, the latter has often been substituted for the former. That those who fought under gen. Grant, had a priority of claim on the government works we all know, notwithstanding having received every penny of their pay as sailors soldiers, &c &c. while so engaged. Indeed many northern men enlisted more for the purpose of having a "free fight" than that of any concern for the freedom of the slave. These, with bounty jumpers,[110] and other deceivers of the government might be counted by tens of thousands if not hundreds of thousands. The government, therefore, in dealing out its patronage, had to take both "wheat and tare" of its own make up, and as chance would offer, when the war was over, they settled, or many of them stopped in those sections which pleased them best. Our own District, from its proximity to the North, has been very largely represented in this way.—They have not been all good, nor have they been all bad. But in any case, they could all show papers why they should have the exclusive right to the employment afore said; and where no papers could be obtained, many a poor fellow has lied all the way from his lips clear through to his back-bone showing his rights, &c. To get employment then, for our own suffering people—more especially those who had not been in the Federal army—(and there were many hundreds in Portsmouth alone—required no small amount of labor and patience. And here again I use the name of the patriotic and humane Clements whose advocacy by letters, and in person before the Secretary of the Navy, and our Representative from this Dis. to the Lower House of Congress and our United States Senator, the Hon. B. F. Lewis was urged with a fervor not inferior to that of the importunate widow.[111] Senator Lewis and congressman Platt, have used their influence with the Secretary,[112] Naval Committee and where ever else they could carry our cause with any hope of success. And I deem it useless to say here the part these trusted Representatives has taken in securing such an amount of labor of all grades from the government, as would fore shadow reconstruction in its truest sense. And however others may differ with these gentlemen in other respects, the interests of the laboring classes have been regarded by them as paramount to all else. It was on the 10th of May 1871 when we were ushered in the presence [and to the] chamber of the Sec. of the Navy by Col. Platt, when his hon. the Sec. attentively listened to all we had to say in regard to our mission as a committee man.[113] And however out of place our English, we done our best, being promised when through that what could, would be done in our case. We then commenced our remarks as follows:

"Mr. Sec. of the Navy:—

Sir,
I would say to your honor, that, at an unusually large meeting called by the citizens, mechanics and laborers of the City of Portsmouth and Norfolk County, on Friday Evening 28th of April,[114] instant, having as its object two purposes; to wit:

Fist: To reorganize the Executive Committee, whose term of office expired on the 18th of last month; and Secondly, to consider what further could be accomplished by way of securing such favors from the general government as would relieve the many hundreds and thousands among us whose present necessities are fast reducing them to a condition of destitution, want, starvation, and all their concomitants. To this we put ourselves to work. Sir, this meeting was organized under the presidency of our excellent Mayor of the City of Portsmouth, and whom I accompany here, he having the double honor conferred upon him of being Mayor of the City, and Chairman of the New Committee, and chosen by that body, while sustained by the great bulk of the loyal masses to present their grievance here.

Sir, you have heard the statements made by the chairman of our Ex. Committee; they are all true; and occupying, as I have the honor to occupy, the second position on that committee, I appear before your honor in common with him, humbly asking that so far as your honor's instrumentalities may go, that you will duly consider our mission by hearing our prayer and answering our request. Sir; born and raised in that community, and having spent a life of nearly fifty years in Virginia slavery, some times in, and often out of the Navy Yard, has rendered me perfectly familiar with that people, and on seeing such a manifest disposition on their part to support that government which freed me and my fellow bondsmen, it is with the greater zeal, I would press the object of our mission upon your honor's respectful consideration. We ask no donation beyond that which, with favoring circumstances, the well muscled arm of the mechanic and laborer can hew out for themselves. But in the absence of these, we shall feel doomed to pass through the ordeal of Reconstruction with no other help or hope than that which leads to despair.

And I would further say,—without, I hope being burdensome to your honor's patience—that the geographical position of our section gives it every advantage over any other territory in our country in point of Naval architecture, navigation &c. The best floating batteries of which any Navy can boast, as compared with our own, were framed and fitted there. The great Eastern in a direct line from England has safely rode at anchor within our waters. And even as by a fatality irresistible to the mariner, he is often driven by stress of weather, hundreds of miles from his line of trade to seek protection behind Cape henry light house, where he is doubly safe within the iron jaws of Fortress Monroe and the Rip-Raps. The Monster of the ocean in Naval war fare (Merrimac) received her well timbered keel and plating there on quick time.[115]

But I do not pretend to inform your honor as to these very natural advantages and facilities, for in days gone by when they should have been ignored, the party in power secured the largest patronage to th[os]e, who, since have invoked the spirit of war to break up the government of these United States.

Sir, the God of nature has bountifully spread forth His Hand in making our sea port the most available in the known world and Congressional legislation with your honor's favoring opinion, should—it seems—constitute this section, what has been long aimed at—the great naval depot of the country.

Sir, we are a community of hardy mechanics and laborers, with our wives and little ones looking to us for support. And we ask these favors for the sake of the sailor and soldier, and for the sake of the citizen who makes both sailor and soldier. And we urge it for all without discrimination. We ask it for the white man because our interests in this particular are identical, and we beg it for the black man for the reason that all the money earned by him, in government Departments, and else where, previous to the rebellion has been turned over to his Master, leaving him nought to subsist upon when the war broke out but the atmosphere by which he was surrounded.

But with this, as with other matter referred to here, I am fully persuaded your honor needs no information from me. Let us indulge the belief that a benign government will, through your great influence, stoop at last and touch our complaint. We do not forget the zeal with which our representative to the Lower house of Congress has labored to this end, and to some extent has been successful, but the demand has so far exceeded the supply, that seemingly all has been unavailing.

And I would say to your honor, in conclusion that we are not here as advocates of any particular clique or party outside of those who have accepted the situation; and these, with us have thrown themselves on the progressive side, declaring it their duty to repair the damages of the past, in strict accordance with the terms of reconstruction And, Sir, it is to be regretted that certain government Officials and others, having failed in taking a broad comprehensive and catholic view of this matter, the government patronage in consequence, has been narrowed down to the

"Rings" "Cliques" &c. And these have been utterly denounced by large and over whelmning majorities of the honest people, as no doubt your honor may have recently seen in the journals of our locality.[116] Having never doubted your honor's devotion to those great over shadowing principles which struck down the tyrant and gave freedom to America, so shall we cherish the hope that you will, at least suggest, and if possible, have put in operation some plan by which the sons of toil may obtain that Bread for which we shall ever pray.

And now we most humbly thank your honor for this kindly interview and most patient hearing: and we leave, in the hope, that your days may, be many, and your administration crowned with abundant success."

While his honor—the Secretary—has sympathised with us, and Col. Platt the mean time endeavoring to bring our case before Congress in its proper light,[117] we have not been able to witness any very material change in the amount of employment given us at this yard beyond such as we then had. But as it is a Naval necessity, the government will soon be compelled to build some where, and it occurs to us that the country should be willing to make of this Section all that could be desired as a commercial port and Naval Station And the North being responsible for the existance of an institution which brought on all the sufferings we now endure, should feel more than willing to second any effort made to redeem one of its oldest Common wealths.

I was elected to the Senate of the first Legislature which assembled (1868) [1869] after the ratification of the Constitution by the people of Virginia. After stating as I have that in consequence of the treachury of many leading republicans,—and I would also add, that of democratic deceptions—it would be useless to ask, what was the political complexion of the Virginia Legislature?—It was democratic, and largely in the majority, but few counties being able to withstand the giant frauds practiced upon them by the old campaigners of democracy. There were no remaining doubts with the members of the Constitutional Convention, (excepting those who "sold out") on the sine die adjournment of that Body, but that amidst the most stubborn opposition that might be shown, we would have carried the Legislature. I have but little to say as to my Senatorial experience.[118] In deed, had I, or any colored member of that body—and there were six of us—been as ornate and forcible in argument as the Sumners or Websters have been in their day,[119] we should have failed in making a single impression on the most liberal minded of the "Only True Republicans," as that was the assumed name by which Democracy carried the State. Other means were employed, but the above was the most potent lever. Senator J. W. D. Bland, who was one of the many killed when the upper flooring of the court-room fell on the heads of the assembled hundreds while they stood in the hall of representatives, was often listened to by the opposite side, and in many cases his speeches,—though not abounding in fluency or depth of thought—would receive from their journals a verbatim report,—apparently,—though greatly altered from what I had known to be his own language. The same also characterized his course in the Constitutional Convention, of which he was a delegate.[120] That he was an intelligent, progressive young man, and one of good social qualities, I presume none will deny. But Senator Bland, from causes well known to us, was not destined to shoulder the responsibilities of an out and out Republican. This young man, whose personal appearance and general make up, I must say, and without flattery, was the most perfect specimen of human mould it has ever been my pleasure to look upon. It is likely he had acquired his knowledge of letters in the darker days of slavery. I have been informed he was a country school Teacher in his Town Ship in the county of Prince Edward, from whence he was sent by his confiding constituents, to Convention and Legislature. He essayed at one time to change his course and stem the current of opposition; but alas! he had drifted so far on the destructive Falls of our political niagara, that, while frenziedly gazing around, he found— greatly to his sorrow—all was lost. I visited his room and sat through the night—laid my hand upon his frigid brow, and mourned "his untimely taking off." I accompanied his remains to his Residence at Farmville, where they were taken possession of by one of the Benevolent Societies, and decently entombed. I was the sole member from Senate or Lower House who followed his remains to their final resting place. A proper respect was paid him by the conservatives, three or four of whom escorted the remains to the junction between Farmville and Richmond; and on returning to the Capitol, offered resolutions of condolence, which,—of course—were unanimously passed. Senator Bland left, to mourn his loss, a young widow, and two small children, for whom the conservatives of the two Houses, and a few republicans, have, I believe, made some provision.

On the heels of Bland's death, came that of Senator Isaiah L. Lyons, of Elizabeth City.—Co. He was a native of New York, having—it is said— graduated there, as practicing physician under Doctor MCuine Smith.[121] He was the only colored member in either branch of the legislature who possessed a routine education. The old adage, that "death loves a shining mark" holds good here. Doctor Lyons, was a very fine looking young man, and must have been—for his good looks at least—very highly appreciated among the more fashionable circles of his city. His family residence was in

Hampton, they* having come there during the war. He had a plentiful flow of good language, though not able to follow his subject from premise to conclusion with any remarkable force of reasoning. While his merit for penetration was doubtful, he was greatly lacking in tersness of style, often rising in his place to address the Chair, as though startled by a frightful dream. He was also sadly defective in analogy, as I have seldom known him to prove any one thing by reference to another. Very frequently his speaking would grate upon the ear. Added to all this, he fell into intemperate habits by which he was not only led away from his Senatorial duties, but contracted a disease which ended his life. In his deportment, Doctor Lyons was a perfect gentleman, and a sound republican. The former may be truly said of Senator Bland, whose courtesy far exceded his republicanism.

We offered resolutions of condolence for Dr. Lyons, similar to those passed for Senator Bland. Senator Riddick white of Nansemond County, who while on leave of absence, was taken sick in New Orleans, died in that city. His death occurred between that of Bland's and Lyons'. He was a conservative.[122] Speaking to Dr. Lyons' resolutions, we said.

> "Mr. Speaker:—Sir, flashing along the wires, comes the deathly telegram of another Senator. By the mysterious designs of an All Wise Providence, another chair is made vacant in this hall, by the sudden taking off of Senator Isaiah L. Lyons.
>
> While lapping the morning dews of youth, and peering at the horizon of man-hood, with advantages to become both good and great, at once the tidings reaches this chamber that Dr. Lyons has gone to his God:—Peace to his ashes! And this—no doubt—is the desire of us all. This vacant chair, as with the other two so recently made here, reminds us that we are all passing away. Mortals can find no shield adaquate to this warfare, not even the virtue and flushness of youth can ward off the messenger clad with immortality. Again we say, peace to his remains. And may his mentally afflicted widow and relatives find consolation in Him, who is the Father of us all."

His remains were forwarded to New York and taken possession of by his relatives, and in due time were buried in great pomp and splendor by the Masonic fraternity of that City.

The following named gentlemen (colored) of the Senate have, in all their Legislative course, proven themselves true to the great principles of the Republican party.

Senators Wm P. Mosel[e]y John Robinson and Frank Moss.[123] Never, save once, have I ever known these gentlemen to differ with me in any very

---

*his family.

important vote, or question affecting the interest of the State, and even then they went with me and carried the bill, when shortly afterwards a reconsideration was called for which resulted in the passage of a measure which their former vote had already killed. The measure in question was called, "The Pennsylvania Central Rail Road Bill." It created great excitement when first offered for the consideration of the two Houses. Distinguished gentlemen from the North were lobbying for its passage, while no less distinguished gentlemen from the South, with warmer zeal opposed its passage. The raddicals claimed it as being a republican measure, and the opposition regarded it as being anti-republican, and ruinous to the State, and greatly so to our own section—"Tide water—.[124] This Bill, or the character of it was well known to rail road men who could at a glance see all its minutia. As to my knowledge of what would have been the result of its passage, when first brought forward, I had as well have voted one way as an other. On all matters, such as Rail Roads, however, more particularly those affecting the interest of our own locality, I have generally consulted the opinion of Senator Walter H. Taylor,[125] the candid conservative. Of course, I could not participate in the debates for the reason that they were not only intricate and mazy; but just as winding as the roads which brought forth these arguments. After having learned the character of this bill, and after seeing, also, that some of the most talented Democratic members of the Senate were pleading for its passage with greater zeal than ever Daniel Webster advocated the fugitive slave Bill, I addressed the following communication to the Editor of the Norfolk Virginian:

"Senate Chamber
Richmond, Va. Feb. 16 th 1871[126]
Ed. Norfolk Virginian:

Sir,—
Having been frequently questioned since the Pennsylvania Central Rail Road proposition came up for consideration in the Legislature, how I expected to vote on that measure, I would briefly state, that in view of the late action taken at meetings held in the cities of Norfolk and Portsmouth, instructing our delegates to use their influence in a given direction to defeat the aims and object of the great Pennsylvania Central Rail Road Corporators, that I was sent here to do the will of my constituents in whatever looked to, and favored their interest as an agricultural and commercial [words missing]. And to protect those interests should be the high duty of those whose sections of the State,—aye, the State itself—are at stake. Being a caulker and not a Rail Road Schemist it is not very likely that I could comprehend all the advantages and disadvantages contained in the Bill. And I feel rather inclined to help raise the Ship of State than sink her any lower. And, Sir, if the sons of Virginia will cut the jugular vein and let flow the

life blood of their own State, I shall not be party to it. Nor do I hope ever to participate in any movement that will further distress my Race by bringing down upon them the trip hammer vengeance of land owners Rail Road contractors and agents, and all that class of merchants who give us employment. And having heard arguments pro and con in both branches of the Legislature touching this matter, the above is the common sense view I have taken of it as affecting our District more particularly. It may be different with other sections more remote from the Seaboard. But I look at it much like our Legislature regards the "whipping-post"—it is all well enough till it comes to my turn. I like all Rail Road enterprises until they begin with running me off the track. I am aware that attempts have been made to convert this into a partizan question, but as I do not see the force of such reasoning, I shall not base any opinion which I may entertain there on. What we want is work and remunerating wages, and other things will follow as matter of course. And I am fairly persuaded that if we insist on taking steps diametrically opposed to the advantages we have, and those we seek, we shall loose the sympathy of that class upon whom we depend for our daily bread. We ask for no other wrights than those belonging to us under the State Constitution. These granted we shall be more than willing to help our people out of any difficulty, whether Rail Roads, or ought else. I speak this independently and risk the consequences. Excuse my poor style, and believe me a friend to all classes and complexions.

      Geo. Teamoh"

The earnestness with which the Democrats worked to get this bill through, very soon convinced me that this poor bleeding Common wealth (Virginia) was either about to be bartered off by an aristocratic junta, who had already bought over what little republicanism we had in the General Assembly, or that there was something in it favorable to what is known as the "lost cause". My first impressions were, no doubt right, for when an amendment to the bill was offered to the effect that the passenger trains, or cars on said road should accommodate equally all persons irrespective of color, or previous condition of servitude, nearly every republican in the Lower House and Senate voted against it—certainly every colored member in the lower houses did so, I believe. It was passed then, with out such amendment reaching the Senate. [127] Having studied, some what, the practical operations of this measure,—the advocacy of Democrats and sale of Republicans,—I at once came to the conclusion that it was "devilish funny" Republicanism. On the Evening before the vote was taken, one of the distinguished "Centrals", who had been for some time "lobbying", came to my room at a most unusual time for any one to receive visitors. The weather being cold, I invited him in, there being a nice grate fire which I had left on going to bed. I am not prepared to say whether this was a lady or a gentleman; certainly the voice was very feminine. I speak of this person however as gendering of the masculine. After the usual introductory civilities had passed, I raised the light and showed him to a seat near the fire. He would see me on a matter of business which he hoped I would regard as private. Having informed him of my ignorance of his mission and that I could not decide either in favor of or against its revelation until knowing its character, he at once drew from the side pocket of his heavy over coat a map checkered with Rail Roads, which when spread out would occupy a space of five square feet, or more. [128] Calling my attention to it, he gave some of the most potent reasons—as seen on paper—why this lion clawed corporation,—whose bank vaults of millions upon millions were tapped in the capitol of Virginia—should have the right of way, by the terms of the bill, through those sections of the State laid down on the afore said map. He argued much in supporting his paper, by way of cheap fare and freight, shortning of distance, convenience of travel, emigration and skilled labor, &c. He apologised for his unseasonable visit by saying, that he had seen a letter in the papers written by me expressive of the will of my constituents as to how I should vote on the bill in question, and that all the Republicans in the Senate having been "reached" but myself, he thought he would interview me at a time and place, when I could not be other than alone, to all of which I answered, saying, I was prepared to listen to whatever he might have to say in regard to the published letter. [129] While displaying his chart, he pitched into Rail Road matters generally, and the Pennsylvania Central, particularly, saying, that it seemed a little out of place that one like myself should have shown the least opposition to the latter, and that if I would consult my individual interest as well as that of the people's I would—after all that has been said and written—vote for the measure. Your constuents—said he—are not as much opposed to it as you might suppose. Softly adjusting the folds of his map and placing it in his heavy portfolio, he drew from the latter a package of green back money consisting of Ten Thousand Dollars, ($10,000) made up of Five hundreds, One thousands, Twenties Tens and hundreds.—It was charming to behold!!—He was certainly an expert at handling notes, and must have been a bank Teller. Before leaving, he counted out Fourty Thousand, which he said had to be applied in another direction, but sooner than loose my vote that amount might very readily be turned over to me, and if I had any doubts about it, all he asked was my assent to the measure, and that before I reached the Senate chamber said amount would be placed within the reach of my control. With the limited knowledge I then had of Rail Roads running through the State, more particularly of those in my own section, the objections which I offered, I supposed to be well founded, which were these:—First it—the bill in question—was presented to republicans as being strictly republican; Secondly to democrats as being decidely democratic; Thirdly, it was advocated by both, and therefore [I] concluded that it could not be much of either; Fourthly, when the amendment was voted down giving colored travellers equal accommodations over said road with the white travelling public;—[130] Fifthly;—That its tendancy was to supplant the present population in many of our counties by giving place to the introduction of a strange class of beings who were to so cultivate the soil—it was said—as to make it double its productions; Sixthly That the displaced inhabitants, would by thousands be driven by stress of circumstances to seek their homes in Africa, or other far off territory; Seventh; That it would not only reduce travel and frate on our own roads, but in the end would annihilate them; Eighth;—That colored men, by hundreds, as well as very large numbers of white men—living in the two cities and surroundings, were soly dependent for support on the wages drawn for their work, performed on these roads;—Ninth; That in consideration of keeping in tact the business employments of other roads, meetings had been called for the purpose of instructing members from this District to use their influence in opposition to the bill. [131]

The above were my principal reasons for refusing my support of the Rail Road bill, of which I have been speaking, the gentlemany expert at note shuffling saying, in the end, that if it required argument to over come my objections, there was no use in talking the matter over any longer. He left and I went to bed.

With my then present convictions, I could not have supported the bill under any considerations, and nothing gave me more supprise than that of hearing, as well as seeing, gentlemen wearing the ermine of statesmen, scholars, and patriots of the dear old Commonwealth, yielding up their bed ridden mother to the rapacious maw of the money king. It seemed to be the last "grab" to plough up Virginia into farm lots, and then sell her from the auction block. And even at the present moment I fail in seeing where those great benefits which were to accrue to the State by the Rail Road in question "comes in at"—to use an ordinary phrase. It was, therefore, in opposition to great inducements, bribes and blandishments that I voted against that Bill in stern obedience to the dictates of my own conscience. [132] And yet I am not prepared to say how far this road might prove beneficial to sections of the State more remote from the sea-board. Theoretic speculations in this matter would not afford me the smallest assistance. A comprehensive view of practical life when well applied by the less erudite, often serves as a science. I am to be judged there fore, according to my vote founded on general views such as given above. My ideas of men are, when they have been called to serve in legislative capacity that they should be actuated by motives too high to be reached by any pecuniary, or other consideration. If a sacrifice must needs be made, let it not be at the unholy expense of severing the last link in the chain of honor connecting man with his God. But some men who had supposed slavery to be eternally lost, were not capable of acting otherwise than they did. While others, nursed in the same faith, and whose tone of honor could not be touched, or suspected beyond their devotion to the "peculiar cause", could not, by any possibility share the deep and unpardonable disgrace of placing a crown of thorns on the weeping brow of their Mother State. The more honest men are not always found in the halls of legislation. If so on their arrival, the vaccine of corruption but too often fevers the moral system, when so much of their former standing in society goes for nothing. I have been sadly disappointed in the average honesty of many great politicians, such as yielded their entire support to the Clays and Calhounds.—I speak of the classic parliamentarians and political leaders of my own State, who, by their recognized means of operating upon the credulity of the less informed,—but more honest—carried the State, not only out of the Union, but after the adoption of a Constitution Republican in form, against the administration; and fearing another chance would never offer, made the sale in "nut-shell" form to those who were able to pay most for it—as I have reason in believing. "To be honest as this world goes"—says Shakspeare "is to be one man picked out of ten thousand."[133] When there was a finale to the Rail Road war, I drew from the post office—in common with other letters which had been addressed to me by friends—a note, enclosed in which was a Fifty Dollar ($50-00) bill, and stating in the former—the words.

> "Geo. Teamoh: I had lost all hope of further honesty being found in those whom we had held as our slaves, you being one of that number. I am an old Virginian and opposed to your politics. Enclosed find Fifty Dollars as a conscious fund donated to yourself.—I am quite relieved of the bad opinion I held regarding yourself of late. You will be none the wiser by trying to find out the author and giver."

There seems to be no dout but that this money must have been given by some one then interested in the afore said bill, whether a member of either branch of the Legislature I can not say, only it would appear to be one who had increased his coffer by a large speculation and a shameful sale; and all at the expense too, of the lashings of a guilty conscience. And it may have been otherwise.

"The mind that broods o'er guilty woes
Is like the scorpion girt by fire:
In circle narrowing as it—glows,
The flames aroundt their captive close;
Till inly searched by thousand throes,

And maddning in their ire,
One, and a sole relief she knows:
The sting she nourished for her foes—
Whoes venom never yet was vain,
Gives but one pang and cures all pain—
She darts in to her desperate brain—
So do the dark in soul expire,
Or live like scorpion girt by fire
So writhes the mind remors hath riven
Unfit for Earth, undoomed for heaven;
Darkness above, despair beneath,
Around it flame, within it—death!"[134]

I am yet left in darkness as to the special object for which the money was given,
only I never tried to return it to any one, fearing rather that complications
and trouble might prove the result. Should these lines ever come within sight
of the donor, I desire to say to him that, while I appreciate the gift to its utmost value, I have but little confidence in his honesty, if he obtained the money
in the way I have supposed; if not, I have no objection to receiving another
Fifty of the same sort, and in the same way.—I am waiting —Box 137, Portsmouth Virginia. You need not register it, just send as you did the other—
anonymously written,—you know. To "blow my own horn", I have been a
pretty good fellow since the Pennsylvania Central was the order of the day;
and "being relieved of the bad opinion you held of me of late," time has left
margin for an increase of confidence to the amount of another Fifty, or more.
Do not fail in sending it.—Mind Box 137. If you have no other bills but such
as "those Ones" backed by three beautiful zeroes, the latter will be still more
acceptable. I shall faithfully comply with any, and all instructions you may
put in the P.S. such as "burn this up after being read" as formally.—See—
137. I hope your family—if you have any—are well, and blessed in basket
and store—mind 137—the place from which I now write, Portsmouth Virginia. Do not regard my selection from Lord Byron as any very serious reflection upon any one but yourself, for when conviction has done its office, I
am very sure you will send that "One" with the afore said "zeroes" behind—
I can almost see it coming now.—In deed, I have just received a letter with
seal unbroken, and I am so hopeful it is the one in question, I shall open [it],
and give it to my readers at once.

"Juniper Swamp, Va. April 2d/72
Dear friend Teamoh: I write hoping to find you and family well: I
want you to write and let me know when our men should come home to be
registered for the May elections. We have about forty in this part of the
swamp who are within easy reach of Deep-Creek. Please send us Twelve,

or Thirteen Dollars by _____who is a trust worthy man, and all
will be well.—He brought it before.
    Very Truly Yours for the cause of freedom
    _____"

How mistaken!! That the above was not the anticipated letter, may be very
clearly seen. With failing faith, however, I shall still be hopeful until despair
has done its work.
    Having served two terms, or two sessions, in the Senate,[135] I again re-
turned to my constituents, humbly submitting my labors to their consideration, which, after being carefully investigated were decided upon more
favorably than I had expected, when considering my great lack of literal education as well as that of parliamentary experience. The great majorities in
city and county, have never failed in supporting me for positions which I
have neither coveted, and could never fill, with any considerable degree of
educational fitness. And here I recognize the mistakes so frequently made
in our choice of those to represent us. We are but too often led in to the belief, that, because a man can read and write, and with all, exhaustless in un-
meaning arguments, that he, a bove all others, is best suited to be assigned
to certain positions.[136] True, this state of things does not attain, to any very
alarming extent at this time; Still, adaptation to the fitness of things "is
more honored in the breach than in the observance". The great Republican
Party of this State and country, of which I shall always be glad to boast as
being a member—but only so long as it keeps the faith—is not exempt
from the sweeping charge of turning its patronage in to the hands of those
least competent to discharge the duties of the position sought and obtained.
Positions, too, of high trust and involving grave responsibilities. No one
doubts—I presume—their devotion to those principles which gave them office, as a war record would seem to justify the government in doubling
compensating them—or at least some of them—for service well performed,
in doing which it has been egregiously imposed upon. No one can look at
our little surroundings here, without recognizing this fact. To meet this
emergency, I believe, a Civil Service Reform Bill, either offered, or
amended by one Mr. Curtis,[137] in the Lower House of Congress is now
pending, as a remedy. But should this bill pass, resulting in the appoint-
ment of a commission on examinations and qualifications for office, I doubt
very much whether anything very tangible could be arrived at, unless such
Bill was so shaped as to suit every body "and the rest of man-kind." Many
of these offices were dealt out in the heat of war, and by bloody bayonets,
and so kept in tact by the Office holders themselves being the leading spirits of the organization known as the "Grand Army of the Republic"—
which is another imposition upon the credulity of the nation and ought to

go out of existance with "the names of conquered portions of our country as at present written on our battle flags."[138] But while saying this, I do not forget that the spirit of its organization, as well as that of the great Union League of America[139] originated out of the very depths of patriotism as an off set to the Ku Klux Clan, which latter body of disguised marauders had instituted a systematic guerilla war-fare through out the southern country, murdering and otherwise persecuting those whom the action of a spirited war between North and South had set free; and this too, after the liberated millions had protected the families of their murderers from the hostile invasion of northern armies, or those who broke the chains of their enslavement. High heaven can but record the deed as one of the darkest ever perpetrated since the creation of Adam!! But the government having captured and brought to condign punishment many of these guilty out laws, and having also added amendment after amendment to the Federal Constitution, down to what is known as the "Enforcement act,"[140] guaranteeing to the enfranchised Race ample protection, just in proportion as our civil rights are vouched safe to us under them, and Society melts back into its wanted serenity, just in that proportion should these protective organizations cease to exist, for when asserting that these are impositions upon the credulity of the nation, I am mindful of some giant frauds practiced under cover of these powerful organizations. "Lo the poor sailor and soldier" have been jointly made the convenient vehicle in which to drive a corrupt trade in politics, as in election times these are generally appealed to from the ascertained fact of their oneness in sentiment. I am no historian; but it would seem that the Fathers broke with England to establish a republican form of government, which at any time, and from any cause, became unendurable, was to be changed, remodified, or so altered as to secure the greatest good to the greatest number. Any connivance, therefore, at the country being ruled, out side of a fair representation of the great body of its citizens, is dangerous to their liberties, and should not be tolerated for a single moment. Having performed their mission as instructed from the "war Office of the nation", they ought, and without delay, strike colors to civil government; and doffing the armor of a cruel and wicked war, banish every semblance of it by ceasing to flare in the face of civilized man the tokens of his capture and subjugation. We are some where told, that the Prince of Pandemonium once announced from his "high" place the following: "When human victims feed the flames, then shines my altars brightest." The better way,—in our opinion,—to memorialize those who fell in the deathly struggle for freedom, would be, admitting such organizations as the G.A.R. are to be disbanded, (and they should be)—to organize a great national party for freedom and equal rights, to be made up of all who fought and all who did not fight in the war which gave freedom to our country. And while we know that the name Republican would seem to cover these grounds, we also recognize the fact that the G.A.R. was founded on Republican principles which principles by said G.A.R., or a considerable portion of them, have been violated in letter and spirit, so that we can no longer confidently look to that source for the purity of Republicanism. Indeed, the great Republican party itself, has not been, at all times, free from suspicion of having done some things wrong in administering to the actual necessities of those late from under the heel of oppression, and millions of other laboring classes of its supporters. We believe the time not very far distant when the ruling party of to day will have to cast about for another shibboleth as a matter of relief from the rotten rut of American, or false democracy, or that system of legislation which swayed the country when faithful Old John Brown, with prophetic vision, predicted, from the narrow planks of a Virginia scaffold, the down fall of a system of hellish villanies which had been supported by every pulpit—North and South—in America, during a space of nearly two and a half centuries. But, this is not the place to dwell upon these matters.[141] I saw then, the better way to perpetuate our reverence for these heroes immortal, is not to be found in false adorations with dangling sword in pompous display, while riding the hobby of "protection to the enfranchised race". But by laying the sword aside. The "race" is now sufficiently apprehensive as to its general and special security under Federal rule; and, while watching our ascending star, we shall endeavor so to demean ourselves as to prove to the nation that although less cared for than the murderous Modocs[142] of the lava beds, our most prominent idea is a fair chance to advance in the scale of being. We are in the progressive, and do not, as yet, like our more highly favored brethren, expect to "sit serenely mild, like Halcyon[143] on the wave, calm and unruffled as autumnal skies, while softest zephyrs fans the waving leaves."—No, not at all. The Republican Party should at once, and without delay, do one of two things, take up another name, or disband its national secret organizations,—My boast of being "proud to be called a member", to the contrary notwithstanding. While admitting, as I have done that these bodies of men may have been of some benefit as an off set to the Ku Klux, it is as palpably before us as the noon day sun, that their pretentions to loyal reconstruction in our Townships, or "county organizations", where the negro vote largely preponderates, have, at every turn of the screw sunk the latter, and thrown themselves to the surface, with the deceptive inscription marked on their brow, "eternal devotion to the negro." It out herods Herod, and plays a game which would baffle the skill of Iago!![144] And what makes it more damnable in practice, if not in conception, is, that after the freed men had voted these men—many of the delegates—to the Constitutional Convention, where, during a term of Five long months they drew the sum of Eight Dollars per diem, on the sine die adjournment of that body, and when they knew all the judge-ships were to be appointed by the Legislature (for they so framed it) they then sold out, declaring that they would not only not support the constitution which they had assisted in making, but did actually "sell out," thus, leaving the negro in a far worse condition than they found him—in the hands of a conservative government, and ruled by Democratic judges through out the state.[145] And they followed up, with a consistancy that would do credit to piracy, for when the convention was called at Petersburg to nominate our first governor under the new constitution, as a "bilging blow" they advocated the claims of Dr. J. D. Harris col. (a very good scholar and a refined gentleman, I admit) as occupying the second place on the ticket;—who, accepting the nomination, killed the ticket off. Though put foward with the evident intention of being defeated, I supported the nomination as a matter of principle, and should do so again,[146] under like circumstances, excepting, always my knowledge of the fraud. We shall now take—as it were—a bird's eye view of some opperations of the G.A.R. in our own congressional District, and whose grand commander is Captain James H. Platt, Jr. Member of the Lower House in congress. If we may speak of the Captain as being an exemplary member of the national organization, justice would seem to demand an investigation of the whole machinery by which it is kept in motion.

Per force of circumstances in the constitutional convention, above referred to, and of which Capt. Platt was a member,[147] I regarded that gentleman, in the out set, as a pretty fair exponent of Republican principles. And I may say he was so considered by most on my side of the house; and I continued to hold him in good esteem until an altercation had taken place between him and the Rev Dr. Thomas Bayne,[148] when Platt, in replying to some remarks made by the Dr. called him a "black scoundrel," or "rascal"—I am not sure which. As "straws show which way the winds blow," I held in mental reservation the proscriptive remark; and as the affair seems to have so elated the Democratic side of the House, I thought some use might be made of it in the future. Since its utterance, it has been often repeated unfavorable to the author. The Captain has done many things contrary to the will and wishes of, many, even moderate Republicans, such as being favorable to the striking out of test oaths and disfranchisements, which were the most powerful levers used by the opposition in breaking down the Republican vote, and so losing the state. He is a good political strategist, and knows well the value of numbers—can concentrate at ease, and plan for a simultaneous attack, but once victor, he loses the care of his men, until old veterans and new recruits are wanted. These clamor for compensation—(Office) before they can again take the field—If one can "talk Platt," set him down for an office—if nothing but "Grant and Wilson," his pay is questionable.

The Captain made a very shrewd dodge while running his canvass for the first Congress which met after the ratification of our State Constitution. It consisted in his silence on the "iron clad" or Test Oath, although many, aye the great majority of his supporters had supposed he would have defined his position on that question at some time during that hotly contested campaign.[149] The presumption, no doubt was, that there were more to be gained by ignoring the measure until after the election, when there would be a chance to support it in Congress, where, in all probability he could champion the bill and thus father the measure to a successful passage, being persuaded mean time that the classes coming under it could never hesitate in their support of its advocate at all future elections. While colored men—for the most part—merely looked at this matter on the surface, I was disposed to sift it down a little, which having done, informed that gentleman on his going to Washington, that if he desired the future support of the republican Party of the Second Congressional District, he could not calculate very favorably for himself while using his influence for the repeal of the above measure. But, as a political juggler can easily baffle the keenest observation, so he, in a few general terms said "it—"meaning the test Oath—"was one of the most damnable measures ever put into any constitution." If so "damnable" why not make of it a canvassing document? O no: there were two sides to please,—the one for the test oath—the other against it,—to all appearance,—but in fact he had figured closely enough to find out that with the republican number actually in favor of its removal and the entire democracy more than friendly to such removal, with eagle eye, he saw at once his future prospects looming in the distance .—He won on that card, nor has his prescience failed him since first calculating his chances for place and power. In my own mind, I cannot perceive in the Captain a high toned, patriotic and magnanimous statesman; such as we would like to see in those who legislate for a community of races. One strong man in the minority, drives him from a just consideration of the rights of the majority, which has been very recently demonstrated in our election here for a member to the House of delegates, myself being in question. Nor was this all,—it was by his appearance in person at Providence Va that I lost the chance of being returned to the State Senate in 1872[,] he, in each case prefering a doubtful white republican of the G.A.R. order.[150] In the latter case, I sacrificed Five hundred Dollars ($500-00) that my people might not be sold, as I thought it due to them from the position they had given me to obtain it. But when informed that a distinguish[ed] personage was present to off set my sum to the amount of Two thousand Dollars ($2,000-00), I considered the game lost. It was consoling however to know that nearly the whole convention was for me, only that the unfaithful few misled a number, who gave way under the majority of dollars. Other indications have gone to show that he is largely under the control of the G.A.R. which organization in his District, has two wings—the white and the colored. I have never belonged to said G.A.R. although during the reign of the Ku Klux, I was a member of the Union League of America, and these wisely disbanded when the Klan had been arrested and brought to justice. I have, it is true, supported the Captain when his chances for Congress have been very doubtful; and after being there, to put him in Republican "traces," I have written him some complementary letters, and I give him the credit of having answered them in a decent style coming within my comprehension; and occasionally accompanied with Patent Office Documents on agricultural science &c. &c. and I believe he has sent similar volumes to his constituents in his District; notwithstanding, for my own part, I should have rather had the gift of a spelling book, or some good English Reader, or both. Hon. B.F. Lewis,[151] United States Senator, once sent me a whole cart load of the above Documents, for which I was very thankful, and returned him a letter accordingly, expressing myself something different from those addressed to the Captain, as I believed the former to be an honest man, and largely possessed of a deep sympathy for suffering humanity in what ever shape it may have appeared. But, I do not measure these gentlemen's patriotism by the franking privilege, or freedom of the Patent Office, for the reason that it would not be a proper standard.—All congressmen seem to have this right, and exercise it, too.

Of all the trials and triumphs through which republicanism may have had to pass in our district since the close of the war, Captain Platt has figured most conspicuously among that element from which it was but natural to suppose he must have drawn his greatest strength. He knew well too how to operate upon the various propensities of all men—their prejudices and passions how to bring—as nearly as may be—in to subjection to his will in fortifying his own position whether as officer of state; congressman or what not. This may be seen—and it is nothing strange now—in Platt's manner of securing every nomination where-ever himself has been in question, or any persons for whom he may have felt to use his influence. If I can make the term apply here he is <u>elastic</u>, readily adapting himself to the circumstances and conditions of all men, as evinced in this congressional district, where, after he had been placed in power by its citizens he distributed offices to those, whom we had every reason in believing had pledged themselves to his support on all future occasions; said parties being disqualified from holding certain high positions to which they have been appointed on moral grounds, and their utter unfitness, arising from an educational stand point. He favors a "civil service reform bill," and yet gives it a black eye; hugs test oaths and disfranchisements to his bosom, and yet has not a word in their favor nor any complaint against them when speaking to a people who would like to know his opinion there on. We could easily endure all these; aye, like a vast number of others we have been, and are obliged to endure them, because this ruling monarch of our district has it clearly in his power to roll our head from the block political. And although forty odd years of our life have been lost to us in slavery; still his rapacious appetite for revenge would not be glutted until we had been brought to grief, and the very lowest depths of poverty.—We know where of we speak. But duty urges with a power which we can no longer resist, to record these facts as truthfully as though we had to take a copy of them to that world whither we are all tending: and even this is so, and I am rejoiced that God has thus arranged it in His providence;—the opinion of others to the contrary not with standing. We throw off the shackles of fear in rising to the dignity of manhood, and although a host was encampped against us, we shall utter our thoughts untrammelled, deeming that we have as greater right to tell the truth, as others claim to deal in deceptions and false hoods, greatly to the injury of a confiding people.

With democracy I have no quarrel, they having acted in strict conformity with their known and recognized principles principles,—which like the laws of the "Meads and the Persians,"[152] admits of no change, and which, should they ever again get control of the government of this country, we may bid fare well to the American Republic and invite the cruelist type of war, desolation and distress. And O how sad the reflection: when in our meditations we see—the would be awfully grand magestic temple of liberty, staggering under the hammering blows of democracy, and finally fall under the light of God's sun only to be immerced in, and reserected out of the blood of millions. Hither the portents point with astonishing significance, moving slowly, but surely onward, frictionizing truth with error until former has been burnished in to a brightness which the demon of democracy can never obscure. But God alone can avert the coming storm. He alone can bring proud and exalted humanity within the comprehension of His great designs, and, after the teachings of holy scripture as a guide to our pathway, in dealing justly the one toward the other, this may be as it always has been His final resort, and in stern keeping with His purpose, that man shall do by his fellow man, as he would have his fellow man do unto him. This—in my opinion—is a law, not only deeply implanted in our nature, but it pervades the very atmosphere of our surroundings, and "rough hew it as we may" justice, though long in delay, will turn up at last. A nation, like an individual, may be its own enemy and not know it—May luxuriate in the Dagon[153] temple, do sacrifice and dance before the gods, until its cloud capped spire shall have been lifted from its firm base by an edict from Him who wills but once, and it is done without retraction. And we pause in the contemplation, and although circumscribed our view, we adjust our glasses for a more distant height as her star approaches its zenith, but all in vain.

We again return to conclude our remarks on Capt. Platt's administration. And let me say just here, that the reader, who may be familiar with our affairs here abouts, might opine, that had I have held a good paying position, under him of whom I now write, it would have suppressed any opinion I might feel to publish, as opposed to the means by which he obtains power. This however, is farthest to the thought as I have long since made solemn declaration that nothing short of physical disabilities, or some other unavoidable cause shall ever prevent me from carrying to account facts with which I have been made familiar from my own personal observation.

Mr. Platt, in keeping with many others of his class of republicans, has no very high appreciation of negro intelligence, beyond what he has no reason to believe, will keep him in congress, or by some means perpetuate his power. While seeking the influence of our more distinguished colored men,— those I mean who could lead the masses in a direction favorable to himself,—Mr. Platt has left unturned no scheme in the accomplishment of his designs. His presence at our churches, grog shops and bar rooms has been frequent in which latter places he has, but too often, for one of his standing, hoisted the glass of bacchical rejoicings at tr[i]umphs in prospect, while participants of the beverage, inspired by free drinks and a plenty of them could find no check for their glorifications in honor of him whom they had unthoughtfully "crowned lord of all". The eagle eyed reporters of the Democratic press, in serving their columns have said many things about Mr. Platt which were not true, leaving the majority of facts unsaid, more particularly those truths which would tend to elevate that portion of colored men whom this gentleman had, by his modus operandi worked into his service. This comes, however, of that systemized opposition which characterizes Republican and Democrat, not withstanding, the latter being doubtful of his (Platt's) sincerity of purpose, has yielded nothing to the negro as his constitutional right—and—possibly never will, while we encourage such men in taking advantage of our enfranchisement. We may—occasionally— persaltum—leap to honorable positions in life, but being destitute of the capacity to serve, such pretentions are only turned into a farce, leaving time to prove that, having uneducated ourselves in the ordanary duties of life, we can no longer hope to return to the wholesome labor of our respective callings without casting back with something of serious reflections as to the deceptions practiced upon us. Because I can caulk a ship, it is no proof of my capacity to navigate the same over the vasty deep; and admitting I could do the latter, it would not demonstrate my fitness for the legal profession. But, I do not dwell here, for availability in framing its own law, will "catch at a straw". We are not forgetful however, or feel to ignore the good that has been accomplished, by whatever means or men, knowing that we have had some faithful souls enlisted in our cause—those who have not regarded the "Grand Army of the Republic" as the ultimatum of their success in life.

Mr. Platt has done nothing to elevate the negro upon the score of the latter's intellectual genious; as I have known some of the most besotted ignoramuses to occupy important official positions, only out of consideration that they could control the vote of the masses in keeping with themselves. Nor has this state of things been a lone confined to the colored classes, for as shown, availability stops at no law when resorted to by a scheming politician. I could, were it absolutely necessary, establish, by incontrovertible facts, as witnessed in my own person the truths contained in the above statements, and only that it would seem insisting on my own claims to certain favorable considerations that I do not put them to record here; notwithstanding I am too sensible of my own disqualifications to push forward any claim founded on educational attainments; for had merit been rewarded in the direction alluded to, the recipients of such favors would have been no question with me, beyond that of loyalty to his profession as a republican. Without any fixedness of purpose, Mr. Platt is a creature of circumstances, and would remind one of a sailer bearing a cargo to any port whither a storm would drive it, and in utter disregard of the laws of trade, profit at all hazards.

Whatever may be, or may have been, the character of Capt. Platt's congressional career, this much may be said of him, that he has faithfully labored to the extent of his abilities in securing the patronage of our government to the benefit of his constituents; and we are not disposed to detract a whit from his great services in this case, as it was not very likely any one sent from this District at the time, could have accomplished more than him; For he was in his seat but a short while, at Washington, when made chairman of the Naval Committee[154]—a position commanding great influence, and one also which afforded him frequent interviews with the Sec. of the Navy. And I must say what every intelligent mind, here abouts will admit, which is, that, through Capt. Platt's advocacy, as well as through other channels, his honor, the Sec. of the Navy, had indulged a very favorable inclining towards the poor of our land, in that he has ordered to work this naval station which, it has been argued, properly belonged to other Sections. I will say here, also, on behalf of his hon. Geo. M. Robeson, Sec of the Navy, that, although having received the gross insult of being fired upon in the City of Norfolk, while engaged both head and heart in the difficult work of reconstruction, he returned to Washington, saying "Father forgive them for they know not what they do", and made no delay in forwarding work to this Navy Yard. True enough, he was down here—possibly,—through the cunning of Platt, as the latter was then driving his Congressional campaign.[155] And this serves as an instance of Platt's influence with that great dignitary. Again: Our Congressman's dealings with the colored men of this city and vicinity have left me greatly in doubt as to his sincerity of purpose. It is well known, in this community, for what object the genl. government saw fit to institute an Executive Committee in each of our Town-Ships. They are charged with great, and very often, grave responsibilities, having more to do in recommending good, and reliable persons as government employes than anything else. The first organization of this character, was made up—nine in number—of this Grand Army of the Republic order. Their jurisdiction was, the Navy Yard, Bouy Yard—Gun Yard, Custom House and whatever else supposed to be with in government limits in the 2d Congressional District.[156] In entering upon the discharge of their duty, Committee was very careful, first of all to apply nature's own rule—"lookout for yourself"—which was very soon agreed upon by this Body. This precedent having been established by the faithful first, all subsequent committees of that character, have adhered to it with a tenacity not very wonderful—all things considered. Committee had its way, day and sway, and when all the Offices and other places, from the clerical pen to the pick axe had been filled, and there was nothing else to be had, the Capt. of the "Post" and host sounds with his gavel, "let out siders in". Accordingly we took our turn, being elected as a committee man. But when we got there every thing was gone, and it was pitiable indeed to see how these wire pulling experts laughed at us "in the sleeve" as we made our way to the Federal departments in quest of employment. It so happened in those days, that a Spanish Bark sprung a leak, and it was asked that she be allowed to go in our Dry Dock for repairs. The request granted, a very large number of caulkers were called in, myself one among them. We had been at work on Spanish bark only a few days when the news got abroad that one, blessed with the three fold honors of being Master Machinist in the Norfolk Navy Yard, a distinguised Officer in the G.A.R. and Dictator to the Executive

Committee had engaged in a conspiracy, "with knowledge afore thought", to rob the general government by fraudulently contracting for some thousands of the best Spanish cegars, then known to be on board of this same Spanish bark. About the time—while the process of thievery was going on—as we had been shortly afterward informed— I was clothed in my over-alls, and at work on this vessel's bottom as she lay in the Dry Dock. Government detectives, or some else, worked this matter up, and it was brought before the United States Court—sitting at Richmond—in legal form.[157] At two successive terms the charge of fraud was established, each jury having returned, a true bill— (guilty) New bonds were found and a third trial motioned for. But during the court in vacancy, strenuous efforts had been made by the Grand Army party to dismiss the cause from further litigation, and so let the accused go free. The third trial was had at the U.S. Court Room at Norfolk, and resulted in the acquital of the party arraigned, quite contrary however from what the public had anticipated. We had never, until the case referred to was brought up for final decision, believed in a familiar saying—"jury men for sale". And although the guilt stood out in bold relief, with the impartial rendering of Judge J.C. Underwood's opinion, the case was indeed dismissed by the jury then sitting, they having failed in finding a true bill.

Having occupied considerable space in attempting to characterize the actions of a class of men,—many of whom by fraud, or assumed patriotism, had wormed themselves in to the graces of the general government,—I again return to a more definite account, or further consideration of my own autobiography.

But thinking I have written quite enough already to furnish a brief history of myself, and having no special desire for writing about ones self, I shall close this volume with a bare allusion to my labors and late circumstances in life. True it is, I have not, in any regular form, observed—in these writings—those rules laid down as a guide for the prose composer; if, however attention has been paid to what has been written, he is a dull scholar and a poor christian indeed who can not perceive and forgive the several errors accompanying this brief sketch of my life. During the eight, or ten years last past, my employment has been varied indeed, having wrought howeve more at my trade—caulking—than anything else. And even at that I could scarcely obtain a living.[158] And it was not until I had been chosen as a representative to the department of State [State Senate] when a chance was given to lay by enough money to purchase a home stead for myself and family. By strictly economising I had accumulated an amount sufficient to justify me in contracting for what was known as Prof. N.B. Webster's estate, or that portion of it situated on the South East corner of Green and Queen Streets, Portsmouth, Va.. The delapidated condition of this property was such as induced Mr. W. to dispose of it at a price far below its then present value; with an additional reason, that, those having rented it from time to time having failed in meeting their payments.[159] While Mr. W. resided in it during the continuance of his college Institute adjoining the same lot, there is every evidence in believing that, as an abode of comfort it had received all the attention of professional skill.[160] And I refer chiefly to his, or what was his, horticultural gardens. Indeed, he had well classified, in a very small space too, flowers, fruits and vegitables. There are twelve rooms in the main building, with an adjoining kitchen containing three rooms. The residence measures Thirty four feet by twenty nine feet square, with a height of Thirty two feet including a brick basement story, some two feet under ground & on which the structure rests. The admeasurement of the kitchen is—height Twenty feet, and Twenty two by Thirteen feet square—flat top. The lot on which this property stands, runs one hundred and fourteen feet on queen Street, and eighty nine on green Street. On the above property, I have, to the present time, paid for its possession in the amount of Eighteen hundred Dollars, ($1800-00) besides having expended over Four hundred dollars ($400-00) in putting it in proper repairs. I also own one nineteenth (1/19) share in the college building adjoining my lot, and which building also did belong to Prof. Webster until, through my agency & others a company was raised to purchase it of him for the sum of Twenty Five hundred dollars ($2500-00)[161] The college, or school building is now fairly the property of said company, they having complied with all the conditions laid down in the bill of sale. At present this college is used—hired from the company—for Public Free School purposes for colored youth. This concludes the present volume of my life, and I would say here, that my only regrets are that it could not be presented—in this age of high literary culture—in a more acceptable style. But ample reasons have been given why it could not have been otherwise than it is. And while suffering from these regrets, I have at least one consoling thought which is, that few of my chances have done better.—Few who have suffered a like term in slavery without the assistance of a living Teacher, have accomplished more. And I am more than thankful to my Heavenly Father, and His Son Jesus Christ the Righteous Who have stood by me in this, as in all other laudable enterprises.

Res ly Yours,

Geo. Teamoh

Oct. 5th 1874

Portsmouth, Va. Feb.

1883

Some twelve years having elapsed since the above was written, and being unwilling it should come before the public with this long space of my record unnoticed, I purpose here to make an addendum, as briefly as I may, in covering the time stated.

My principal object in purchasing the Webster estate—or a part of it— was, that after I had searched the city inquest of a suitable place where the largest number of colored familes resided, I might by some means, in addition to my own, plant a school for the education of as many children as were in that School District. This property had been lying idle for several years, or it at least had been occupied by non-paying tenants. I am now speaking of *Prof. N.B. Webster[162] whose residence stands on the corner of Green and Queen Streets with college adjoining. Having spoken with him concerning the purchase, he was steadfast at Five Thousand Dollars ($5000-00) for the whole estate, or Twenty five hundred Dollars ($2500-00) for ether the college building, or his residence. I soon negotiated with him for the latter, and paid the price asked. Restless as to the School Building, and fearing it might fall into other hands than those friendly to the Race, I at once organized a club of some Eighteen, or Twenty members,— all col of course—and purchased that also. This I did, fearing the public Free School Supt. for col. might fail in securing a building with ample room for at least Four hundred pupils, it being, then when organized the only school in a city where there are from seven, to Eight thousand col inhabitants.[163] The college building being purchased, or while the books were open for subscribers, I took a one twentieth share, and very soon after another to the same amount, Forty Dollars, it being twenty Dollars ($20-00) to the share.[164] In addition to this, each member was required to pay an assessment of one Dollar and a half ($1.50cts) per month, which gave the Association the building inside of three years and a half. And, but for the tardy organization of the Pub. Free Schools for col, this property might have paid for itself in far less time. An East room in it has always been reserved for the meetings of benefit Societies &c and which paid about Twelve Dollars ($12-00) per month. The pub. F. School commissioners held it about five years, paying Forty five Dollars per month; thus realizing from rents alone, in one year, the handsome sum of Six hundred and Eighty four Dollars ($684-00) making a total amount of rents for five years, Three thousand four hundred and twenty Dollars ($3420-00) In placing this matter on

*Prof. N.B. Webster, School No. 47, Charlotte St. Res. 45 Ch St[.] Norfolk, Va

record, I do so to show how unjustly I have been treated, not only by those of my Race, for whom I have ever sought to do most, for reasons which it is not necessary I should explain here— others as well, as the following will show. But I shall state those reasons at once. And they are to be found in politics, which I care but little to introduce here, for the reason that the <u>domain is unbounded</u>[165]

Through State obligations, and the great charities of the North, a new School building has been erected to substitute the one of which I have spoken above, the Peabody fund—as it has been alleged, having been most shamefully shaved to complete it—being the most generous elemosynary gift it has, so far as I know, ever received. It has been running now, about four years, I think to this—1883. As I can not speak of the character of the above school without losing my mental balance, I shall waive that consideration at present, substituting a line of thought which has been rekindled since I commenced these writings. Let me say, however, that the P.F. School for col,[166] in this city, has been, from the commencement tought by relatives of the "Old Masters," and are so being taught to day—Feb 20th/ 83.

But to my "line of thought," and then I shall go on with my politics and close up.

Religion at the South a farce with the white churches, and two thirds of the colored churches.

The above caption is the basis of a subject upon which no one should dare enter without duly considering the relation-ship existing between him and his God, should his object be that of seeking intelligent and reliable information. Indeed he should put himself in a position to realize all that mortals may, or can know—of spiritual matters. In a word, he ought to be an evangelically converted christian, and live, if he so elects, without having any church to control his thoughts or actions.

"He is the freeman whom the truth makes free",
And only to his God will bow the knee;
Live in the Savior's love and onward move,
To his heavenly home in worlds—above.

To such distinguished Divines as the Rev. Joseph Cook[167] of Boston, Mass. whose deep subsoil plough is now tearing up the bottom layer of infidelity and false adoration in this country, by showing, in panoramic view the dark spots yet uncovered on the missionary field in America, I have not the least to say. Nor yet to the lamented Wm Lloyd Garrison,[168] who called the country's church, and made it stand its ground Then argued not, but knocked it instant down. These patriot souls had no question as to the Fatherhood of God and the Brotherhood of man—"One God, one brotherhood, one grave" say they. A few days ago it was my fortune to meet a white minister of the gospels, whose name here, it is unnecessary to give, since all or nearly all of his persuasion—Wesleyan Methodist—are of the same opinion with himself. [169] Our conversation turning on the Sacriments and rites of the Several churches here abouts, said I "Rev.—Suppose Christ, as in His day when among men should disguise himself so that He could not be distinguished from an ordinary mulatto, came to your church, and while the officiating priest were offering the sacred emblems, rise from His place among the people in the gallery of all colors and proceeding forward to the altar and there meekly neel to receive the offering, I ask, what disposition would be made of Him?—I am supposing now, that He is only known to the minister as an ordinary negro-mulatto, for the Jew you know are several—some of them—shades lower than many of our *Blue eyed Negroes.*"

Said he, "I should ask pardon on knowing who it was, and I am well aware He would grant it." "Then" said I, "you would not hand Him the cup although there was nothing could be seen to distinguish Him from the blue eyed Saxon, only that yourself, and the audience—possibly—knew that the subject was tinged with the sixteenth drop of African— Negro—blood coursing through His veins?"—I do not know that I should at the time of which you speak, but I would, as I have frequently done, administer our Lords Supper to Him, or any that might offer themselves for the purpose, after the white members had been served" was his reply.

Qu. "Then you would not serve Our Savior in the first case, as the question was put?" Ans "No, but I would under the last circumstances." Query—"Are you a missionary of the gospels in the denomination to which you belong?"—Ans— "I am". Quer.—Suppose you establish a church in some part of Africa, and its membership consisting of two, or three hundred Negroes in addition to about five, or six white Missionaries, would you then make the same distinction as here?"—"Undoubtedly, I would" he replied.—Quer. On what grounds?—Ans. "color, of course" Ques—How about the blue eyed Negro, suppose he should put in an appearance, and desiered to commune at the *white table*? Certainly, you could not object on the grounds of color, for I am now giving you a blue eyed Negro whose complexion is whiter than was Henry A. Wise,[170] and many others of our tan colored statesmen?" Ans. "I shall write out my opinions on that subject in due time, and I think you will approve of my course as a missionary.—We parted.

Another Wes[leyan] minister attacked from a different quarter

Quer:—Rev. Sir:

"Are you a Wesleyan methodist Minister?" Ans. I am. Do you believe
any distinction on account of color, should be made at the communion table, between the two Races—black and white? Ans. "I do"—Quer.—"on
what grounds?" Ans. "color.— Qu. Suppose then, some great calamity
should over take us at the very hour when the offerings should be made,
and the darkness and surrounding circumstances were such that you be
driven to administer the emblems throug an opening barely large enough to
pass the bread and wine—you on one side—your communicants on the
other side, and so mixed up that you could not, by any possibility tell the
one from the other of these two complexions. Ans.—"If we had discharged
our duty up to that very fatal moment, there would be no necessity of delivering it to any one". Ques. Suppose this state of things should continue
through several sacrimental seasons, and when you could discharge this
very holy obligation, how then?" Ans. Well—when it comes to that, I think
I should assume the responsibility of accommodating all without regard to
color &c." Quer.—"What is the color of my spirit?"—Ans—"I do not
know". Qu. Then what the color of your spirit? An. "I do not know that
either." Qu."Can your Rev. tell me then, what is the color of God's spirit,
or whether a spirit has any colour"?—Ans. "White,—as opposed to black—
seems to have been given us as emblematic of purity, innocence, simplicity,
&c &c, and which, I believe, constitutes a very large part of the Creator's
make up, whether that be of Bodily parts, or otherwise. Mind, I do not say
He is white, or black."

Quer—"Have you ever studied chemistry to any considerable extent?
Ans. Not sufficient to rely on any knowledge I may have gathered in that
direction. Quer.—Then you are acquainted, I suppose, with metaphysics,
which teaches, I believe, the science of mind. Ans.—While I may be prepared, in some sort, to argue the general proposition as to the hue of the
two Races, and the difference in mental and physical capacity of these, I
candidly admit that few, other than the professors themselves, of those ab-
struse sciences, know but little about them; nor are they all essential in the
Study of Divinity. They are, however, some times introduced in theological exercises, but not in regular course. Quer Then your Rev has never
taken them up, or been compelled to do so, as routine lessons?—Ans.
"never-never" It will be very readily seen that the above questions have not
been, in the least, evasively answered, but stand out in bold relief, showing
to what a great depth of infamy—if that is the word—the Wesleyan M.E.
church has fallen since by being established by its great founder, John Wes-

ley.[171] And that church is, and can only be a synagogue of Satan, where Christ, nor His followers, are allowed to partake of those sacred emblems in commemoration of His sufferings and death, to save a world exposed to all the wrath of God. And this is that great besetting sin which befouls the skirts of full two thirds of the white churches of this country, the majority of them being found in the Southern States. And I do not know of a single denomination—religiously speaking—known as African, or colored church of the same faith and order where this inhibition is practiced upon any human being of the many millions of those who believe in Christ our Savior. I here make an exception of those known as "close communionists" although, each of these have their seperate communion tables. I now finish this section in Our Blessed Lord's own words—"For if ye do this to one of the least of these my little ones, ye have done the same unto me". Having shown, as I believe I have, the pretentious character of our white churches—who after all can not support an argument against the power of truth—I shall now have some what to say as to our col churches.

The great Protestant Church of America, with hands dripping with the blood of the Negro, have at least, tought the latter something. It tought a servile and cowardly fear which, being woven in the ligaments of its religious teachings, was given to the Negro as a genuine article though secondhanded. He was raised on the milk of subjugation, cowardice—fear. And so deeply are these wrought in his nature, that to look beyond the pale of hewer of wood and drawer of water, seems to be attended with insurmountable difficulties, even with the great majority of those who have passed through college life. I know we strive hard to give the denial to this, but its presence is proof against its removal. One who is the son, or daughter of two blue eyed Negroes, may only realize this in proportion to blood measure—sixteenth drop—but that he feels it to a greater or less extent, there is but little doubt. I know of but few colored men in this country who, it seems, have shaken off this fearful incubus entirely. And strange to say, it is more noticeable in many who were free born than in the ex slave.[172] The mongrels—Indian and Anglosaxon,—partake less of this character. I know of a tonsorial artist, or barber, who is nearly white, and for fear of giving offence to his Anglosaxon patrons, he resorts to a shop where colored a lone have their shaving done, to have the same performed on himself.

Whether taken in his wild and savage condition, or recently brought under the laws of christian civilization, the native african seems to carry with him an admirable independence of mind and body, and when educated up to what is known as his historical orgin, he shows the same unpretentious manliness characterizing all other peoples, he being a stranger to the <u>milk of fear</u> which like many other inherited principles, it takes two, or three generations to work off. I regard it, therefore, as only being structural in so far as the Negro's raising and surroundings are concerned, and no further—It is inherited, and if gotten rid of at all, as shown, it must be done so by time.[173]

Hence the col. churches, in spite of the well cultured training which seems to characterize very many of their pulpit orators, continue to rotate as it were—in their accostomed sphere with out showing any visible signs of mental independence,[174] they having acquired a kind of a fixedness of imitative forms, differing from genuine spirituality in that the latter carries with it all that was gained by youthful intellectual training, when, and where the faculties were left untrammelled and free, being a stranger to all fear, excepting that of a parental or religious character, and these should be held responsible accordingly. Then the Negro,—or the existing race here—in his most advanced state of civilization, christian and literal culture, while he may not be chargeable for any constitutional defects of his nature, arising from birth and bondage, he never-the-less feels himself hedged about, under the circumstances named, in a manner, which is almost imperceptible to his keenest observations, or his nicest faculties of detection. The chafing chain galls in any effort we make to strain away from what seems to be the growth of nature. Still, in many of us, to all appearance, this state of mind, body and soul, does not exist; and more especially is this so with those of us who have been reared in the same schools with the whites. I regret to say however, that among many of the former, ripe as they are in scholar-ships, they fall far below the average of whites of the same class, in any business transactions of dealings with their own Race. Or I mean to say that the whites are truer to the demands of suffering humanity growing out of advanced thought, christian enlightenment and the forces of educational training, than we are who were born and reared under the circumstances named—taken as a whole. As shown, I was born with the peculiar characteristics so marked in those of similar birth, and which I can not deny, for

> There is grief in conception with the party conceived,
> While clouded with fear and madly —aggrieved
> At the chains that await, to ring in the —jails,
> Till despair does its work at the annual sale.

After the lapse of nearly a half centuary, since his disinthralment, it has taken the Negro of the West india Islands nearly that whole period barely to reach the edge of a pure christian civilization. No one may say, that he has not been learned, and thoroughly educated by the most distinguished Masters of all the sciences known to the "big books", or authors of them. Neither may it be said, that he has been at all hampered in any pursuit he may

have made in distinguishing himself as a gentleman, a scholar, and one well
fitted to the difficult task of giving shape to the most perfect form of civil
government known among men.—I have often met such, and with much
surprise, I have generally found them occupying, not very enviable situa-
tions on Shipboard, either in the American, or English service, where they
but seldom rate beyond that of able seaman, musician, & the majority being
waiters, &c &c—A few have been serving here as public and private school
teachers. And, as a general thing, few of our American taught colored
scholars can compare with them, as the Westindian, received a thoroughness of training even in his primary departments which is more than sufficient to over balance all, or nearly all that is acquired by the diplomated
graduates at the Ham[p]ton Normal Institute in Virginia.[175] And yet for
all that may be said or shown, favoring his (Westindian's) statesman like
qualifications to plan, and build up a government based upon christian civilization, when the test is applied, the result is a failure. Nor is he—the
Westindian such as spoken of—very select, even in his marriage relations,
if we are to determine, or judge of the people of these Islands from what is
known of the great majority of them, who take to themselves wives in this
country; for if the "survival of the fittest"[176] be an established doctrine, we
have very little warrant in believing that the results of such unions would
be regarded as any material advantage to posterity, for, from all the indications, these living parents are not the fittest to survive, as the offspring of a
higher culture, and, it would seem that their children can not be; which, as
shown, brings us to confront what shall be their posterity, on a very unfavorable platform. The doom of such, to the "third and fourth generation,"
therefore, should surprise no one who has given this matter the smallest attention, as the case seem to be a construction—if not strictly—of the passage
of scripture referred to. It is very true, that in passing through the ordeal
of a higher stage of christian enlightenment, the subjects of these Islands
had—possibly—besides the liberal sentiment of an aristocratic government,
to cover their way,—also, the purest culture of the age to teach in their
schools, and otherwise force by moral suasion the absolute needs of a people, against whom the fates have so sternly fixed themselves. Very true, in
the beginning of their freedom, that maddened spirit which leaps out of the
dark throat of war, as opposed to educating these people, just as all others
had been educated, found no favor in the British parliament; but on the
contrary, they were at once shielded by the strong arm of the law, and, as
though repenting for the past, in that poor distressed and despised people,
Great Briton, without delay, recognized the "Fatherhood of God, and the
Brother hood of man". By its additional amendments to the Federal constitution, the U.S. government has done, theoretically for the Negro, what

the British government has accomplished for him practically—a thoroughness of scholarship adaptable to all the vocations of civil life; and—allowing for his poverty—if he has not improved in the science of government, it is an argument in favor of the opinion advanced.[177] The American Negro obtained his freedom under the most unfavorable circumstances, as out of a government of forty odd million there were but few willing to shoulder his cause, and not even then until he had been called on the field to lift the country from off the hip of the enemy; and which, when accomplished, he was again relegated or transferred, into the very hands of that maddened power bristling, as with forked lightning revenge upon the Negro, more particularly, who were party to its defeat. Bowie-knife, shot-gun, revolver and the bludgeon, have been made the convenient substitutes for whatever may be named as a means of raising the Negro from his iron bed of sorrow, up to a plane of intellectual culture, independent man-hood and a fair chance in the race of life. This malicious and revengeful spirit, born of slavery, by cunningly devised political trickery did—when the late civil war had ended and an honorable surrender was supposed to have been made—promise ample protection to the Negroes who had so largely contributed to the slaughter of the <u>flower of the South</u>. Under martial law, we had the humane and unbroken services of our Northern friends, male and female, white and colored, as School Teachers. These people—and God bless them all—done much by way of literal instructions and in teaching us, as far as practicable those well defined laws of civil life. They not only believed in our Adamic origin and oneness with the Races, but like them they held we were susceptible of as high a degree of educational attainments and refined culture as any other people—all things considered. These Teachers—many of whom had waded through the red fires of a sanguinary civil war to reach down the Samaritan hand and touch our complaint,—with the deepest pity in the soul, came and laid their offerings at our feet. Being refused shelter and association with their own race—the whites—we invited them to our cabins where, amidst the great object of their mission they seem to have been perfectly at home. At once taking in the situation, there was nothing found to dampen their zeal. And although the detached forces of the guerrilla marauders had sent these Teachers anonymous letters with skull and cross bones marked there in and accompanied with threats as to what would prove the result of their teaching these Negroes to read and write, still, instead of being deterred, or in the least intimidated, these threats furnished a new inspiration to a more zealous prosecution of their duties in the great uncultivated field of missionary labor upon which the eye of pity wase then looking. To this end Christ died, John Brown was hung, Garrison was cast about with ropes, Phillips pursued with deadly hate of the nation, Sumner slaughtered on the senate floor of the country, Lincoln shot and later Garfield meeting a like fate. Nor were these heralds of Emmanuel's cross[178] ashamed in the least to enter the huts and cabins of the most unsightly, ignorant, degraded and repulsive of my race, in futherance of their holy cause, as with more than Roman devotion to the Madonna they nursed, and instructed the objects of their care until Reconstruction had opened the Public Free Schools. They assembled with us in our churches and instructed at our Sabbath Schools. And although they had stood through the most bitter proscriptions and social ostricisms, on their retirement from a well fought field which they had conquered, they had no words of reproach for the enemy, but they were followed by the prayers and tears of the wards of their labors, and even, their enemies had to praise them for their courage after driving them from the State But, thanks to the God of our Fathers, they had accomplished their mission before returning to their distant homes, as an evidence of which, many of the little waifs that came under their first instructions could read well and write before these God appointed missionaries left us. And where ever they may be at their respective homes, may the same holy spirit inspire them on and on in the calling of the gospel of Jesus Christ until we shall all meet in a different world from this and reap the full reward of all their labors for the oppressed. Reaching now the close of life, and closing also on these writings, I might say more, but not less on behalf of the nation's friends who wrought out our freedom. And although dragged down to poverty and without a shelter, shut out, even from government employ after placing white men—supposed to be loyal Republicans—in distinguished positions where they have amassed fortunes,—I am only satisfied that they shall meet me at another place than this. I am not mad at them, but rather pray for them that they may see in time the giant wrongs they have perpetrated upon an ex-slave who has never had five minutes schooling in all his life. Besides my efforts in the missionary work, I have done much, as shown, in securing justice to the Negro, employed by the government. I have, also, from a practical knowledge of the trade, prepared a document, showing the cause of early decay and preservation of the wooden war batteries of our Navy. This I forwarded to his Hon. Wm. E. Chandler, Sec. of the Navy whose reply was as follows

"Navy Department
Washington 12th March 1883

Dear Sir,
    I have read with great interest your valuable remarks upon the proper means of preservation of the wooden ships of the Navy. Your record as a

practical caulker gives your opinions great weight upon all matters concerning the operations of that trade and the materials used.

I have referred your communication to the Bureau of Construction and Repair which is charged with the construction and preservation of men-of-war.

Thanking you for expressions of personal regard and for the interest which you have envinced in the Naval branch of the public service, I remain Very Respectfully

W.E. Chandler[179]

Sec of the Navy"

It was quite a lengthy document covering some seven or Eight pages foolscap in M.S.

Under such a paper, I had thought to ask his hon.—Sec of the Navy, to give me some employ, but on considering the political modus operandi through which a petition of the kind had to pass before reaching the hon Sec. and aware also that I had not only led the colored voter in to the support of the Republican party, but that I had been always found giving advice to my former fellow bondsmen in that direction, there was no use in making application on the grounds of competency. However, on looking back I have all for encouragement and nothing to regret for a single step I have taken in defending the rights of my race, or others who were not so identified, and if the former have not been sufficiently intelligent in rising to a just appreciation of these disinterested labors on their behalf, the fault does not rest exclusively with themselves as being fearless independent thinkers. And although, I have not been very concise or conclusive in showing the cause, yet the judicious reader will find a basis for meditation in what has been already advanced on that subject—fear. Having, as I have shown, been requested to write out a synopsis of my career, I was rather slow in entering upon the arduous work; the further I proceeded, however, the more I felt to pursue the task, to the end that I might be satisfied in my own person, the possibilities of the Negro doomed to slavery, while the desecting knife of cruel barbarism had been whet, as it were, upon the bleached bones of our sires and grand sires, & waiting to be crimsoned with the blood of the severed arm of any Negro who had aspired to spell, or read, or write the name of God on paper. Yes, my white brethren, you have done us badly. And you may again garner up and hug to yourselves all that may be acquired by the intellectual culture and wealth of ages; all that the dark spirit of oppressions may offer as a reward for your obedience to its mandates, and thus again, with blind inspiration and a false devotion bow to the Molochs, the Ahiuns and the Ashtoreths,[180] with a pleasant sail over the sea of life, but remember this, you will be burdening posterity with a debt of your own contracting, piling upon your children and their children's children a condition of torments from which—happily for the country—it has just been delivered.—Be wise in time. Besides demonstrating the capacity or possibilities of the Negro brain which acquired its knowledge of letters under the most adverse circumstances, these writings, unclassic and unscholarly as they may be, will have the merit of pointing out to the authors of lingual science or pure English composition, that faculty of the educational powers most necessary to be guarded, assuring all,—mean time—that I have never read anything in a book known as "English grammar" the study of which might have aided me in condensing much that would almost seem to be superfluous. And now, after the most intense application to these studies, I am only left to the cold charities of the world, while around me stalks in Princely pride the beneficiaries of my labors. And now, O God, and ye spirits immortal, close around me and help me offer prayerful thanks to Him who gave me being and early pointed to the quick-sands in the lane of life—direction to thought and nerve to pen, And now I lay my course and cause at the bleeding feet of His own dear Son, Jesus Christ the Righteous.

Yours,
Geo. Teamoh
Completed, June 27th 1883

SUPPLEMENT

Thinking it well to state, in as brief terms as I may, what has contributed most largely,—within the last decade,—to my present misfortunes, the inquiring, and candid reader will, no doubt, pardon me for further intrusion on his, or her patience. Indeed I had intended something like the following to be inserted in the body of my former work, but as I could not very accurately anticipate occurrences reaching down to the times in which I now write,—I am, as it were forced to make this addendum from that and other considerations.

Never having drank a dollar's worth of intoxicating drinks in all my life, during many years I have been—among my people, more especially— a strenuous advocate of temperance and was chosen by the Grand Lodge of Virginia in 18   as a delegate to the Right Worthy Grand Lodge, Independent Order of Good Templary which convened that year at Cardiff, Wales,

England: To prevent a drain on the Grand, and Subordinate Lodge's Treasury, I declined the journey and addressed a proxy letter to a lady citizen of that place, a Miss or Mistress Collins I think it was. However, the minutes reported a faithful discharge of her duty as a proxy member[181] Very soon after the "war for the Union" I assisted here in organizing the "Union League of America" as an off set to the bloody clans, known as "Kue Klux". A methodist minister, however, choosing to use the Chas. Sumner council—of which I was a member—as a "catch penny", I soon with drew from it and formed a Thad. Stephens [Stevens] Lodge.[182] Let me say here, as a matter of justice to the founders of this League, that its recognized existance greatly assisted in keeping the enemy at bay, amidst the many riots resulting from a civil war in which the Negro was made the central object of persecution.

It is much to be regretted that I can not speak more favorable of those ministers who formally held our pulpits here as by Divine authority. While making the necessary allowance for their deficiency in theology, and educational abilities, it has been quite remarkable with me how shrewdly they had set a side the great cause of temperance. It is not, however a very difficult matter to assign reasons for this—they feared the loss of patronage and member-ship. Once in a great while, one speaks out on the subject, but they work very stiffly in the harness, as a general thing, so much so that their words fail in carrying conviction. One of the most noticeable of this class of Ministers was stationed here during the four years ending some time in the Spring of the present year—1883.[183] It is known, that in previous years great censure had been brought on the pulpit of the country as a result of its reticence on the very important subject of temperance. With reluctant recognition of the necessity of clerical action being taken in the matter, and per force of public opinion, many of these were driven in to the issue, and quite a large number, like new converts, became co-laborers with the old veterans, who for so many years had been fighting down the monsterous evil of intemperance. What I have, in another section of these writings, termed "imitative forms" should not be lost sight of by those who would read me through. Having exhausted our patience in calling the attention of our clergy to take part with us in arresting the spirit of intemperance which was then, as now,—leading our youth down to destruction, we succeeded in securing the temporary service of the minister to whom allusion has been made. Being well aware that the white churches had now entered upon the work in good earnest and that it was also the hope and desire of that venerable and good man, Bishop   Paine that his ministers should encourage and give countenance not only to the cause in question, but that historical clubs, literary associations, and whatever other institutions looking to our progress and elevation in life, should also come under the fostering care of the church as far as practicable, to that end we worked hard. When a temperance meeting had been called at the A.M.E. church of which he was then pastor, he read a M.S. dissertation on temperance, the poverty of which it is not necessary I should speak of here, considering he was famed, among the less informed as a scholar. The Venerable Bishop, himself had assisted in person in the infant organization of the historical club which was composed chiefly of the best material we had at our command. Keeping on the trail of the minister referred to, we find him, first slyly conniving with politics in, what was, and is known as the "Mahone movement"[184]—now in favor of it and now against it. And now since it is supposed to control State politics and several of his communicants (col) having obtained offices under the government by their alliance with it, he is found with the successful party. He takes the most intelligent and monied of these, and organizes a joint Stock Association to be known as the "Tide Water Trust Company".[185] The place of meetings, at first was in his church, he being a member of that Tide Water &c body. There were some Eighteen (18) of them, all having subscribed one hundred dollars each. At a time when it was not possible to prolong his stay here, and when he had, as he thought, artfully concealed the intent and purpose of engaging in real estate enterprises with those of his Company, my Residence was about to be sold on a mortgage claim. His party, or club bought it, and on my knowledge of this minister being a member, I had supposed my chances of instantly vacating the premises not to be so bad, after all, as I informed my wife that her minister was the leading spirit and that in all probability some favor would be shown me; in all of which she heartily acquiesced. This high apostle of real estate brockerage, however, was the first to motion for a total vacation of the property and within the shortest legal limits. This I should have thought nothing of, had I not been at the time on the most intimate friendly terms with the man. If there is latitude in his discipline for all this, or half of it, it would seem that amendments are in time.

I have never disputed the right, and do not now, which the company had to purchase the property. What I would show is, the unmanly and unchristian part taken by a supposed-to-be minister of the gospel in stepping out side of what is a holy calling, to deal in Stock jobbing even at the risk of driving a poor man out of house and home. If we must have an African Church,—and I am opposed to the term—let us by all means save it from further shame by relieving it of all such Judas as this whickering penurious preacher And I told him to his head that he was a Judas if guilty of the charges alleged and which he did not deny. "Take neither purse nor script for your journey" does not weigh with such men and when priest craft of this character has been brought to light, and where it has been known, as in his case it is, that his object is to make permanent residence where he can make the most money, let him be at once dropped from the ministry and take his chances with the devotees to mammon. His name is on their—Tide Water Trust Company's books—Secrecy being one of his leading traits, I doubt very much whether his Bishop and others, will ever be any the better informed than they now are, or otherwise. I have thus furnished my readers with a specimen brick of many of those who, are sent down here as missionaries to build up society—to build up a people to the honor and glory of the great God of heaven, and His Son Who has shouldered our cause and without script & briberie borne it to a triumphant victory. "Go ye and do likewise".

With all I have said, I rejoice to see that the Rev Bishop recognizes the necessity of giving us master builders in our pulpits, as he has recently given us a young man of whose piety, education and christian qualities generally, I am informed, there can be no doubt. I have heard him only once. Our opinion is, that he can cope with the most refined pulpit oritor—white or colored, now in this place.

And so with zion Baptist Church whose minister runs a newspaper press, and besides being a good elocutionist, he is at once a scholarly Editor as his "Virginia Baptist Companion"[186] will show. These instances in the history of our progress not being among the least to be considered, I may be pardoned for giving mention here, although patent.

Whatever may follow as unwholesome or other wise—in the history of these, at present shining lights—as the results of birth and condition, of course, we know not, but leave time, which is no less a true recorder than a just rewarder, to show this nation, and then send down to posterity the possibilities of the Negro born under the <u>fearful</u> whip of American Slavery.

In much of the above writings I have, no doubt, over estimated my ability as a prose composer.[187] If, however, it may be considered an unusually long, and poorly contrived production, even that would be more than is deserved when brought to the light of critical examination. This is perhaps, the last book that will ever be written by the untought Negro of this country, and espicially so in the State of Virginia And although, many the dark spots that linger along my highest skies of intellectual thought—many the erroneous paths through which I have wandered while in full view of the labored summit I sought to reach, still,—unshod, and as with bleeding feet I pressed my weary way over the flinty rocks of life which have been so amply bridged for others of my race—I have fallen far short of its fruitful fields. Never-the-less, I rejoice while recognizing the wide spread hand of missionary charity which has been so liberal, so humane and christian in lifting from many of my race the dark clouds of ignorance and superstition, and can only trust that this good work will be pushed forward with a zeal commensurate with the cause.

ENDNOTES

Introduction

[1]Virginius Dabney, *Richmond: The Story of a City* (Garden City NY: Doubleday & Company, 1976) 216-18; *A Full Account of the Great Calamity, Which Occurred in the Capitol at Richmond, Virginia, April 27, 1870, Together with a List of Killed and Wounded* (Richmond VA: Ellyson and Taylor, publishers, 1870) 12-14, 46-49; "Terrible Calamity," *Richmond Daily Whig*, 28 April 1870, p. 1; "The Calamity of Yesterday," *Richmond Daily Whig*, 28 April 1870, p. 2. Teamoh later visited the mortally wounded Bland as he was dying; he also took part in Bland's funeral.

[2]Virginius Dabney, *Virginia: The New Dominion* (Garden City NY: Doubleday & Company, 1971) 1-125; Thomas J. Wertenbaker, *Norfolk: Historic Southern Port*, ed. Marvin W. Schlegel (Durham NC: Duke University Press, 1962) 3-47; Marshall W. Butt, *A Brief History of Norfolk Naval Shipyard, Portsmouth, Virginia* (Portsmouth VA: Public Information Office, 1956) 1-4; Marshall W. Butt, *Portsmouth under Four Flags: 1752–1970* (Portsmouth VA: Portsmouth Historical Society, 1971) 4-11; Brent Tarter, ed., *The Order Book and Related Papers of the Common Hall of the Borough of Norfolk, Virginia, 1736–1798* (Richmond VA: Virginia State Library, 1979) 11-12.

[3]Wertenbaker, *Norfolk*, 48-73; Dabney, *Virginia*, 146-54.

[4]Wertenbaker, *Norfolk*, 74-94; Butt, *Portsmouth*, 23; Tarter, *Order Book*, 15-17; *The Norfolk Directory* (Norfolk: Augustus C. Jordan and Company, 1806) 57-60, passim; *Return of the Whole Number of Persons within the Several Districts of the United States* (Philadelphia: Childs and Swaine, 1791) 50.

[5]Dabney, *Virginia*, 200-20; Wertenbaker, *Norfolk*, 95-187; Butt, *Norfolk Naval Shipyard*, 6 and *Portsmouth*, 27-32; H. W. Burton, *The History of Norfolk, Virginia* (Norfolk: Norfolk Virginian Job Print, 1877) 13-14; idem, "Model of *Delaware* Returned to Yard for Museum," *Service to the Fleet* (Norfolk Navy Yard paper), 2 April 1954, p. 3; John C. Emerson, Jr., "The Steamboat Comes to Norfolk Harbor (1815–1825)" (typescript in the Sargeant Memorial Room, Norfolk Public Library), p. 169; Commander A. W. Ashbrook, *The History of Our Navy Yard* (pamphlet in Marshall W. Butt Library, Portsmouth Naval Shipyard Museum, dated 1927), p. 5; Wayland Fuller Dunaway, *History of the James River and Kan-*

awha Company (New York: Columbia University Press, 1922) 164-88; Nelson Morehouse Blake, *William Mahone of Virginia: Soldier and Political Insurgent* (Richmond VA: Garrett & Massie, Publishers, 1935) 24-33; J. B. D. DeBow, ed., *The Seventh Census of the United States: 1850* (Washington D.C.: Robert Armstrong, Printer, 1853) 258; William S. Forrest, *Historical and Descriptive Sketches of Norfolk and Vicinity, Including Portsmouth and the Adjacent Counties, during a Period of Two Hundred Years* (Philadelphia: Lindsay and Blakiston, 1853) 271. Forrest mentioned the difficulty of obtaining an accurate census count in a seaport with many transient seamen, and he claimed that in 1840 seamen on U.S. vessels in port were counted while in 1850 they were not counted. Just before the Civil War, railroads operating out of Richmond were carrying much more freight than the recently completed Norfolk and Petersburg Railroad.

⁶David R. Goldfield, "Disease and Urban Image: Yellow Fever in Norfolk, 1855," *Virginia Cavalcade* 23 (Autumn 1973): 34-41; Wertenbaker, *Norfolk*, 188-97; Butt, *Portsmouth*, 34-35; Col. William H. Stewart, ed., *History of Norfolk County, Virginia, and Representative Citizens* (Chicago: Biographical Publishing Company, 1902) 75.

⁷Wertenbaker, *Norfolk*, 116-44, 185-86; Butt, *Portsmouth*, 29, 36; Joseph C. G. Kennedy, *Population of the United States in 1860; Compiled from the Original Returns of the Eighth Census* (Washington: Government Printing Office, 1864) 519; Forrest, *Sketches of Norfolk*, 331-416. See also Eugene Ferslew, compiler, *Vickery's Directory for the City of Norfolk to Which Is Added a Business Directory for 1859* (Norfolk VA: Vickery & Company, 1859).

⁸Wertenbaker, *Norfolk*, 197-206; F. N. Boney, *John Letcher of Virginia: The Story of Virginia's Civil War Governor* (University AL: University of Alabama Press, 1966) 99-113.

⁹*Return of Persons* (1791), 50; *Seventh Census* (1853), 258; *Population of the U.S.* (1864), 519; Wertenbaker, *Norfolk*, 126; Richard D. Wade, *Slavery in the Cities: The South 1820–1860* (New York: Oxford University Press, 1964) 262-66, 278-80; Miss Mildred M. Holladay, "History of Portsmouth" (typescript within a larger work compiled by John C. Emerson, Jr., and entitled "Some Fugitive Items of Portsmouth & Norfolk County History," dated 1948) (Portsmouth, 1936) 185-86, 302. Miss Holladay's work appeared in episodes in the *Portsmouth Star* during the year 1936. The original is in the Sargeant Memorial Room, Norfolk Public Library.

¹⁰*Seventh Census* (1853) 258; *Population of the U.S.* (1864) 519; Wertenbaker, *Norfolk*, 126; Claudia Dale Goldin, *Urban Slavery in the American South, 1820–1860: A Quantitative History* (Chicago: University of Chicago Press, 1976) 52-53; Tommy L. Bogger, "The Slave and the Free Black Community in Norfolk, 1776–1865" (Ph.D. diss., University of Virginia, 1976) 161-99; Ira Berlin, *Slaves without Masters: The Free Negro in the Antebellum South* (New York: Random House, 1974) 248-49. The 1850 Census Population Schedules, Slave Schedules, County of Norfolk, State of Virginia, p. 149, lists Nathaniel Nash as the owner of twenty-six adult males and three adult females.

¹¹Bogger, "Black Norfolk," 200-82. See also the above-mentioned volumes by Berlin, Goldin, and Wade. For recent studies of black life in another antebellum seaport, see Michael P. Johnson and James L. Roark, eds., *No Chariot Let Down: Charleston's Free People of Color on the Eve of the Civil War* (Chapel Hill: University of North Carolina Press, 1984) and their *Black Masters: A Free Family of Color in the Old South* (New York: W. W. Norton & Company, 1984).

¹²Gerald W. Mullin, *Flight and Rebellion: Slave Resistance in Eighteenth-Century Virginia*

(New York: Oxford University Press, 1972) 140-55; Wertenbaker, *Norfolk*, 126-27, 197; Bogger, "Slave Community in Norfolk," 107-60; Stephen B. Oates, *The Fires of Jubilee: Nat Turner's Fierce Rebellion* (New York: Harper & Row, 1975) 15, 49, 93, 110-11; Clement Eaton, *The Freedom-of-Thought Struggle in the Old South* (New York: Harper & Row, 1964) 92-93, 102-103, 137, 260; Willard B. Gatewood, Jr., *Free Man of Color: The Autobiography of Willis Augustus Hodges* (Knoxville TN: University of Tennessee Press, 1982) xxvi.

[13]John W. Blassingame, ed., *Slave Testimony: Two Centuries of Letters, Speeches, Interviews, and Autobiographies* (Baton Rouge: Louisiana State University Press, 1977) xvii-lxv; F. N. Boney, ed., *Slave Life in Georgia: A Narrative of the Life, Sufferings, and Escape of John Brown, a Fugitive Slave* (Savannah GA: Beehive Press, 1972) ix-xii; Forrest, *Sketches of Norfolk*, 417-19. A chamber-of-commerce type, Forrest assured his readers that

> our coloured people, the slaves particularly, are generally happy and contented. They are entirely free from those cares and troubles which necessarily grow out of the responsibilities and duties of life, that devolve on those upon whom they depend for support. This statement will apply especially to those who are held in servitude, and who, of course, constitute the principal portion of the blacks here. Very many of them seem as free as any beings on the face of the earth; having, generally, liberal, kind, and indulgent owners, who allow them many privileges and who look anxiously to their welfare, providing for them comfortable lodging-rooms, sufficient clothing and a full quantity of wholesome food. . . . It is also quite observable, that there are not a few who prefer their present state of subjugation to their owners, to an unqualified freedom.

[14]George Teamoh, "Geo[.] Teamoh's Autobiography," passim; George Teamoh and Elizabeth Smith marriage registration, 6 May 1863, vol. 164, p. 41, Twenty-Second Registration 1863, Suffolk-Worcester Counties, Registry of Vital Records and Statistics, Department of Public Health, Boston, Massachusetts; The 1850 Census Population Schedules, for Free Inhabitants, Portsmouth in the County of Norfolk, State of Virginia, p. 163 (Josiah and Jane Thomas and family); personal property tax records of Josiah Thomas, 1843, Portsmouth, Norfolk County, Virginia State Library, Richmond.

[15]Teamoh, "Autobiography" 1-116; 1850 Census, Free Inhabitants, Portsmouth, Norfolk County, Virginia, p. 163 (Josiah and Jane Thomas and family); personal property tax records of Josiah Thomas, 1843, Portsmouth, Norfolk County, Virginia State Library, Richmond.

[16]Teamoh, "Autobiography" 116-57, 251.

[17]Ibid., 158-201. For other examples of local legal proceedings freeing fugitive slaves, see Stanley W. Campbell, *The Slave Catchers: Enforcement of the Fugitive Slave Law, 1850–1860* (Chapel Hill: University of North Carolina Press, 1968) 133, 141; and especially Donald Martin Jacobs, "A History of the Boston Negro from the Revolution to the Civil War" (Ph.D. diss., Boston University, 1968) 115.

[18]Teamoh, "Autobiography" 202-31 (quote on page 212); Larry Gara, *The Liberty Line: The Legend of the Underground Railroad* (Lexington: University of Kentucky Press, 1961) 61-66; *Seventh Census* (1853), p. 50; Jacobs, "Boston Negro," 82; Robert D. Brown, *Massachusetts: A Bicentennial History* (New York: W. W. Norton & Company, 1978) 147, 173-75.

[19]Teamoh, "Autobiography" 231-33. See also Arthur May Mowry, *The Dorr War: The*

Constitutional Struggle in Rhode Island (New York: Chelsea House Publishers, 1970).

[20]Teamoh, "Autobiography" 233; Jacobs, "Boston Negro," 85-291; Oscar Handlin, *Boston's Immigrants, 1790–1865: A Study in Acculturation* (Cambridge MA: Harvard University Press, 1941) 100-101, 180-82; *Population of U.S.* (1864), pp. 225, 444; James Oliver Horton and Lois E. Horton, *Black Bostonians: Family Life and Community Struggle in the Antebellum North* (New York: Holmes & Meier, 1979) 1-13.

[21]Teamoh, "Autobiography" 233-46; Jacobs, "Boston Negro," 83-323; Elizabeth Haflin Pleck, *Black Migration and Poverty: Boston, 1865–1900* (New York: Academic Press, 1979) 27; Benjamin Quarles, *Black Abolitionists* (New York: Oxford University Press, 1969) 32; Adams, Sampson & Company, *Boston Directory 1860* (Boston: Damrell & Moore, 1860) 416; William Edward Farrison, *William Wells Brown: Author and Reformer* (Chicago: University of Chicago Press, 1969) 402; George A. Levesque, "Inherent Reformers—Inherited Orthodoxy: Black Baptists in Boston," *Journal of Negro History* 60 (October 1975): 521-25. See also Levesque, "Black Boston: Negro Life in Garrison's Boston, 1800-1860" (Ph.D. diss., State University of New York at Binghamton, 1976). For a long time Pitts served as a deacon in the African (First Independent) Baptist Church, and from 1868-1871 he listed William Wells Brown as a partner in his clothing store at 24 Brattle Street.

[22]Teamoh, "Autobiography" 199; Horton and Horton, *Black Bostonians*, 97-114; Jacobs, "Boston Negro," 265-323; Irving H. Bartlett, *Wendell Phillips: Brahmin Radical* (Boston: Beacon Press, 1961) 175. Earlier in 1842 fugitive slave George Latimer was arrested in Boston and returned to Norfolk, Virginia, but only after a huge protest that led to enactment of a personal liberty law in Massachusetts in 1843.

[23]Teamoh, "Autobiography" 246-47; Teamoh-Smith marriage registration, 6 May 1863, Vital Statistics, Boston; Horton and Horton, *Black Bostonians*, 42; J. G. Randall and David Donald, *The Civil War and Reconstruction* (Lexington MA: D. C. Heath, 1969) 89, 514-32. The black Twelfth Baptist Church was thrown into a heated controversy when Thomas Teamoh, George's half brother, brought his former wife out of bondage, separating her from her current husband in slavery. Some members accused Teamoh of adultery.

[24]Clement Eaton, *A History of the Southern Confederacy* (New York: Macmillan, 1954) 1-60; Emory M. Thomas, *The Confederate Nation, 1861–1865* (New York, Hagerstown, and London: Harper & Row, 1979) 37-66; Richard N. Current, *Lincoln and the First Shot* (Philadelphia and New York: J. B. Lippincott, 1963) 103-81; Roy P. Basler, ed., *The Collected Works of Abraham Lincoln*, 9 vols. (New Brunswick NJ: Rutgers University Press) 4:332.

[25]Ralph A. Wooster, *The Secession Conventions of the South* (Princeton: Princeton University Press, 1962) 139-54; Boney, *Letcher of Virginia*, 91-147; Emory M. Thomas, *The Confederate State of Richmond: A Biography of the Capital* (Austin and London: University of Texas Press, 1971) 3-14; Randall and Donald, *Civil War and Reconstruction*, 180-89, 227-42.

[26]Wertenbaker, *Norfolk*, 207-209.

[27]Butt, *Portsmouth*, 34-43; Wertenbaker, *Norfolk*, 212-16; Virgil Carrington Jones, *The Civil War at Sea*, 3 vols. (New York, Chicago, and San Francisco: Holt, Rinehart, and Winston, 1960-1962) 1:86-97, 385-437; Randall and Donald, *Civil War and Reconstruction*, 442-44.

[28]T. Harry Williams, *Lincoln and His Generals* (New York: Alfred A. Knopf, 1952) 87-115; Shelby Foote, *The Civil War: A Narrative*, 3 vols. (New York: Random House, 1958-

1974) 1:414-15.

[29]Wertenbaker, *Norfolk*, 217-21; Richard G. Lowe, "Francis Harrison Pierpont: Wartime Unionist, Reconstruction Moderate," in Edward Younger and James Tice Moore, eds., *The Governors of Virginia, 1860–1978* (Charlottesville: University Press of Virginia, 1982) 36-38; Hans Louis Trefousse, *Ben Butler: The South Called Him Beast* (New York: Twane Publishers, 1957) 140; Wertenbaker, *Norfolk*, 222-27; Butt, *Portsmouth*, 45-47.

[30]Trefousse, *Ben Butler*, 1-64, 107-21; Benjamin F. Butler, *Butler's Book: Autobiography and Personal Reminiscences of Major General Benjamin F. Butler* (Boston: A. M. Thayer & Company, 1892) 733. For comments concerning idealism of this type in the officer corps of the Union Army, see William C. Harris, "The Creed of the Carpetbaggers: The Case of Mississippi," *Journal of Southern History*, 40 (May 1974): 202. For a different view stressing the racism and antiblack prejudice of Union officers and soldiers, see Leon F. Litwack, *Been in the Storm So Long: The Aftermath of Slavery* (New York: Alfred A. Knopf, 1979) 128.

[31]Butler, *Butler's Book*, 256-63; Trefousse, *Ben Butler*, 78-79; Benjamin Quarles, *The Negro in the Civil War* (Boston: Little, Brown and Company, 1959) 58-61.

[32]Randall and Donald, *Civil War and Reconstruction*, 370-98.

[33]Quarles, *Negro in the Civil War*, 60-64; Wertenbaker, *Norfolk*, 220-21; Litwack, *Been in the Storm So Long*, 45-59.

[34]Alrutheus Ambush Taylor, *The Negro in the Reconstruction of Virginia* (Washington: The Association for the Study of Negro Life and History, 1926) 137-41; Dudley Taylor Cornish, *The Sable Arm: Negro Troops in the Union Army, 1861–1865* (New York: W. W. Norton and Company, 1966) 266-67; William Preston Vaughn, *Schools for All: The Blacks and Public Education in the South, 1865–1877* (Lexington: University Press of Kentucky, 1974) 8-12.

[35]For details on the difficulties of escape and the determination of blacks to restore family and marriage ties, see Litwack, *Been in the Storm So Long*, 167-87; Clarence L. Mohr, *On the Threshold of Freedom: Masters and Slaves in Civil War Georgia* (Athens and London: University of Georgia Press, 1986) 99-119. For examples of the concerns of federal officials at the refugee camps, see Herbert G. Gutman, *The Black Family in Slavery and Freedom, 1857–1925* (New York: Pantheon Books, 1976) 370-73, 267-69, 412. The conditions in the contraband camps, of course, could be quite grim. For an example of such conditions, see Fred Harvey Harrington, *Fighting Politician: Major General N. P. Banks* (Philadelphia: University of Pennsylvania Press, 1948) 104.

[36]For comments on contrabands and freedmen around Fort Monroe marrying and formalizing family ties, see Gutman, *Black Family*, 412-14.

[37]Lowe, "Francis Harrison Pierpont," 38-40; Jack P. Maddex, Jr., *The Virginia Conservatives, 1867–1879: A Study in Reconstruction Politics* (Chapel Hill: University of North Carolina Press, 1970) 27-28, 37-41; William Larsen, "Virginia," in David C. Roller and Robert W. Twyman, eds., *The Encyclopedia of Southern History* (Baton Rouge: Louisiana State University Press, 1979) 1285.

[38]Walter L. Fleming, *Documentary History of Reconstruction: Political, Military, Social, Religious, Educational and Industrial, 1865 to 1906*, 2 vols. (Cleveland: Arthur H. Clark Company, 1906-1907) 1:401-403, 407-11; Patrick W. Riddleberger, *1866: The Critical Year Revisited* (Carbondale and Edwardsville: Southern Illinois University Press, 1979) 176-201;

Eric L. McKitrick, *Andrew Johnson and Reconstruction* (Chicago and London: University of Chicago Press, 1960) 421-47. There was also a riot on 16 April 1866 in the Norfolk-Portsmouth area. See John Hammond Moore, "The Norfolk Riot 16 April 1866," *Virginia Magazine of History and Biography* 90 (April 1982): 155-64. This violence erupted when local blacks marched in celebration of the senate's override of President Johnson's veto of the Civil Rights Bill. Several blacks were killed and several were wounded.

[39]Hamilton James Eckenrode, *The Political History of Virginia during the Reconstruction* (Baltimore: Johns Hopkins University Press, 1904) 68-86; James Douglas Smith, "Virginia during Reconstruction—1865-1870—A Political, Economic and Social Study" (Ph.D. diss., University of Virginia, 1960) 41-61; Richard G. Lowe, "Republicans, Rebellion, and Reconstruction: The Republican Party in Virginia, 1856-1870" (Ph.D. diss., University of Virginia, 1968) 204, 228-88. In the state as a whole, the calling of the convention was endorsed 107,342 to 61,887. For the vote totals for both the state and Teamoh's district, see *Documents of the Constitutional Convention [1867–1868] of the State of Virginia* (Richmond: printed at the Office of the New Nation, 1867) 53-56.

[40]*Journal of the Constitutional Convention of the State of Virginia, Convened in the City of Richmond December 3, 1867, by an order of General Schofield, Dated November 2, 1867, in Pursuance of the Act of Congress of March 23, 1867* (Richmond: printed at the Office of the New Nation, 1867 [*sic*]) 28-29; Richard L. Hume, "Membership of the Virginia Constitutional Convention of 1867–1868: A Study of the Beginnings of Congressional Reconstruction in the Upper South," *Virginia Magazine of History and Biography* 86 (October 1978): 463-70.

[41]Patricia Hickin, "Henry Horatio Wells: The Rise and Fall of a Carpetbagger," in Younger and Moore, *Governors of Virginia*, 49-55; Maddex, *Virginia Conservatives*, 60-85; Norfolk *Virginian*, 7 July 1869, p. 1; "Returns of July 6, 1869 Election Portsmouth City and the County of Norfolk," in Mss. Election Record No. 428, Virginia State Library, Richmond.

[42]Norfolk *Virginian*, 17 May 1869, p. 1; 13 May 1871, p. 1; 18 February 1871, p. 1; John F. Stover, *The Railroads of the South 1865–1900: A Study in Finance and Control* (Chapel Hill: University of North Carolina Press, 1955) 99-121.

[43]"Statement of the Whole Number of Votes Cast in the City of Portsmouth in an Election for Members of the House of Delegates of Virginia, Held Pursuant to Law, the First Tuesday after the First Monday in November, 1871," in Office of the Secretary of the Commonwealth Election Returns 1870-1871 (State Delegate) Abstracts. Mss. No. 3, Virginia State Library, Richmond.

[44]Norfolk *Virginian*, 2 November 1870, p. 1; 14 November 1871, p. 1.

[45]Deed Book 6, pp. 359-61, Office of the Circuit Court, City of Portsmouth, Virginia; Norfolk *Virginian*, 14 November 1871, p. 1; 15 November 1871, pp. 1-2; 20 November 1871, p. 1.

[46]James Tice Moore, *Two Paths to the New South: The Virginia Debt Controversy, 1870–1883* (Lexington: University Press of Kentucky, 1974) 5-6; *A Compendium of the Ninth Census June 1, 1870* (Washington: Government Printing Office, 1872) 356; Wertenbaker, *Norfolk*, 247-70.

[47]*Compendium of the Tenth Census (June 1, 1880)*, 2 vols. (Washington: Government Printing Office, 1882) 1:317; Wertenbaker, *Norfolk*, 271-74; Maddex, *Virginia Conservatives*, 143-65.

[48]Wertenbaker, *Norfolk*, 273-77.

[49]Deed Book 6, pp. 403-405, Office of the Circuit Court, City of Portsmouth, Virginia: letter of Ms. Rosa M. Wells and Dr. Walter T. Galliford (assistant superintendent for instruction, Portsmouth Public Schools) to Richard L. Hume, 2 August 1983.

[50]Deed Book 14, p. 346, Office of the Circuit Court, City of Portsmouth, Virginia; "Centennial Anniversary Emanuel African Methodist Episcopal Church Portsmouth, Virginia 1857–1957" (n.p., n.d.) in Ester Wilson Memorial History Room, Portsmouth Public Library, Portsmouth, Virginia; Stanley P. Hirshson, *Farewell to the Bloody Shirt: Northern Republicans and the Southern Negro, 1877–1893* (Bloomington: Indiana University Press, 1962) 251-55; Vincent P. DeSantis, *Republicans Face the Southern Question: The New Departure Years, 1877–1897* (Baltimore: Johns Hopkins University Press, 1959) 217-21.

[51]Moore, *Paths to the New South*, 45-92.

The Autobiography of the *Autobiography*

[1]Peter Kolchin deserves my thanks for urging me to begin work on Teamoh; this essay's earliest incarnation appeared in his Harvard graduate course in Reconstruction historiography. I would also like to express my appreciation to the Virginia Center for the Humanities and Public Policy; to the University of California at Irvine for giving me the opportunity to present some of this material at their Autobiography and Self-representation Conference in March 1990; Hoda Zaki, John McGuigan, and Peter Wallenstein; my colleagues at the Center for Afroamerican and African Studies, University of Michigan; to the committee that granted me a CASS-Ford Foundation faculty award, which allowed me to purchase some of the photographs for this volume; Lynn Weiss, for eleventh hour research; Valerie Kivelson and William Paul.

[2]My great-uncle, George Teamoh; his son, George "Sonny" Teamoh; his son, George Teamoh III; and his son, George Teamoh IV.

[3]The three other siblings were Edward, Lottie, and Aurelia (Swiggett).

[4]Dorothy Sterling may be best known now for her anthology of black women's writing, *We Are Your Sisters: Black Women in the Nineteenth Century* (New York: W. W. Norton, 1984).

[5]When I finally asked the provenance of this chest, my grandmother told me she had bought it at a pawn shop. "Wingo," the name of a long-gone and broke magician, is crudely painted on the inside lid.

[6]My grandmother never revealed her age. Going through her things after her funeral, we found various official documents, all with crudely altered birthdates.

[7]That Sarah married a black man, in a doubly tabooed act (miscegenation of white woman and black man), may be more intriguing. On the other hand, without the census record immediately before me, I cannot be sure that she was identified as such—which may only mean that she was not legally white (a curious enough designation).

[8]This rupture may have led to the Bailey-Teamoh feud my great-aunt recalls, or may have been precipitated by some internecine clan warfare; in any event, Maggie remembered the injunction that should they, the children, see a member of the opposition on the street, they were

not to speak.

⁹Although seasoned historians are well aware of this fact before commencing research, I was horrified to learn that the 1890 census records were destroyed by fire. Thus an additional method of confirming Edward's relation to George is unavailable.

¹⁰Teamoh describes the purchase of this homestead in his autobiography (134-35). A boarder, Harris, lived with the family as well. His first name may have been Littleton; it cannot be deciphered with accuracy.

¹¹Waldo Martin and Peter Wallenstein, personal communications, University of Virginia, summer of 1989.

¹²Edward Teamoh was listed as a thirty-year-old man in the 1900 census.

¹³As George Teamoh's marriage to Elizabeth Smith of Boston took place in 1863 and was terminated by Civil War's end, I am assuming that Edward was not the product of Teamoh's northern life. Thanks to my coeditors, Nash Boney and Richard Hume, for locating this second marriage's certificate; see n. 27.

¹⁴In these directories the names of African-Americans were distinguished from those of their Caucasian compatriots by an asterisk. Though dictated by racism, this practice would make matters of identification easy—for both contemporaries of Teamoh and latter-day historians— for it was and is well known that certain Southern families have both black and white branches. I found Riddick a common name for both African- and Euro-American Virginia families.

¹⁵In 1874–1875 both a George Teemer, laborer, and a George Teamoh, caulker, are listed in Sheriff and Chataigne's city directory for Portsmouth; they reside in the same area. To confound matters, fifteen years later George Teemer, *caulker*, has an address on First Street. Should the 1890 Teemer be the same man as the original George Teamoh, that would mean the former senator lived into his seventies.

¹⁶Teamoh did not include the copybook covers in his pagination. When microfilming, the Library of Congress used a numbered counter during the reproduction of the Woodson papers; thus this film "page" is numbered 000236.

The 1839 date written on the cover of this volume precedes the interior one given by Teamoh by some thirty-one years. Either Teamoh completely got the year wrong, which seems unlikely, or he wrote in materials dated decades before. Another possibility could stem from a similarity of handwriting—that is, an earlier owner's script may have resembled Teamoh's. Coincidentally, Teamoh does write at one point that he kept a journal for the year 1839 (p. 56); that volume has not been located.

¹⁷See the title pages of the narratives of Douglass, William Wells Brown, Harriet Jacobs, and Henry Bibb, among the well-known works, for evidence of this apparent obsession with authorship. Fugitives were chiefly concerned with asserting their literacy, as reading and writing were believed to be beyond the slave's legal and intellectual ken. See also Rafia Zafar, "Franklinian Douglass: The Afro-American as Representative Man," in Eric Sundquist, ed., *Frederick Douglass: New Literary and Historical Essays* (New York: Cambridge University Press, 1990) 114-15.

¹⁸Frederick Douglass, *Narrative of the Life of Frederick Douglass, an American Slave, Written by Himself*, ed. Benjamin Quarles (1845; Cambridge MA: Harvard University Press, 1960) 23.

[19]See Orlando Patterson, *Slavery and Social Death* (Cambridge MA: Harvard University Press, 1982) 5, for an explanation of this term.

[20]Frederick Douglass, *My Bondage and My Freedom*, ed. William L. Andrews (1855; Urbana and Chicago: University of Illinois Press, 1987), 28.

[21]Douglass's birth year of 1818 was established by Dickson J. Preston. See Preston, *Young Frederick Douglass: The Maryland Years* (Baltimore: Johns Hopkins University Press, 1980) 31-34.

[22]Teamoh refers to letters written by him and published in various newspapers. One letter, protesting racism in the New Bedford caulking trade, led to the rehiring of black workers. See p. 209.

[23]Frederick Douglass had only minimal aid. Sophia Auld, his initially sympathetic mistress, became convinced by her husband of the danger of slave literacy. See Douglass, *Narrative*, 63-64.

[24]Antislavery editors and amanuenses, who were responsible for the publication of the bulk of the slave narratives, encouraged the recitation of nothing but the facts; such patronizing, if good, intentions could lead to a sameness among stories. Douglass's break with the Garrisonians stemmed from his desire to escape these boundaries. See John Sekora, "Black Message, White Envelope: Genre, Authenticity and Authority in the Antebellum Slave Narrative," *Callaloo* 10 (1987): 482-51.

[25]See Harold Bloom, *The Anxiety of Influence: A Theory of Poetry* (New York: Oxford University Press, 1973) 5-16.

[26]Newbell Niles Puckett, *Black Names in America: Origins and Usage*, ed. Murray Heller (Boston: G. K. Hall, 1975). Examination of lists in Ihechukwu Madubuike, *A Handbook of African Names* (Washington D.C.: Three Continents Press, 1976) and Ogonna Chuks-orji, *Names from Africa: Their Origin, Meaning, and Pronunciation*, ed. Keith E. Baird (Chicago: Johnson Publishing Company, 1972) yields no homologous name. Nevertheless, Lemuel Johnson, of the University of Michigan, noted the similarity of the name Teamoh to words found in the Dru language of Liberia; he also pointed out that "Tiemoko" is the name of a character in the novel *God's Bits of Wood*, by Senegalese writer Ousmane Sembene. Lemuel Johnson, personal communication, 10 February 1990.

[27]See the marriage license for George Teamoh and Elizabeth Smith dated 6 May 1863; Teamoh there gives his parents' names as David and Lavinia (n. 8, p. 173).

[28]Robert B. Stepto, *From Behind the Veil* (Urbana: University of Illinois Press, 1979) ix.

[29]Regarding authenticating documents, see ibid., 3-4. Teamoh includes the letters of others as well. Another literate slave, George Cooper, a friend of Teamoh and the reluctant slave jailer of Sallie Teamoh, is represented by a missive he sent to her frantic husband (131). Cooper also shared with Teamoh letters from slaveholders seeking new purchases (145-48).

[30]Teamoh's experience with kindly Europeans is one echoed by any number of slave writers—some, like William and Ellen Craft, would take up residence abroad. Compare James Baldwin's account of a visit to Switzerland nearly one hundred years later; children there still cried out "To wit mankind was made so dark." Baldwin, "Stranger in the Village," *Notes of a Native Son* (1955; New York: Beacon Press, 1957) 161-62.

[31]Many slaves did return to their Southern home states after the war, if only to reunite with their families. William L. Andrews writes that the postbellum slave narrative breaks significantly with its prewar ancestors, most notably in the depiction of slavery. See Andrews, "A Poetics of Afro-American Autobiography," in Houston A. Baker, Jr. and Patricia Redmond, eds., *Afro-American Literary Study in the 1990s* (Chicago: University of Chicago Press, 1989) 85-86.

[32]See, e.g., Richard L. Hume, "The Membership of the Virginia Constitutional Convention of 1867–1868. A Study of the Beginnings of Congressional Reconstruction in the South," *Virginia Magazine of History and Biography* 86 (October 1978): 461-84.

[33]See David Howard-Pitney, "The Enduring Black Jeremiad: The American Jeremiad and Black Protest Rhetoric, from Frederick Douglass to W. E. B. Du Bois," *American Quarterly* 38:3 (Bibliography 1986): 481-92.

[34]Douglass, *My Bondage and My Freedom*, 248.

Geo. Teamoh's Autobiography

[1]Born in 1817(?) on a plantation on the Eastern Shore of Maryland, Douglass experienced a slave life similar to Teamoh's, but he escaped in 1838, fifteen years earlier than Teamoh. Douglass worked hard and became a self-made businessman in the best American tradition. An outstanding orator, he attacked slavery relentlessly and soon became a prominent abolitionist, known widely in Europe as well as America. In 1845 he published the short but succinct *Narrative of the Life of Frederick Douglass: An American Slave, Written by Himself* (Boston: The Anti-slavery Society, 1845), and in 1855 and 1881 he published expanded, more introspective versions of his busy life. In 1847 in Rochester, New York, he began the newspaper *The North Star*, which was soon renamed *Frederick Douglass' Paper* and remained in circulation for seventeen years. During the Civil War he helped recruit blacks into the Union army and after the war he championed suffrage and civil rights for all black Americans. After the collapse of Radical Reconstruction, he held several Republican patronage jobs with the federal government, and he capped off his distinguished career as U.S. minister in Haiti from 1889 to 1891. He died in 1895, universally recognized as a pioneer in the struggle for black equality.

[2]Another fugitive slave and, like Douglass, the son of a white father and a slave mother, Brown was born in Kentucky around 1815. After being hired out to work on a steamboat and in a printer's shop in St. Louis, he escaped in 1834. Just as ambitious and industrious as Douglass, he pursued formal education, including the study of medicine, but he finally found success as a professional writer. He published poetry, novels, plays, travel literature, and biographies, but he concentrated on black history, and his *Narrative of William Wells Brown A Fugitive Slave, Written by Himself* was published in 1847, just two years after Douglass's *Narrative*. He too joined the abolitionists and spoke eloquently against slavery and he also traveled widely overseas.

John Sella Martin was another black abolitionist, but he was not as well known as Douglass and Brown. He was born a slave in Charlotte, North Carolina, in 1832 and worked for masters in Georgia and Louisiana before finally escaping in 1856. He studied for the ministry in Detroit and in the late 1850s served a church in Buffalo, New York, before coming to Boston where he was interim pastor at the Tremont Temple and then minister at the African Baptist Church on Joy Street. His sermons on Nat Turner drew large crowds, and he championed the

Republican party from this pulpit too. During the Civil War Martin moved to Washington, D.C., where he gained even wider prominence as a leading black minister. He strongly supported the Union war effort and Abraham Lincoln's reelection in 1864, and he toured Great Britain for the American Missionary Association seeking funds for freedmen's relief.

[3]This refers to Frederick Douglass's second autobiography, *My Bondage and My Freedom. Part I.—Life as a Slave. Part II.—Life as a Freeman* (New York and Auburn, NY: Miller, Orton & Mulligan, 1855).

[4]This large tract lay three miles north of Portsmouth in 1824 and originally belonged to the Portsmouth parish, hence the name "the glebe." In 1802 John Thompson bought it at public auction for $22 an acre. The Norfolk County Land Book for 1824 listed 237 acres of high ground valued at $3,654 (for which he paid a tax of $2.94). Thompson operated a brickyard, hired bricklayers, and was involved in general construction and rental activities—often under the business title of Thompson and Latimer. He lived in Portsmouth on the corner of North and Middle streets, which was almost on the river. He owned considerable other real estate in town as well as a productive farm and a brickyard at "the glebe." The federal manuscript census of 1840 (population schedule) listed him as a white male seventy to seventy-nine years old and the owner of ten slaves—eight males, two in the ten to twenty-four-year-old bracket and the rest older, and two adult females (p. 121). On 27 July 1847, Thompson died at age seventy-nine, and his will was probated in Norfolk County. He left five buildings and lots in town and twelve slaves to his wife Elizabeth; three buildings and lots in town and five slaves to his daughter Maria Baird; and an additional "two story framehouse and lot" to a nephew. He further ordered his "plantation usually called the glebe" to be sold. Thompson was a self-made man and widely admired. He served as a justice of the peace and then as a state legislator. Much later his grandson, John Thompson Baird, was elected mayor of Portsmouth. In his will Thompson had added a codicil in 1844 leaving the youngster his books (Will Book 6, Virginia State library, 234-37).

[5]The manuscript census of 1830 listed Joshua Silverthorn as a resident of the city of Norfolk and head of a family consisting of one white male twenty to twenty-nine years old, two white females twenty to twenty-nine years old, one white male under five, one white female under five, and one female slave ten to nineteen years old (p. 320). On the first page of his manuscript journal (preceding p. 1), Teamoh made the following entry:

> Please correct mistake in the name which I
> have given as "Silverthrog." It should be
> "Silverthorn." The plantations hands
> pronounced it right—Silverthorn.
>   Geo. Teamoh

In the text of the journal itself Teamoh corrected the name to read Silverthorn.

[6]John Thompson's will was written on 21 May 1841 and probated on 16 August 1847; it listed only three female slaves—Phoby Ann, Lamey, and Ira. Susan was no longer present among the Thompson slaves.

[7]The slaves Thompson willed to his daughter Maria Baird in 1847 were George, Haney (possibly a female), Nelson, Phoby Ann, and Joshua. The latter may well be the "Old Uncle Joshua" Teamoh quotes.

[8]When Teamoh married in Boston in 1863, he listed his parents as David and Lavinia.

See 6 May entry, volume 164, page 41, Twenty-second Registration, 1863. Suffolk-Worcester, Registry of Vital Records and Statistics, Department of Public Health, Commonwealth of Massachusetts, Boston.

[9]Hampton is located in Elizabeth City County, and Needhams do appear in the county records, but there is no way to identify for certain the family of Jane Needham.

[10]Her first husband is probably the "J. Winslow" listed as a twenty-seven-to forty-five-year-old resident of the little city of Norfolk in the manuscript census of 1820 for Norfolk County (p. 103). His family included a wife twenty-six to forty-five years of age and nine children or young dependents plus five slaves. Her second husband, Josiah Thomas, appears frequently in official records for Portsmouth. In the manuscript census of 1830, he is listed as head of a household of nine whites and five slaves (p. 336). One of the two male slaves between ten and twenty years of age must have been Teamoh. In the 1840 census (p. 123) he is listed as head of a household of eleven whites and five blacks. The male slave ten to twenty-four years of age must have been Teamoh. The more detailed census of 1850 listed Josiah Thomas, age forty-eight, as a ship joiner born in Virginia and included his wife Jane, age fifty-seven, and daughters Jane (nineteen), Caroline (seventeen), and sons twenty-nine and twenty-six years of age, who were given as ship carpenters (p. 163). (The sons' first names started with J, but the rest of the letters were indistinct.) The accompanying slave census of that year listed his four slaves, and the thirty-six-year-old male mulatto must have been Teamoh (p. 32). The Personal Property Book for the town of Portsmouth in Norfolk County in 1840 listed Josiah Thomas, his one slave who was more than sixteen years of age, and the tax of 33¢ right beside the much larger holdings of John Thompson (which partly explains how Teamoh came to be hired out to a neighbor). *The Portsmouth Directory, 1861–1862* listed Thomas as a joiner who lived on South Street between Dinwiddie and Washington streets, right in the middle of town.

[11]The bloodiest slave revolt in American history erupted in Southampton County, Virginia, before dawn on Monday, 22 August 1831. It lasted only two days, but Nat Turner and his followers cut a bloody swath through the county, leaving some sixty whites dead. The white counterattack that crushed the rebellion probably killed several hundred blacks in Southampton County. The lingering white anger and fear radiated out through the South, bringing a brief reign of terror to the black masses. Nearby Norfolk and Portsmouth had sent volunteers to help crush the rebellion, and whites in both communities remained angry and apprehensive. See Stephen B. Oates, *The Fires of Jubilee: Nat Turner's Fierce Rebellion* (New York: Harper & Row, 1975).

[12]Many whites in Virginia had always opposed education for blacks, but others took a more casual approach, and strict laws came slowly. In 1805 the legislature forbade overseers of the poor to require that owners of black orphans teach them. Not until April 1831 (a few months before Nat Turner's rebellion) was a law passed prohibiting free blacks from gathering to learn reading and writing. Anyone who gathered with slaves to teach them for compensation could be fined up to $100. These laws were not very systematic, and whites sometimes ignored them anyway. In 1853 authorities in Norfolk briefly jailed Margaret Douglass, a white, for operating a school for free blacks that charged three dollars per quarter per student. Around the same time in Lexington, an eccentric professor at the Virginia Military Institute named Thomas Jonathan Jackson (later known as "Stonewall") taught black children at a Presbyterian Sunday school free of charge and faced no more than the grumbling of a few townspeople.

[13]William Blackstone's *Commentaries on the Laws of England* (four volumes published in the 1760s) and the writings of William Shakespeare, John Milton, and John Knox (the founder

of Scottish Presbyterianism) were all well known. "Jeffreys" probably refers to George Jeffreys, first Baron Jeffreys of Wem, who was named lord chief justice of England in 1683. In the declining years of the Stuart Monarchy, he directed some of the most flagrant legal lynchings in the history of Anglo-Saxon law. As one scholar has said, his conduct in criminal trials was "disgraceful," but in other, less politicized areas his opinions were sound and judicious, and they were often studied respectfully. The only other possibility for "Jeffreys" is Francis Jeffrey, Scottish writer and critic, who edited the *Edinburgh Review* from 1803 to 1829. This journal was widely read on both sides of the Atlantic and would have been available in a growing urban area like Norfolk-Portsmouth.

[14]Jesse Nicholson was born in the interior of Virginia in 1759. He served throughout the Revolutionary War as an infantryman, participating in many battles such as Germantown and Brandywine. As a captain he led a Virginia regiment in one of the decisive attacks that forced Cornwallis to surrender at Yorktown. He settled in Portsmouth after the war, became postmaster during President Jefferson's administration, and retained the post until his death on 26 September 1834. He was also a county surveyor, an ordained minister serving the local Methodist Church, and the teacher of young boys at the first private school established in Portsmouth. Often he wrote out books in longhand for his students while operating the post office on High Street, the town's main thoroughfare. A distinguished-looking fellow, he always dressed in the old style—velvet coat, knee breeches, silk stockings, and silver buckled shoes, with his hair tied in a queue with a ribbon. He was widely respected in the community, and he was buried with honor in the Methodist churchyard as local volunteer companies paraded amidst great throngs of mourners. As late as 11 May 1904, the *Portsmouth Star* described the handsome monument that marked his grave.

[15]John Walker was born in England in 1732, and after early careers as an actor and a teacher he became a famous lexicographer and philologist. His *A Critical Pronouncing Dictionary and Expositor of the English Language* was first published in 1791 and went through many later editions in England and America. It continued to be reissued after Walker's death in 1807 and rivaled Noah Webster's *An American Dictionary of the English Language* (1828), even in America.

[16]A native of New Hampshire, John Emerson Worcester graduated from Yale in 1811. After a few years of teaching, he settled into his long career as a lexicographer. In 1830 he published his *Comprehensive Pronouncing and Explanatory Dictionary of the English Language*. This began a series of dictionaries that rivaled Webster's throughout the antebellum period. Worcester also edited *The American Almanac and Repository of Useful Knowledge* from 1831–1842, but most of his energies were devoted to his dictionaries until his death in 1865.

[17]Unfortunately, this journal has disappeared.

[18]President Martin Van Buren, a Democrat, served from 1837 to 1841, but was defeated for reelection in November 1840 by William Henry Harrison and the Whigs.

[19]Located at the corner of Main and Church streets, French's Hotel was one of Norfolk's finest. Soon it was renamed the National Hotel, and Stephen A. Douglas stayed there in August 1860 while campaigning for the presidency. Mr. Carrington is not positively identifiable.

[20]The manuscript census of 1840 listed J. Capheart as a resident of the city of Norfolk, age twenty to twenty-nine years and the head of a household that included one adult white female, three white children, six free blacks, and one elderly female slave (p. 185). The more detailed census of 1850 listed John Capheart (age forty-nine) as a constable (p. 77). Also included in

his family were Elizabeth (age thirty), Mary Capheart (twenty), John (ten), William (seven), Virginia (five), Emogene (three), Julie (one), and Margaret (eighteen). William S. Forrest's *Norfolk Directory* for 1851 listed J. Capheart as a police officer residing at 13 South Church Street, near the river (p. 49). In 1851 he went to Boston and tried unsuccessfully to return fugitive Frederick "Shadrack" Jenkins to his master in Norfolk. In August, while in Boston, Capheart described his duties in a short article entitled "An Exalted Profession" in the August 1851 issue of *American Missionary* (p. 75):

> It was part of my business to arrest all slaves and free persons of color, who were collected in crowds at night, and lock them up. It was also part of my business to take them before the Mayor. I did this without any warrant, and at my own discretion. Next day they are examined and punished. The punishment is flogging. I am one of the men who flog them. They get not exceeding thirty-nine lashes.
>
> I am paid fifty cents for every negro I flog. The price used to be sixty-two and half cents. I am paid fifty cents for every negro I arrest, and fifty cents more if I flog him. I have flogged hundreds. I am often employed by private persons to pursue fugitive slaves. I have been thus employed since 1838. I never refuse a good job of that kind.

[21]Several men with the name William Collins appear in the antebellum records of Norfolk and Portsmouth, but Teamoh is referring to William B. Collins, who was listed in the Norfolk County census of 1850 (p. 127). A native of Virginia and a resident of Portsmouth, Collins was a forty-four-year-old bricklayer. He and his thirty-four-year-old wife Lucy Ann (also a native Virginian) had nine children. The oldest, William, age seventeen, worked as a clerk, probably in his father's establishment. His father, William B. Collins, owned thirteen slaves, nine of whom were adult males, and they too probably labored in the growing business. The Personal Property Book for Portsmouth in Norfolk County in the same year listed him as owning six slaves older than sixteen and one older than twelve plus a horse and a metal clock (total tax $2.59). On 6 January 1851, the Norfolk *American Beacon* mentioned that William B. Collins attended a meeting to organize a local insurance company. Clearly, he was doing well.

[22]When John Thompson died in 1847, he left twelve slaves to his wife Elizabeth (see n. 4). Among these blacks were "Peter Cutler" and "Peter." When Elizabeth Thompson died in 1854, her will was also probated in Norfolk County, and Peter Cutler was still part of her estate. One of these two Peters was probably the "uncle Peter" whom Teamoh mentions.

[23]At the very tip of the peninsula between the York and James rivers, Fort Monroe was a large, seven-sided, brick bastion encompassing sixty-three acres of land on the seashore of Elizabeth City County near the town of Hampton. Some sort of crude fortification had existed there almost from the beginning because it was the natural defensive site for the whole strategic Hampton Roads area. The experienced French had added a few facilities during the Revolutionary War, but work on the permanent fort only began in 1819. Officially named in 1832, it was almost completed by 1834 at a cost of almost two million dollars. From 1837 to 1845 it underwent considerable repair and modification, and limited construction work continued right up to the beginning of the Civil War. The garrison was small, mostly guards and court-martialed soldiers who, along with gangs of slave laborers, did the hard labor necessary to build and maintain the huge structure. Such backbreaking work was truly "hard time" for soldiers and slaves alike. An artillery school also operated at this bastion, which was fortified on all sides and thus too strong for the rebels to seize in 1861. In the spring of 1862, it served as the springboard for George McClellan's massive Union offensive, which swept up the peninsula to the outskirts of Richmond before being turned back by Robert E. Lee's counterattacks. After the Civil War Jefferson Davis was imprisoned at secure Fort Monroe.

The hiring agent was probably William Laughton, an Elizabeth City County entrepreneur. On 30 September 1835, he signed a deed confirming a loan of $400 and put up twenty shares of stock in a local toll bridge company, half ownership of the slave Tony, an iron chest, and a hair sofa as collateral. The same year the county's Personal Property Book listed him as an "auctioneer" (often a euphemism for a slave trader) and acknowledged his payment of the sixty-dollar license fee on 25 November. He is listed in the census of 1840 for Elizabeth City County as a white male sixty to sixty-nine years of age who lived alone with no slaves (p. 114). The *Virginia 1840 Census Index* erroneously lists him as William "Saughton."

[24]More than a mile out from Fort Monroe in the main part of the narrow channel from the Chesapeake Bay into Hampton Roads lay Rip-Raps, a large shoal. Here the government determined to further strengthen the Hampton Roads defenses by constructing an island of stone topped with a small fortress. Work began in 1819, and ton after ton of rocks gradually built up an island that reached six feet above high tide in 1826. Then, after a year's delay to allow the mass to settle, a fort was built and named for John C. Calhoun, secretary of war under President Monroe. Further settling of the increasingly heavy mass required major reinforcement of the foundations during the first half of the 1830s, and additional work continued sporadically for the rest of the antebellum period, when Fort Calhoun threatened to cost almost as much as the much-larger Fort Monroe back on shore. When the Civil War began, the Union also retained possession of this artificial island, hurriedly renaming it Fort Wool. Slaves dreaded being assigned to hard labor on this barren, isolated island of rock only a few feet above the swirling waters rushing in and out of Hampton Roads with the tides.

[25]Rip-Raps, or Fort Calhoun, was a little more than a mile southeast of Fort Monroe and about three miles northeast of Sewells Point, which was on the Norfolk side of Hampton Roads a little farther in from the Chesapeake Bay and just a few miles east of the mouth of the Elizabeth River.

[26]Thomas Riley (or Reilly) was a prominent businessman early in the century. In 1817 he invested in a new steam grist and sawmill on King's Wharf. Colonel William H. Stewart's *History of Norfolk County, Virginia, and Representative Citizens* (Chicago: Biographical Publishing Company, 1902) 341, mentions "the imposing Riley residence, at the northeast corner of Riley and Holt streets, at one time known as 'The Retreat for the Sick,' with its large grounds, paved walks and trees, all protected by massive brick walls." This is in the Briggs Point area near Newton's Creek. H. B. Bagnall's article "The Old Custom House," in the Norfolk *Ledger Dispatch* on 5 July 1911, mentions "the large building on the southeast corner of Main Street and Market Square, owned by Mr. Thomas Reilly."

[27]The manuscript census of 1830 for Norfolk County (Briggs Point area) names Isaac Fuller as head of a household of "free colored persons"—a male twenty-four to thirty-six years of age, two males less than ten, two females less than ten, one female twenty-four to thirty-six years of age, and one female a hundred or older (p. 404). Ten years later the census of 1840 for Brooke County (in far western Virginia) listed Isaac Fuller as head of a household of three free blacks, a male fifty-five to one hundred years old, a male ten to twenty-four years old, and a female less than ten years of age (p. 214).

[28]A crowd of 20,000 people poured in from Maryland, North Carolina, Richmond, and Petersburg to witness the launching of the powerful seventy-four-gun ship-of-the-line *Delaware*, which had been under construction for three years. Spectators crowded into the Navy Yard and spilled over to the opposite shore and onto the frigates *Guerriere* and *United States* and the storeship *Alert*. At 10:30 A.M. on Saturday, 21 October 1820, the great ship—a bat-

tleship of its day—glided into the Elizabeth River as the crowd roared a welcome. Over the years the *Delaware* served as flagship of the American fleet's Mediterranean and Brazil squadrons. She frequently came home to Norfolk—see n. 33—and there on 20 April 1861 she was scuttled and burned by Federal forces when they evacuated the Navy Yard before the rebel troops took it. An accurate, detailed model of the *Delaware* is on display at the Shipyard Museum in Portsmouth, Virginia.

[29]James S. A. Bigham served as a private in Company F, First Regiment of Virginia Foot (Infantry) and appeared on the muster roll in Mexico on 30 April 1848 (Stewart, *History of Norfolk County*, 66). This man seems to be the S. A. Bigham who appeared in the Personal Property Book for Portsmouth in 1840 and 1841, and it is certainly the Jas. S. A. Bigham listed in the Personal Property Book for Portsmouth in 1850 as a white male older than sixteen and paying no tax. The James Bigham listed in the 1850 census as a forty-eight-year-old constable in Portsmouth is probably the same person again, the fellow who earlier directed Teamoh's work at the shipyard and then went to war in Mexico (p. 182). The manuscript census for Richmond in 1820 listed Samuel Bigham as head of a household that included a white male at least forty-five years old, a white male sixteen to twenty-six years old, one slave, and one free black (p. 170). The younger white male might well have been Samuel Bigham, or more likely Samuel Bigham's son of the same name who later moved to Portsmouth, but this identification cannot be verified.

[30]Twelve Mannings are listed in the 1840 census for Norfolk County. Of the two residing in Portsmouth, Teamoh probably referred to Nathl. Manning (page 119), who headed a family consisting of males thirty to thirty-nine, twenty to twenty-nine, and five to nine years of age; one female thirty to thirty-nine, two females five to nine, and one female under five. Manning also owned a female slave thirty-six to fifty-five years old, a female slave ten to twenty-four years old, and three slave children. He is described as engaged in "manufactures and trades." The dry dock was located at the southern end of the hundred-acre Gosport Navy Yard, and the nearby engine house containing the pump was part of a larger structure that also housed the blacksmith shop and the foundry.

[31]The manuscript census for Norfolk County for 1840 listed Thomas Simington as head of a household in Portsmouth consisting of a male thirty to thirty-nine years old, a male under five, a female twenty to twenty-nine, a female five to nine, a female under five, and one female slave ten to twenty-three years old (p. 132). Simington is described as engaged in "manufactures and trades." The Personal Property Book for Portsmouth in 1840 listed Thos. Simington as a white male more than sixteen years of age who paid no tax. The Norfolk *American Beacon*, 29 August 1842, described a recent meeting of the mechanics of Portsmouth (p. 3). These white workers complained about undue interference by U.S. naval officers in the technical aspects of shipbuilding, and they condemned the substitution of "Negro laborers" for white mechanics at the shipyard.

[32]The name is written indistinctly and is not positively identifiable.

[33]The *Delaware* had been built at the Navy Yard—see n. 28—and on 17 June 1833 it returned to enter the brand-new dry dock. A week later the *Constitution* was the first vessel to enter the twin facility at the Boston Navy Yard. The Gosport dry dock at Portsmouth had been authorized by Congress in 1827, and construction began in November of that year under the direction of designer Francis Grice. The finishing touches were added in March 1834 after the *Delaware* had departed. Five hundred thousand cubic feet of granite went into the 314 by 100 foot structure, which was drained by eight powerful, steam-driven pumps. The first large

dry dock in the Western world, it cost slightly less than a million dollars, and it was seized intact by rebel forces in April 1861.

[34]Joseph Gorham is listed in the 1870 manuscript census for Elizabeth City County in the Old Point Comfort District as a sixty-two-year-old black day laborer (p. 44). He is also included in the column marked "Male Citizens of U.S. of 21 years of age and upwards"—a first for former slaves. His family included his wife Sally—sixty-five years old, black, and a housekeeper—and four children, Fanny, John, Sally, and Susan Blake. A good number of black Robinsons appear in this county in 1870, but no elderly John Robinson. A little later a black John Robinson represented the county in the state legislature. However, he was a graduate of Hampton Institute, a lawyer, and a large property holder and thus pretty clearly not the old freeman Teamoh had known for so long.

[35]William H. Hunter is listed in the 1850 census for Norfolk County as a thirty-five-year-old "collector" with a thirty-one-year-old wife and six children (p. 32). Forrest's *Norfolk Directory* for 1851 listed him as a "city collector" with an office at 38 Bank Street, and Elliott and Nye's *Virginia Directory* of 1852 listed him the same way. More likely Teamoh is referring to William F. Hunter, who operated a shipyard at the end of Nebraska Street in Norfolk. *Scientific American*, 21 December 1895 (63:25, p. 392), referred to him as a "ship joiner" who in 1821 built America's second ocean-going steam vessel, the 281-ton, 50-horsepower *New York*. The Norfolk *Beacon*, 28 October 1822, carried an advertisement for her Norfolk to New York run that included a sketch of the vessel. Or he may have meant W. H. Hunter, who was listed in the 1840 census for Norfolk County as head of a family of nine white males— one thirty to thirty-nine years old, one twenty to twenty-nine, six fifteen to nineteen, and one under five (p. 187). He also presided over three females—one forty to forty-nine, one twenty to twenty-nine, and one under five. His household also included one free black ten to twenty-four years old, one male slave under ten, twelve male slaves capable of shipyard work, and only three female slaves. Twenty-one members of this overall group were listed as employed in manufactures and trades.

[36]Peter Teabo—evidently the Peter Teabeault to whom Teamoh referred—is listed in the 1830 manuscript census for Norfolk County as head of a family of three white males—ages sixty to seventy, fifty to sixty, and forty to fifty—and one white female, forty to fifty years old (p. 311). Also included are five slaves—one male under ten, two males ten to twenty-four years old, one male fifty-five to 100, and one female thirty-six to fifty-five years old. In 1840 Peter Teabo is listed in the Norfolk County census as a white male sixty to seventy years old who owned two slaves, a male under ten and a female thirty-six to fifty-five years old (p. 144). The Personal Property Book for Portsmouth in 1831 listed Peter Teabo as claiming one white older than sixteen, no slaves, three free blacks, and two horses, with a total tax of 87¢. Two years later the three free blacks were replaced by three slaves older than sixteen and the two horses dwindled to one, making a total tax 81¢.

On 1 June 1854, the Norfolk *Beacon* described caulkers gathering at the Gosport Navy Yard and resolving "to cease work until the Department increased their pay to such amount as would justify them in returning to their vocations." They wanted three dollars a day, the same wage earned by workers at other naval yards.

[37]According to the *General Register of the United States Navy and Marine Corps (1782 to 1882)*, edited and published by Thomas H. S. Hamersly (Washington, D.C., 1882), p. 569, William P. Piercy was commissioned a midshipman on 15 March 1815, a lieutenant on 28 April 1826, and a commander on 29 March 1844. He died on 14 July 1847. Mrs. Henrietta Piercy, the widow of Commander William Piercy, was mentioned in the Norfolk *Southern*

Argus on 18 October 1852. Letters from Commander Piercy to the secretary of the navy indicate that he was ill the last few years of his life when he resided in Portsmouth.

A ship "lying in ordinary" is one that is out of commission.

[38]The *Constitution*, one of the navy's most famous ships, remains in commission today in Boston harbor, where she was originally launched in 1797 as one of six powerful new frigates. She served well in the undeclared naval war with France in 1798 and then was put in reserve at Charleston. She then served with distinction in the naval campaign against the Barbary pirates and returned in 1807 to Boston, where she underwent repairs. In 1809 she became the flagship of the North Atlantic Squadron. During the War of 1812 she captured or destroyed nine British merchant vessels and five warships. The *Constitution*'s dramatic, one-on-one victories over the British frigates *Guerriere* and *Java* fired the pride of the new nation. After the war she underwent extensive repairs and returned to service in 1821 as flagship of the Mediterranean Squadron until 1828. She was declared unseaworthy in 1830, but a public clamor led to extensive repairs at Boston from 1833 to 1835, when she was recommissioned again. She served as flagship of the Mediterranean Squadron for three years and then as flagship of the South Pacific Squadron for two more years until 1841. She remained in home waters in the Hampton Roads area for several years and then in April 1844 began a thirty-month voyage around the world.

The *Constitution* was at the Gosport Navy Yard early in March, so Teamoh probably worked aboard her before this long voyage. He is a little late in his estimates of the period in which he labored on the ship. The *Constitution* later returned to duty in the Mediterranean and then performed antislavery duty along the coast of West Africa. In 1855 she was decommissioned again, and she was almost seized at Annapolis by rebel forces when the Civil War began. She was rebuilt in 1871 and recommissioned in 1877 but never again served as a combat vessel, and she returned to decommissioned status in 1882. Recommissioned again in 1931, she visited the harbors of the nation she had served for almost a century and a half. In 1934 she returned to Boston where she remains today, America's oldest commissioned warship.

[39]The *General Registry* indicates that Samuel Forrest, a native of the District of Columbia, was made a purser (officer in charge of money on a ship) on 8 October 1836 and that he died on 15 March 1860 (p. 259). It also indicates that Bushrod W. Hunter became a midshipman on 1 November 1827, a lieutenant on 28 February 1838, went on reserve status on 13 September 1855, resigned from Federal service on 23 April 1861, and became a lieutenant in the Confederate Navy (p. 371). On 17 July 1842, he was the officer in charge of the *Constitution* and signed the log "B. W. Hunter, Lt."

[40]This may be Benj. (middle initial indistinct but not W) Palmer, listed in the manuscript census of Portsmouth in 1850 as a thirty-year-old "Clerk U.S.N.Y." with a wife and one young child (p. 129). The Norfolk *American Beacon* on 6 April 1843 listed B. W. Palmer as a member of the committee of thirteen appointed to commemorate the death of Melzar Gardner, editor of the *Portsmouth Chronicle*. The *Official Records of the Union and Confederate Navies in the War of the Rebellion* (Washington, D.C., 1900) series 1, vol. 10, pp. 657-58 indicated that on 26 May 1864, B. W. Palmer was commanding a Confederate battery on the James River.

[41]These events occurred early in 1843. Melzar Gardner, a native of New England, had been editing the *Portsmouth Chronicle* for less than a year as an organ for white working men who had long opposed competition by slave labor in places such as the Gosport Navy Yard in Portsmouth. Inevitably he clashed with more conservative interests; and on 30 March at Ferry Wharf in Norfolk, Gardner had a heated argument with Mordecai Cooke, Jr., a twenty-five-

year-old lawyer. They wrestled around; Cooke raised a stick but lost it before he could strike. Gardner pulled a small, double-barreled pistol from his pocket. Cooke seized him, and in a brief struggle the pistol fired, sending a bullet through Gardner's heart. A hearing was held, and Cooke posted $10,000 bail. In June he was tried in the Superior Court and acquitted by a jury. Meanwhile, Gardner's widow Martha and their children went back to Massachusetts. The local papers gave very little coverage to the embarrassing incident, reporting only the barest details. Mordecai Cooke, Jr. remained in the city of Norfolk and was listed in the manuscript census of 1850 as a lawyer with a wife and three young children, six slaves, and real estate worth $5,000. His father, Mordecai Cooke (Sr.) was a very distinguished lawyer and planter residing in Portsmouth at a large home on Dinwiddie Street near the corner of County Street. A power in the local Whig party, colonel of the Ninth Brigade of the local militia, the owner of more than fifty slaves, active in the highest levels of local society, the colonel's influence may at least partly explain the very limited publicity given his son's bloody encounter with Gardner. The Norfolk *American Beacon* on 31 March 1843 furnished a brief summary of the killing and on 6 April described a rally of Gardner's supporters in which resolutions were passed denouncing the killing and demanding "the administration of justice."

[42]The manuscript census for the City of Norfolk in 1850 listed John G. Colley as a fifty-year-old "Ship Builder" with real estate worth $21,000 (p. 107). He had a wife named Elizabeth (age forty-five) and four sons from seven to twenty-two years old. The slave census of 1850 listed him as the owner of twenty-nine slaves— nineteen adult males, three adult females, and seven children. This unbalanced labor force was ideal for a shipyard. Stewart's *History of Norfolk County* mentions that John G. Colley operated one of the seven Norfolk shipyards that constructed ten canal boats in thirty days for the Virginia and North Carolina Transportation Company (pp. 29, 383). Forrest's *Norfolk Directory* for 1851 listed J. G. Colley as a shipwright operating at 30 East Widewater Street (now Water Street and always the main waterfront thoroughfare in Norfolk) and residing at 17 Holt Street (p. 50). For Hunter, see n. 35.

[43]The manuscript census of 1850 listed no William Graves in Norfolk County. The Norfolk *American Beacon* mentioned on 1 November 1851 that W. A. Graves and Brother had built the hull of a new steam ferryboat and on 4 September 1852 they had taken over Hunter's old yard, which contained a marine railway. Forrest's *Norfolk Directory* for 1851 listed (p. 58) Graves and Bro. as shipwrights at 66 East Widewater Street, while *Vickery's Directory for the City of Norfolk* (1859) listed (p. 69) Wm. A. Graves as a shipbuilder operating a marine railway and sawmill at 66 East Widewater and residing at 28 South Duke Street. Stewart's *History of Norfolk County* mentions "W.H. Graves' marine railway," which built the *Lady Davis* with funds subscribed by patriotic Confederate women (p. 76). This small vessel was captured by Union forces before launching, renamed the *Endeavor*, and was used for coastal survey work. Steward's and Dey's *Norfolk City and Business Directory for 1866* (Baltimore, 1866) carried a large advertisement by "William A. Graves, Marine Architect, and Draughtsman, Ship Builder, Spar Maker, and Calker," who was still listed at 66 W[ide] Water Street with a "Marine Railway, Saw & Planing Mills."

[44]The manuscript census of 1840 for Norfolk City listed N. Nash as head of a family of four white males—one under five, two fifteen to nineteen, and one twenty to twenty-nine— and two white females—one under five and one twenty to twenty-nine years old (p. 189). Also included in the household are seven slaves—three males ten to twenty-three, two males twenty-four to twenty-five, one female ten to twenty-three, and one female thirty-six to fifty-four. Eight persons are listed as in "manufactures and trades." The census of 1850 showed much progress (p. 92). Nathaniel Nash is listed as a thirty-six-year-old, native Virginia "ships carpenter" with $9,000 worth of real estate and twenty-nine slaves, each adult and all but three of the males

capable of shipyard labor. Nash's wife, Mary F., was thirty years old, and they had six children: Alexina (eleven), John H. (nine), Nathaniel (seven), Mary F. (five), Emma H. (three), and Miles (one). Forrest's *Norfolk Directory* for 1851 listed "Nath'l Nash" as a shipbuilder with a sectional marine railway located at 48 East Widewater Street and a home at 113 East Main Street (p. 69). *Vickery's Directory for Norfolk* (1859) located Nash's shipyard and sawmills at 60 East Widewater Street (p. 96), as did Stewart's and Dey's *Norfolk Directory* for 1866 (p. 60). "Mr. Miles" probably refers to Issaac H. Miles, who was listed in the manuscript census of 1850 for Norfolk County with $2,000 in real estate. His wife, the forty-four-year-old Elizabeth Ann, and his seven children, ranging in age from two to twenty-two, were all native Virginians. Forrest's *Norfolk Directory* (1851) listed him as a shipwright at Herbertsville who resided at 21 West Freemason Street in Norfolk City.

[45]The manuscript census of 1840 for Portsmouth listed John W. Murdaugh as head of a family of three males—one under five, one ten to fourteen, and one thirty to forty—and five females—three five to nine, one ten to fourteen, and one forty to forty-nine (p. 128). Also included are twenty slaves—six males, including one child under ten, and fourteen females, including six children under ten. Murdaugh was captain of the Portsmouth Dragoons, and in this capacity he entertained distinguished visitors such as Andrew Jackson at his home on Crawford Street only a block from the river. A prominent lawyer, he served several terms in the state legislature in the 1830s, and as late as 12 January 1897, the *Norfolk Virginian* referred to his services to Norfolk County. Late in the 1830s he established a newspaper in Portsmouth, the *Clay Banner and Naval Intelligencer*. He died at the age of forty-three of what the Norfolk *American Beacon*'s 22 November 1842 obituary described as "hemorrage of the bowels." His funeral at Portsmouth's Episcopal Church drew a large crowd. Murdaugh's cousin, also named John Murdaugh, assumed direction of the *Clay Banner*, but soon he too died.

[46]The manuscript census of 1840 for Portsmouth listed Hollis Amidon, age thirty to thirty-nine, as head of a family and engaged in "manufactures and trades" (p. 117). Also included in the household were five males fifteen to nineteen years old, one female under five, and one female twenty to twenty-nine. He also owned two female slaves, one under ten (probably one of Teamoh's children) and the other twenty-four to thirty-five years of age (probably his wife Sallie).

[47]Vernon Eskridge was a Methodist minister who lived in Portsmouth with his wife and three children. He served as chaplain at the navy yard, and the Norfolk *American Beacon* carried periodic notices of his performing marriages in the surrounding community as well. The manuscript census of 1850 for Norfolk County listed him as a forty-seven-year-old "clerk" residing in Portsmouth, the owner of $1,500 worth of real estate and five slaves (p. 254). When the yellow fever epidemic hit in 1855, Eskridge stayed at his post. Another local minister, James Chisholm, wrote: "Mr. Eskridge and myself are the only resident ministers who can go abroad and visit the sick, the dying and the bereaved," but soon both contracted the disease and died. In September 1855 Chaplain Eskridge succumbed at the Naval Hospital in Portsmouth. The quotation appears on page 300 of Miss Mildred M. Holladay, "History of Portsmouth" (1936 typescript within larger work compiled by John C. Emmerson, Jr., which is entitled "Some Fugitive Items of Portsmouth and Norfolk County History" and dated 1948). It is located in the Sargeant Memorial Room, Norfolk Public Library.

[48]John Lindsay was listed in the 1840 manuscript census for Elizabeth City County as the head of a family of three white males—one under five, one five to nine, and one thirty to thirty-nine—and three white females, one five to nine, one twenty to twenty-nine, and one fifty to fifty-nine (p. 107). His household also included one female slave ten to twenty-three years of

age, with one person engaged in "manufacture and trades." The manuscript census of 1850 for Elizabeth City County is more precise (p. 55). John Lindsay was listed as a forty-six-year-old carpenter along with his thirty-five-year-old wife Mary and his ten-year-old son George and seventy-eight-year-old Margaret Keating. He is located in the Old Point Comfort District surrounding Fort Monroe, a rather thickly settled area of the county with a concentration of clerks, soldiers, masons, hotel keepers, carpenters, and other nonagricultural workers. It was also the only area with many inhabitants born outside Virginia. With the exception of the town of Hampton, the rest of the county was very rural.

[49]Not positively identifiable.

[50]The manuscript census of 1850 for Henrico County listed Solomon Davis as a thirty-one-year-old resident of Richmond and a native of London, England (p. 407). His wife Ann, age twenty-four, was a native of South Carolina, and they had two children, Esta (five) and Ansel (three). Davis is described as a "trader." The *Richmond Directory* of 1852 listed him and his brother Benjamin Davis (1807–1879) under another broad term, "auctioneer." The *Richmond Directory* of 1859 spelled it out more clearly as "Negro trader." Six of Richmond's fourteen slave traders listed in 1859 were located on Locust Alley, between Franklin and Main streets, in the heart of the city. Solomon Davis died on 26 April 1876 and was buried in the city's Jewish cemetery by his wife, Anna Abrams Davis. (N.B.: Davis's wife was referred to as "Ann" in the census data and "Anna" elsewhere.—ED.)

[51]The manuscript census of 1850 for Henrico County listed Henry Rosenfield as a thirty-seven-year-old Richmond merchant born in Germany (p. 337). His wife Sabina, age twenty-five, was also a native of Germany. Also in the household were Isaac Rosenfield, his thirty-two-year-old brother and partner in the dry goods business, along with Fanny Rosenfield (twenty-two) and Sigmund Hirsh, a twenty-three-year-old merchant; they too were natives of Germany. The *Richmond Directory* of 1852 listed "Rosenfield, H & Bro. dry goods, 173 Broad," and the *Richmond Directory* of 1856 placed the Henry Rosenfield residence on 4th Street between Grace and Franklin streets in a respectable neighborhood where Confederate Secretary of the Treasury Christopher G. Memminger lived during the Civil War. The Richmond *Daily Dispatch* regularly carried advertisements for "Great Bargains" in "my entire stock of Dry Goods" by "H. Rosenfeld, 175 Broad Street"; see, for example, page 1 of the 17 January 1853 issue. Rosenfeld was born on 4 July 1813 and became an American citizen on 11 July 1843, as did his wife Sabina a decade later. She was born in Dornheim, Bavaria, on 20 October 1823 and died in Richmond on 26 June 1864. Rosenfeld took an active role in the life of Richmond's sizable Jewish community, which was mainly of German background. He buried his wife in the same cemetery where the Davis brothers were later buried; and then, as the Yankee army closed in on Confederate Richmond late in 1864, he and his family ran the blockade and settled in New York City. One son, Sidney Rosenfeld, became a successful playwright at the turn of the century and another son, Monroe Rosenfeld, had some success as a songwriter.

[52]The *Richmond Directory* for 1856 listed on page 151 "Howell & Messler, boat builders, opposite Tredegar Iron Works." Charles Howell resided not far away on Cary Street and John Messler nearby on Byrd Street. The *Richmond Directory* for 1852 located John Messler's boat-building facility on the Basin, a manmade lake in the middle of town that covered almost four blocks between Canal and Cary streets and from Eighth past Eleventh streets to the huge Gallego Flour Mill. It was part of the James River and Kawawha Canal system, which began about a mile downstream in eastern Richmond near Rockets and ran westward through town and all the way out into the Shenandoah Valley beside the James River. In Richmond barges and small ships could wait at the Basin for cargoes or repair work. Much of the inoperative canal system

remains along the riverbank in Richmond, but the Basin was long ago filled with earth and reclaimed as valuable urban real estate. For a clear map of the antebellum arrangement, see Emory M. Thomas, *The Confederate State of Richmond: A Biography of the Capital* (Austin: University of Texas Press, 1971), between pp. 22 and 23.

[53]Not positively identifiable, but he may be the "colored" blacksmith Henry Banks listed in *Boyd's Directory of Richmond City* for 1869 (p. 43) and residing in the rear of 2205 East Franklin Street. Another "colored" Henry Banks, a "farm hand," is also listed in this directory.

[54]The manuscript census of 1850 for Henrico County listed Henry R. Smith as a resident of Richmond, a native of New Jersey, and a thirty-eight-year-old shoemaker (p. 244). His wife Rebecca was thirty-three, and they had six children: Mary Susan (ten), born in Virginia; Margaret Ann (nine) and Emma Jane (seven), both born in New Jersey; John Henry (five) and David (four), both born in New York; and Parnell (two), born in Virginia. The *Richmond Directory* of 1856 listed "Smith, Henry, vendor in 2nd Vegetable Market, stall No. 9; res[idence] near Fairfield race course" (p. 216). This may be the same individual, but there is no way to be certain.

[55]On 11 May 1852 the Norfolk *American Beacon* described the launching of the *Currituck* the previous day. Built by the Page and Allen Shipyard in Portsmouth in less than six months, it was a sleek sailing vessel 140 feet long, 31 feet wide, and displacing 620 tons. It was constructed to carry cargo speedily and was launched smoothly before a large, enthusiastic crowd. The local owners were Captain James Cornick, John D. Gordon, S. W. Paul, Captain Seth Foster (her skipper) and "Messrs Hardy & Bros," and it was named for the latters' home county just across the border in coastal North Carolina. William S. Forrest's *Norfolk Directory for 1851–1852* listed "Hardy & Bro. shipping and com[mission] merchants, 96 & 98 W[ide] Water, shook [barrel or box] factory, Town Point, near end Main" (p. 59). The Hardy wharf facilities were among the best in the area. On 22 May 1854 the Norfolk *Argus* cited the *Currituck* for aiding a ship in distress, the *Black Hawk*.

[56]Much earlier, around the turn of the century, one Seth Foster had been mayor of Norfolk. However, the manuscript census of 1850 listed only one Seth Foster, an Ohio-born farmer living in Boone County in the far western part of the state. But Teamoh was correct: Captain Seth Foster lived in Mathews County, which jutted out into the Chesapeake Bay only forty miles north of Norfolk. Though he was missed by the census—perhaps because of a voyage— he appeared in the Account Book of Baldwin Foster, Merchant, 1849–1850, 1868, Mathews County, Virginia (microfilm, Virginia State Library, Richmond). Page seventy-nine lists "Cpt. Seth Foster" followed by six entries, several dealing with "power of attorney," a necessary device for a man of property who sailed the seas.

[57]City Point was located far upstream from Norfolk—sixty-five miles as the crow flies— where the Appomattox River flows into the James River (modern Hopewell). The Norfolk *American Beacon* on 15 June 1853 announced that the *Currituck* was loading at City Point and had comfortable staterooms for ten to twelve passengers as well as space for light freight on a voyage to Bremen, Germany. This announcement ran continuously until 9 July, when the vessel apparently departed.

[58]Virginia's manumission laws changed over time. Before the Revolution manumission could be accomplished only by an act of the legislature. In 1782 masters were allowed to free slaves by will or deed, but in 1805 freed slaves were required to leave the state within a year, though some exceptions were made. Beginning in the 1830s many efforts were made to increase the

restrictions and to discourage emancipation, but the legislature enacted no significant new laws. Always a major consideration was the loss of a very valuable piece of property, especially with owners such as the Thomases, who were far from wealthy.

⁵⁹The American Colonization Society was fairly active in the upper South and did send some free blacks and manumitted slaves to Liberia on the west coast of Africa, but in all less than 15,000 American blacks returned to their ancestral continent. In 1850 Senator Daniel Webster of Massachusetts voted for a tough new federal law requiring the return of runaway slaves hiding anywhere in the nation. This move was part of a complex sectional deal—the Compromise of 1850—that held the Union together, but it drew the bitter condemnation of the growing abolition movement, which was especially vigorous in the New England area. To white moderates in the 1850s, Webster's vote was a brave, statesmanlike action; to slaves such as Teamoh and their abolitionist allies, it was a gross betrayal.

⁶⁰Not positively identifiable. Diggs was a fairly common name in antebellum Mathews County, but there is no way to isolate the second mate of the *Currituck*. Forrest's *Norfolk Directory for 1851–1852* listed a Wm. Diggs as a "ship carpenter" living on Virginia Street, but he is only another possibility.

⁶¹Not positively identifiable.

⁶²The *New-York Tribune*, Saturday, 12 November 1853, under "Marine Journal: Arrived" stated: "Ship Curribuck [*sic*], (of Norfolk,) Foster, Bremen 48 days, with mdse. and 216 pass. . . . Sept. 29, in the North Sea, experienced a heavy gale from W. Oct. 18 lat. 47, lon. 40, encountered a severe gale from N.W., which continued for 6 days. . . . 2 deaths on the passage."

⁶³In lower Manhattan near Greenwich Village, Thompson Street ran for eight blocks from Canal Street uptown to Fourth Street at Washington Square, right through an area where some blacks had settled.

⁶⁴Erastus Dean Culver was born in Champlain, Washington County, New York, on 15 March 1803. He graduated from the University of Vermont in 1826 and after further study began to practice law in 1831. He moved to Greenwich, New York, and served in the state legislature from 1838 to 1840. He served as a Whig in Congress from 1845 to 1847. By 1851 he had become a prominent New York City lawyer while residing in nearby Williamsburg. The *New York Directory for 1853–1854* listed him and George W. Parker as practicing law at 289 Broadway (p. 166). From 1854 to 1860 he served as the second judge of the city court of Brooklyn, and during the Civil War he was President Lincoln's minister to Peru. After the war he practiced law again and in 1887 became president of the Greenwich Bank in his home county of Washington. He died there two years later on 13 October, and the *New York Times* carried his obituary in the 16 October edition on page 5. The "Court of Kings Bench" that Teamoh mentioned did not exist in 1853. He may have meant a local court in Brooklyn that was located in Kings County or perhaps New York City's maritime court, which was established in 1853. The "Legal Notices" sections of the *Times* and the *Tribune* do not mention the Culver-Teamoh case in November 1853. Actually, what probably happened (as the narrative suggests) is that the lawyer Culver negotiated directly with Captain Foster who, not wanting to have his ship delayed by litigation, simply "settled out of court," paid up, and departed.

⁶⁵See n. 10.

⁶⁶See nn. 37 and 38. Almost certainly Teamoh worked on the *Constitution* in Norfolk har-

bor and Hampton Roads before it departed on its voyage around the world in April 1844. When it returned, it docked at Boston on 28 September 1846. Lt. "Pat Murphy" is possibly John M. Murphy, who became a midshipman on 18 February 1841, resigned in 1852, and became an acting lieutenant in 1862. During 1843 the log of the *Constitution* was often kept by an officer whose signature appears to be "J.h. Murphy," and this is probably Teamoh's "Pat Murphy."

[67]As stated in the Introduction, New Bedford, Massachusetts, was a refuge for fugitive slaves, and in 1850, 7 percent of its population of 16,443 was black. On 19 January 1854, on page 4 of the New Bedford *Daily Evening Standard*, under the caption "Southern Chivalry!," a long article was reprinted from the *Tri Weekly Globe* of Portsmouth, Virginia. The Virginia editor bitterly criticized New Bedford for harboring and actively protecting several Portsmouth slaves who had escaped to New Bedford by stowing away on a Yankee merchant vessel. He concluded: "There are some 1800 negroes in New Bedford, the greater portion of them runaway slaves, whom the white population of about 19,000 villains protect and encourage."

[68]Examination of extant copies of the New Bedford *Daily Evening Standard* from 1 August 1853 through 31 May 1854 failed to reveal Teamoh's article, but he may have meant the New Bedford *Republican Standard*, a weekly no longer available in a complete run.

[69]As stated in the Introduction, Burns was a runaway from Virginia who was extradited back to slavery in the spring of 1854, but only after local and federal troops overcame the resistance of a crowd of thousands of Bostonians determined to resist the hated Fugitive Slave Act of 1850.

[70]The *New Bedford Directory* of 1852 listed "Concert Hall, 19 1-2 Purchase street" (p. 43).

[71]Lindley Murray was born in Pennsylvania in 1745. He practiced law and became a wealthy merchant in New York City. He retired in 1783 and moved to England, where he lived quietly until his death in 1826. There he wrote a series of books on reading and grammar that eventually went into more than two hundred editions and sold almost two million copies. His *English Grammar* (1795) was revised and elaborated upon in *An English Grammar* in 1818, and this work became his most influential and famous one. Until around 1850 his books were the best known in the field, but then other authorities such as Peter Bullions emerged. Born in 1794 in Scotland where he was raised and educated, Bullions came to America in 1817 and the following year was ordained a Presbyterian minister in New York state. He held clerical and academic positions in various parts of the state over the years. He published a series of textbooks including *Principles of English Grammar* (1834), *Analytical and Practical English Grammar* (1851), similar works on Latin and Greek grammar, and a *Latin and English Dictionary* in 1862, only two years before his death.

[72]Neither Pritlow of New Bedford nor Tatum, an earlier black resident of Portsmouth, Virginia, is identifiable. One free mulatto family of Pritlows lived in Hampton, Virginia, in 1850. The manuscript census for Elizabeth City County listed Wilton, a twenty-seven-year-old male, Mary, a thirty-seven-year-old female, Henrietta (four), and Joshua (two), and they were all natives of Maryland (p. 50). James Pritlow might well have been related to this family, which lived just across Hampton Roads from Portsmouth, the city from which he escaped. Other free blacks named Pretlow in nearby Isle of Wight and Sussex counties were substantial landholders.

[73]The *New Bedford Dictionary* of 1852 listed "Waterman[,] Nehamiah, auction, mart 52

and 54 Union, corner South Water, h[ome] 110 Middle" (p. 171).

[74]The manuscript census of 1850 for Bristol County, Massachusetts, listed William Bush as a 50-year-old laborer living in New Bedford (p. 233). He was a native of Virginia. His wife Lucy (forty-eight) was from Maryland, and their eight children—Susan (twenty-five), James (twenty-four), Mary (twenty-three), Louisa (twenty-one), Martha (nineteen), Josephine (seventeen), Anna (fourteen), and Andrew (twelve) were all born in the District of Columbia. The *New Bedford Directory* of 1856 listed Wm. Bush as the proprietor of a boarding house at 6 Coffin Street (p. 67).

[75]The *New Bedford Directory* of 1852 on page 159 listed Daniel Stowell as a "caulker" with his home west of Dartmouth Street. Benjamin is the only other male Stowell listed. The manuscript census of 1850 for Bristol County, Massachusetts, on page 453 identified Daniel Stowell as a 71-year-old "calker" in the Dartmouth district with real estate worth $1,600. This census on page 366 also listed Columbus Stowell as a 34-year-old "calker" living in New Bedford. These may well be the "caulking contractors" Teamoh referred to as "the Stowell Brothers," for no other Stowells are listed in this occupation.

[76]The *New Bedford Directory* of 1852 noted six Cannons as "caulkers"—Frederick, George, Elisha, Philip, Plummer, and William C.—and the latter four have business addresses listed. One of these is probably the "Mr. Cannon" with whom Teamoh dealt. There is, of course, no way to identify "a colored man . . . by the name of _____ Brown."

[77]Thomas Wilson Dorr was born in Providence on 5 November 1805, the son of Sullivan and Lydia Allen Dorr. Well-to-do, he attended Phillips Exeter Academy and graduated from Harvard in 1823. After studying law in New York, he began his practice in Providence in 1827. He never married, but he had a long political career. He began this career as a Whig in the state legislature in 1834, but he soon became a Democrat. The government of Rhode Island was very conservative: many adult males could not vote; the legislature was seriously malapportioned; and no formal constitution had ever replaced the antiquated colonial charter. Dorr became the leader of the "People's Party," which sought sweeping reform. In 1842 the Dorrites, unwilling to accept half a loaf, established their own government to challenge the regular state government. Overreacting, the regular state governor declared martial law and directed wholesale arrests. Some minor clashes occurred, and the Dorrites retreated in disarray. In October 1843 Dorr gave himself up at Providence, where in April 1844 he was convicted of treason and sentenced to solitary confinement at hard labor for life. He went to prison in June, but aroused public opinion forced a general amnesty, and he was released a year later. In 1851 Dorr's civil rights were restored, but his health had failed, and he lived quietly in retirement in Providence until his death on 27 December 1854. His own ambitions had been frustrated, but many of the reforms he honestly championed made their way into the fabric of Rhode Island's government.

[78]Teamoh had two younger half-brothers in Boston in 1855: Thomas Teamoh, a twenty-four-year-old waiter from Norfolk, Virginia, whose slave parents were David (Teamoh's father) and Rebecca, and John William Teamoh, a twenty-eight-year-old waiter from Petersburg, Virginia, with the same parents, David and Rebecca. This information is contained in the marriage registration books, volume 128, Eighteenth Registration, 1859, page 68 and volume 137, Nineteenth Registration, 1860, page 135, Suffolk-Worcester Counties, Registry of Vital Records and Statistics, Department of Public Health, Commonwealth of Massachusetts, Boston. On 13 July 1859, Thomas Teamoh (twenty-eight) and Margaret E. Patterson (twenty)—both "col'd" and from Norfolk—married. Her parents were the slaves Robert and

Margaret. On 26 October 1860, John William Teamoh (thirty-three) and Florence P. Gault (thirty-two)--both "col'd" and she the daughter of Samuel and Jan Gault of Norfolk—married. Both ceremonies were performed by Leonard A. Grimes, a free black from Virginia who became the most aggressive and activist black minister in Boston while leading the Twelfth Baptist Church.

[79]The manuscript census of 1850 for the Seventh Ward of Boston listed Mace Tisdale as a sixty-six-year-old white merchant, a native of Massachusetts, with real estate valued at $155,000 (p. 1). The *Boston Directory* of 1856 described Tisdale as "merch. 5 Chatham row, house 51 Chauncy" (p. 333) and listed him as a director of the New England Bank (p. 421). The *Post*, Beals, Greene & Co., was a daily Democratic paper costing eight dollars annually; the *Courier*, E. B. Foster & Co., was a daily Whig journal costing eight dollars annually. It also ran semi-weekly and weekly editions.

[80]As stated in the Introduction, Coffin Pitts was a tailor who was active but not highly visible in the black movement in Boston. He often gave new blacks jobs in his business. The manuscript census of 1850 for the Fourth Ward of Boston listed Coffin Pitts as a fifty-five-year-old black "Trader" (p. 132). The *Boston Directory* of 1856 says simply of Pitts, "c'othing, 29 Brattle, house 67 Joy." The modern Government Center has obliterated old Brattle Street, which began at Court Street and ran eastward for several blocks toward Quincy Market. The modern Black Heritage Trail runs for six blocks along Joy Street, which in the antebellum period was part of an area north of the Boston Common informally called "Nigger Hill." A good number of blacks like Pitts had concentrated along a few streets in this general area, which also contained well-to-do white neighborhoods designated part of "Beacon Hill," hardly a slum then or now.

[81]As stated in the Introduction, William Cooper Nell was a leading Boston black. An intellectual as well as an activist, he generally championed black rights. Especially interested in formal education for blacks of all ages, his greatest triumph came when Boston integrated its school system in 1855, the year Teamoh arrived in the city. In that same period Nell published a pamphlet, *Service of Colored Americans in the Wars of 1776 and 1812* (1851), and a book entitled *The Colored Patriots of the American Revolution* (1855). The book told of black military heroes, but it also described the general black struggle for equality. Nell was active in the underground railroad, and he also supported many organizations encouraging speeches, debates, and other intellectual activities for blacks in Boston. He was one of the cofounders of the Adelphic Union Library Association in 1838, and this is probably the "Lyceum" Teamoh mentions.

[82]Probably the most famous white abolitionist was William Lloyd Garrison of Boston (1805–1879). Certainly the most famous black abolitionist was Frederick Douglass (see n. 1). These two talented leaders split in the 1840s. Nell usually (but not always) backed the radical, uncompromising Garrison, and Douglass did not. In the fall of 1853 Nell and Douglass clashed openly in a debate before a black audience in Boston.

[83]Wendell Phillips (1811–1884) was a leading American reformer. One of the elite, he graduated from Harvard in 1831, and after three years at the Harvard Law School he began his practice in Boston. Early he joined the abolition movement. He spoke frequently and eloquently for the cause of American blacks, usually following Garrison's leadership. On several occasions his speeches were so passionate and denunciatory that he was almost mobbed, but his aristocratic look, graceful manner, and persuasive voice made him a popular orator. Pierre Dominique Toussaint L'Ouverture was the privileged slave of an indulgent master on the French island of Santo Domingo. Suddenly in 1791 a bloody slave insurrection erupted, and by 1794

he emerged as a brilliant general and the real leader of a new black nation—Haiti—the second republic to be born of revolution in the Americas. Early French efforts to regain control failed after heavy fighting, and these setbacks had much to do with Napoleon's giving up his dreams of an empire in the New World and selling the huge Louisiana Territory to the United States. However, through trickery the French captured L'Ouverture. He was taken to France where he died in prison; but, like Nat Turner, he became a martyred hero to American blacks.

[84]During the late 1840s the black community in Boston established the Histrionic Club for men and women interested in dramatics. Many of its performances were written by William C. Nell, who was in the process of writing two works on blacks during the early years of the Republic. One black hero was Deacon Cyrus Foster, a scrappy, colorful old-timer who lived on a federal pension for his military service during the Revolutionary War. He talked frequently of his and other blacks' heroic deeds. A clothier and a deacon in the African Baptist Church, Foster was respected as something of an oral historian, and some of his reminiscences found their way into Nell's publications.

[85]On 6 May 1863, the marriage registration book, volume 164, Twenty-second Registration, 1863, Suffolk-Worcester Counties, Registry of Vital Records and Statistics, Dept. of Public Health, Commonwealth of Massachusetts, Boston, recorded the marriage of George Teamoh, "col'd. Boston clothes dealer," age forty-six, a native of Norfolk, Virginia, parents David and Lavinia (second marriage) to Elizabeth Smith, age thirty-six, a native of Baltimore, Maryland (third mariage) (p. 41). Like his brothers, Teamoh was married by the Reverend Leonard A. Grimes.

[86]The manuscript census of 1850 for Norfolk County listed Spencer W. Grant as a resident of Portsmouth (p. 163). A native of the District of Columbia and forty-five years old, he was described as a "Ship carpenter." His wife, Mary A., was listed as forty-four years old and also a native of the District of Columbia. Their five children were Robert (fifteen and a "Student"), Edward (fourteen), Georgiana (nine), Richard (seven), and Alice (four). Their household included three boarders—a "Ship carpenter" and his wife, and a "Cooper." The Grants owned no slaves in 1840 or 1850. Mr. Grant died late in 1865, and his will was probated on 10 December. In Will Book 1, July 1858–November 1883, Clerk's Office, Hustings Court, Circuit Court Building, Portsmouth, he simply directed that his debts be paid and all his property be left to his "beloved wife Mary A. Grant" (p. 73). The following year, 1866, in the Land Book, 1864–1869, Clerk's Office, Hustings Court, that property, designated lot 299, was valued at $2,500—$1,300 for the land and $1,200 for the house (p. 19). By 1875 Mrs. Grant had died too, and (in the Land Book, page 25, 1870–1879, Clerk's Office, Hustings Court) the "Mary Ann Grant Est[ate]" was described as: lot 299 at the corner of Clifford and Effingham, total value $1,800 and lot 259 at the corner of Clifford and Green, total value $450.

[87]See n. 54.

[88]See n. 48.

[89]The City of Richmond Business Directory and City Guide, compiled by Mills and Starke in 1866, in the "Colored Directory" section lists "Bowe, Charles, 100 n. 3rd" (p. 97). In 1869 Boyd's Directory of Richmond City listed "Bowe Chas. (c) [for colored] livery stable, 100 n 3d" (p. 52). Two other black Bowes were listed: Moses, a barber, and Reuben.

[90]During the spring and summer of 1866, President Andrew Johnson split with Republicans in Congress over how best to return the former Confederate states to the Union. The president supported a policy of rapid restoration in which the freedmen played no role. Re-

publican Congressmen, in contrast, became increasingly concerned that Johnson's program was too lenient on former rebels and that a more stringent policy—one designed to preserve the fruits of the Union victory gained at Appomattox by giving the vote to the former slaves—was needed. Following their overwhelming victory in the congressional elections of 1866, the Republicans in Congress passed several Reconstruction Acts. The first of these, passed on 2 March 1867, abolished the civilian governments established by Presidents Johnson and Lincoln in ten of the former Confederate states and divided the region into five districts, each under the command of a military official. According to the provisions of the first supplemental Reconstruction Act of 23 March 1867, authorities in each of these districts—including the first military district of Virginia—were to enroll new electorates, which were to select delegates to conventions to frame the new state constitutions required by Congress for the readmission of the yet-unreconstructed former Confederate states to the Union. This new electorate was to include the freedmen; it was not to include certain groups of disloyal southern whites. For the text of the first two Reconstruction Acts, see U.S., *Statutes at Large*, 14:428-29; 15:2-4. For a summary of the struggle between Johnson and Congress, see Eric N. McKitrick, *Andrew Johnson and Reconstruction* (Chicago: University of Chicago Press, 1960) 274-375.

[91]Francis H. Pierpont (who spelled his surname Pierpoint until he changed it legally to an older family spelling in 1881) was born near Morgantown, Virginia, in 1814. A businessman and lawyer, Pierpont was a Whig, a Unionist, and a supporter of Abraham Lincoln in the 1860 presidential election. Following the secession of Virginia on 17 April 1861, he was a key organizer of the convention that met on 11 June at Wheeling. That body—composed of delegates from some twenty-six counties in western Virginia—elected Pierpont "provisional governor," and he then organized its Unionist members into a legislature, creating thereby the state of West Virginia. Following West Virginia's admission to the Union on 20 June 1863, Pierpont, as noted in the Introduction, moved to Alexandria, where he became governor of the "restored" state of Virginia—that is, the counties of that commonwealth which had come under Union control. Following the collapse of the Confederacy at Appomattox on 9 April 1865, he moved to Richmond and became governor of Virginia. He acted in that capacity until replaced by a military commander under the provisions of the Reconstruction Act of 2 March 1867. For details on Pierpont, see Charles H. Ambler, *Francis H. Pierpont: Union War Governor of Virginia and Father of West Virginia* (Chapel Hill: University of North Carolina Press, 1937).

The military commander to whom Teamoh referred was actually John M. Schofield. He assumed command of the First Military District on 13 March 1867. A native of New York, Schofield was a graduate of the military academy at West Point who had risen from the rank of lieutenant to that of major general during the war, in which he had served in Missouri, in William T. Sherman's Atlanta campaign, and with George H. Tommas in Tennessee. A "moderate" Republican in politics, he got along rather well—too well in the opinion of some Republicans—with a number of Virginia's leading whites. After leaving Virginia shortly before the ending of military Reconstruction there, Schofield served as secretary of war, as the superintendent of the United States Military Academy at West Point, and as commanding general of the United States Army. For details on Schofield, see John M. Schofield, *Forty-Six Years in the Army* (New York: Century Company, 1897); James M. McDonough, *Schofield: Union General in the Civil War and Reconstruction* (Tallahassee: Florida State University Press, 1972).

[92]Some 300 Republicans met at the African Church on Broad Street in Richmond on 17 April 1867 to organize their party for the election of delegates to the constitutional convention authorized by the Reconstruction Acts. About fifty counties and cities were represented. Most

delegates were from districts that contained large numbers of freedmen among their electorates, and some three-quarters of the delegates were blacks. James Hawxhurst, a Unionist from New York state who had settled in Fairfax County in 1846, presided over the two-day meeting. The platform that was adopted seemed too radical to some whites, who coalesced around John Minor Botts—a former Whig and longtime Unionist—and called for a second convention to meet in Charlottesville on 4 July. This intraparty strife, characteristic of Virginia's Republican party throughout the Reconstruction era, was healed, at least temporarily, only after powerful outsiders (including Senator Henry Wilson of Massachusetts) got leaders of the party's contending elements to meet on 16 June at the home of Francis Pierpont. There, a new convention was authorized; it assembled in Richmond on 1 August and reaffirmed the April platform. For detail on these activities, see Hamilton James Eckenrode, *The Political History of Virginia during Reconstruction* (Baltimore: Johns Hopkins University Press, 1904) 8, 47, 68-69, 72-74, 77-79; James Douglas Smith, "Virginia during Reconstruction, 1865–1870—A Political, Economic and Social Study" (Ph.D. diss., University of Virginia, 1960) 43-48; Richard G. Lowe, "Republicans, Rebellion, and Reconstruction: The Republican Party in Virginia, 1856–1870" (Ph.D. diss., University of Virginia, 1968) 250-77. In Teamoh's district, the *Norfolk Virginian*, 18 April 1867, p. 2, commented briefly on the bitter factional divisions at the initial Republican meeting in Richmond.

[93]Teamoh was nominated as a convention delegate at a Norfolk County Republican convention that assembled at Getty's Station in the First District of Norfolk County on 11 October 1867. See the *Norfolk Virginian*, 12 October 1867, p. 1. At that meeting two white Republican candidates—James H. Clements and Luther Lee, Jr.—were also nominated (and later elected) as Republican delegates from the District of the City of Portsmouth and the County of Norfolk. The manuscript census of 1870 for Jackson Ward of Portsmouth listed Clements as the postmaster of Portsmouth and a former machinist (p. 10). He was married with two sons; he was thirty-nine years of age; he was a native of the District of Columbia; and he held property valued at $2,000. The 1870 manuscript census for Pleasant Grove Township of Norfolk County listed Lee as a thirty-seven-year-old collector of the United States Customs with no property (p. 29). It indicated that Lee, like his wife and two sons, was a native of Virginia. However, General Schofield, who was apparently correct, identified him instead as a native of New York who had served in the 20th New York Cavalry during the war. See Richard G. Lowe, "Virginia's Reconstruction Convention: General Schofield Rates the Delegates," *Virginia Magazine of History and Biography*, 80 (July 1972): 347.

[94]Members of the Constitutional Convention of 1867–1868 assembled at the Hall of the House of Delegates in Richmond on 3 December 1867. They finished their work and adjourned on 17 April 1868. A total of 104 of the 105 delegates elected to the convention took part in its deliberations. The calling of the convention was endorsed by 107,342 of the 169,229 voters who had cast ballots in the election, which commenced on 22 October 1867, on whether to hold a convention. A total of 225,933 voters (120,101 whites and 105,832 blacks) were eligible to participate in this election, in which delegates to the proposed convention were also selected. See *Documents of the Constitutional Convention of the State of Virginia* (Richmond: Office of the New Nation, 1867 [sic]) 51-52.

In Teamoh's district (the city of Portsmouth and the county of Norfolk) the convention carried by 3,221 (309 whites and 2,912 blacks) to 1,091 (1,090 whites and 1 black). "Abstracts (Referendum and Election of Delegates) to the Constitutional Convention," MSS Election Record No. 427, Manuscript Division, Virginia State Library, Richmond. Almost exactly a quarter of the convention participants—some twenty-four delegates—were black, the majority of whom represented tidewater constituencies. For detail on the delegates see Lowe,

"Virginia's Reconstruction Convention," 341-60. A useful listing of delegates—along with the constituencies they represented, can be found in Cynthia Miller Leonard, comp., *The General Assembly of Virginia July 30, 1619–January 11, 1978: A Bicentennial Register of Members* (Richmond: Virginia State Library, 1978) 504-507.

[95]Jonathan Catlett Gibson was one of the two delegates from the district of Fauquier and Rappahannock counties. A native of Culpeper County, he graduated from the University of Virginia in 1851. During the war, Gibson served as an officer in the 49th Virginia Infantry. After the adjournment of the convention, he resumed the practice of law in his native county. See Lowe, "Virginia's Reconstruction Convention," 356; 1870 manuscript census returns, Culpeper County, Virginia, First District, Catalpa Township, p. 32.

[96]Thomas Bayne, one of two delegates from the district of Norfolk City, was constantly the target of conservative ridicule. A vocal radical, Bayne was a former North Carolina slave who had escaped in 1855. Like Teamoh, Bayne, a practicing dentist, had lived in New Bedford, Massachusetts, after leaving the South. He was apparently singled out for criticism by conservatives because of his radical oratory and his flamboyant style of dress. The 1860 manuscript census returns for Bristol County, Massachusetts, Fourth Ward, City of New Bedford, listed Bayne as a thirty-six-year-old dentist with property worth $1,400 (p. 243). It also indicated that he was a Maryland native. The 1870 manuscript census returns for Norfolk County, Virginia, Third Ward of the City of Norfolk, listed Bayne as a dentist, a North Carolina native, and a person with property valued at $346 (p. 27). For details on Bayne, see Lowe, "Virginia's Reconstruction Convention," 349n; idem, "Republican Party in Virginia," 252-53.

[97]Eustace Gibson, Jonathan's brother, represented the district of Giles and Pulaski counties. Born in 1842, Gibson, a lawyer, reached the rank of captain in the Confederate Army before retiring from the service in 1863 to recover from wounds. He later settled in Huntington, West Virginia. Still active in politics, he became speaker of the West Virginia House of Representatives and a United States Congressman. See 1870 manuscript census returns for Culpeper County, Virginia, Catalpa Township, First District, p. 33; *Biographical Directory of the American Congress, 1774–1971* (Washington: U.S. Government Printing Office, 1971) 998. Even in death, the Gibson brothers were remembered fondly by Democrats as vocal critics of radicals in the convention. See the obituary of Eustace Gibson in the *Richmond Dispatch*, 11 December 1900, p. 4.

[98]For a discussion of the background and voting patterns of the black convention members, see Richard L. Hume, "The Membership of the Virginia Constitutional Convention of 1867–1868: A Study of the Beginnings of Congressional Reconstruction in the Upper South," *Virginia Magazine of History and Biography* (October 1978): 477-78. See pages 481-484 for a list of the twenty-four black delegates.

[99]The "test oath" and "disfranchisements" that Teamoh mentioned (Article 3, Section 7, and Article 3, Section 1, Clause 4 of the new constitution respectively) were the most hotly debated issues in the convention. Orrin E. Hine, an outside white radical who represented the district of Fairfax County, led the effort to disfranchise significant numbers of Confederate sympathizers and to require all future officeholders to take an oath, swearing that they had never voluntarily supported the rebellion. Republicans tended to support Hine on both of these issues during the convention, although some did vote against several of his most radical efforts to limit the rights of southern whites. Conservative leaders, such as the Gibson brothers, of course, opposed any efforts to enfranchise the freedman, to limit the voting rights of some groups of southern whites, and to restrict the right of former Confederates to hold office.

Hine's determined effort to punish former rebels perhaps resulted from his being driven out of Bowling Green, Kentucky, by a secessionist mob after returning one of the three ballots cast in that community for Abraham Lincoln in the presidential election of 1860. Whatever the source of his actions, however, he was successful in getting most of his oath and disfranchisement proposals through the convention, only to have General Schofield judge some of them to be too revolutionary. The general therefore required separate votes on the two articles noted above. The election took place on 6 July 1869. At that time, the constitution was ratified by a vote of 210,585 to 9,136. The two clauses of the document voted on separately, however, were defeated—the disfranchisement clause in a vote of 124,360 to 84,410 and the test oath by a margin of 124,715 to 83,458. See Schofield, *Years in the Army*, 402-403; Eckenrode, *Political History*, 125; Hume, "Membership of the Virginia Convention," 466.

Like voters throughout the state, voters in Teamoh's district endorsed the constitution—in this instance by a vote of 5,547 to 182 (with 2,493 whites and 3,236 blacks casting ballots). But unlike the statewide electorate, voters in the city of Portsmouth and the county of Norfolk also endorsed both disfranchisement of former Confederates and the test oath—disfranchisement (Article 3, Section 1, Clause 4) by a vote of 3,447 to 2,097; the test oath (Article 3, Section 7) by a vote of 3,451 to 2,098. See "Returns on July 6, 1869 Election Portsmouth City and County of Norfolk" in MS Election Record No. 428, Manuscript Division, Virginia State Archives.

[100]The *Southern Opinion* was a weekly paper owned and edited by Henry Rives Pollard. His brother, Edward A. Pollard, was editor of the *Daily Richmond Examiner* and the most popular wartime historian of the Confederacy. See Thomas J. Pressly, *Americans Interpret Their Civil War* (Princeton: Princeton University Press, 1954) 64-66. For examples of the unflattering cartoons depicting Republican delegates to which Teamoh referred, see the issues of 11 January 1868, p. 1 (Thomas Bayne) and 21 March 1868, p. 1 (Orrin E. Hine). The paper's 14 March 1868 issue carried a lengthy poem on its front page that insulted black delegates Thomas Bayne (see n. 96), Lewis Lindsay (of the District of the City of Richmond), and James W. D. Bland (of the District of Prince Edward and Appomattox counties) in particular and made the following disparaging remarks about the convention's entire contingent of black delegates:

> . . . if you'd look upon the floor,
> You'd see some twenty blacks or more,
> Who mostly sit with hands on lap,
> All dreaming o'er the treasury pap;
> And are receiving as their pay
> The sum, eight dollars every day.

Pollard's firey writing style enraged others besides Teamoh. On 24 November 1868, he was shot and killed by one James Grant, the brother of a woman Pollard had allegedly wronged (with admitted "playfulness and exuberance of style") in comments in his paper concerning "the elopment of a daughter from her parents' control, to pursue a fugitive or truant husband." Grant was put on trial for the shooting; the jury returned a verdict of not guilty. See Edward A. Pollard, *Memoir of the Assassination of Henry Rives Pollard. Prepared by His Brother, Edward A. Pollard* (Lynchburg: Schaffter and Bryant, Printers, 1869) 3-7, 29; *The Norfolk Virginian*, 9 March 1869, p. 1.

[101]Notices concerning Ku Klux Klan activities—in both Virginia and the South in general—first appeared in the paper on 4 April 1868, and they continued for several weeks. In the 4 April announcement concerning the Klan actions in Richmond, it was asserted that

great numbers of these strange but significant documents [Klan warnings] printed in black and red ink, upon paper stamped "K.K.K.," have been circulated over the city, blowing about in people's faces, falling down the chimneys, and fluttering in upon persons sitting at their desks.

It is also reported that the Convention is in great fear and trembling, a copy of another order being found upon the desk of every Radical delegate, black and white.

It was, the newspaper continued, also "rumoured that several of the negro delegates are missing, and that the Convention will adjourn immediately, *sine die*, as the K.K.K. has hinted that it desires the Capitol for the headquarters of the Richmond Division." In concluding comments on the Klan in Richmond, the paper claimed that the "negroes of the city—men, women, and children—have taken a healthy alarm."

The Ku Klux Klan—a conservative terrorist organization that used force and violence against black and white Republicans in the post-Civil War South—first appeared in Pulaski, Tennessee, during the spring of 1866. It actually had little impact on the course of Virginia's reconstruction. Several newspapers did attempt to encourage Klan expansion into Virginia during March and April 1868, the period to which Teamoh makes reference. But because conservatives gained control of the state following the ratification of the new constitution in the election of 6 July 1869, there was little need to control the Republican votes cast by the freedmen. The degree to which Virginia was free of Klan activity during its years of reconstruction thus made it unique among the former Confederate states. See Allen W. Trelease, *White Terror: The Ku Klux Klan Conspiracy and Southern Reconstruction* (New York: Harper & Row, 1971) 65-68.

Ben Johnson (1573–1637) was an English dramatist and a contemporary of William Shakespeare.

[102]The work of drafting the new constitution was done mainly in committees. Twenty standing committees were established on 12 December 1867. Some eighty-nine positions on these twenty bodies (including the twelve chairmanships) were secured by southern whites; thirty-two (including the eight remaining chairmanships) given to outside whites (delegates native to areas outside the Confederate states who had entered Virginia during or after the war). Although the twenty-four black delegates made up about a quarter of the convention's membership, they got only thirty-one committee positions, and no standing committee was chaired by a black. Teamoh was therefore correct. Key decisions about the wording of particular articles in the new constitution were generally made by white Republicans. Teamoh himself secured two committee appointments—one on the Committee on the Executive Department of Government and one on the Committee on Agricultural and Industrial Interests and Immigration. See Hume, "Membership of the Virginia Convention," 464; *Debates and Proceedings of the Constitutional Convention of the State of Virginia, Assembled at the City of Richmond, Tuesday, December 3, 1867: Being a Full and Complete Report of the Debates and Proceedings of the Convention, Together with the Reconstruction Acts of Congress and Those Supplementary Thereto, the Order of the Commander of the First Military District, in the Convention, and the New Constitution*. Vol. 1 (no other vols. published) (Richmond: New Nation, 1868) 60.

For details on Clements and Lee, see n. 93. Teamoh ran third among a group of thirteen who received votes for convention seats in his district. Clements led with 2,769 (126 white and 2,643 black), Lee was next with 2,760 (117 white and 2,643 black), and then came Teamoh with 2,219 (74 white and 2,145 black). See "Election of Delegates to the Constitutional Convention," 101.

[103]Clements chaired the Committee on Taxation and Finance. He was also a member of the

Committee on the Elective Franchise and Qualifications for Office. See *Debates and Proceedings*, p. 60.

[104]By 1871 the local Republican party in the district of the city of Portsmouth and county of Norfolk had become badly factionalized. This division, in part, was the result of frustrations arising from the statewide conservative victory in the elections of 6 July 1869, in which conservatives defeated the two "radical" articles proposed for inclusion in the new state constitution, gained control of both houses of the state legislature, and elected their candidate, Gilbert C. Walker, governor. In addition, as Teamoh noted later, the party was divided between local supporters of two national Republican organizations—the largely black Union League (which Teamoh had organized in the area) and The Grand Army of the Republic, which was controlled largely by whites who had only recently arrived in the Norfolk vicinity. Finally, the party was also divided, within the city itself, between the supporters of William H. Lyons (the former president of the Portsmouth City Council) and Philip G. Thomas, the city's mayor.

A good part of this factionalism was focused on patronage matters, but it also resulted in part from racial tensions within the community's biracial Republican party. In noting this fact, the *Virginian*'s Portsmouth correspondent asserted (10 November 1871, p. 1) that a few years ago "negroes were easily led by the whites in the Radical party, but now . . . they are demanding the control of the party here." As a result of all this infighting, Teamoh was not renominated for the senate seat he then held. That nomination went instead to Matthew P. Rue, an outside white farmer from New Jersey (1870 manuscript census returns, Norfolk County, Virginia, Turner's Creek Township, p. 52), who was then elected to that body.

Teamoh ran instead for a seat in the House of Delegates, and he was even opposed in that race by a second Republican candidate, a southern white named James W. Brownley. Brownley was a thirty-six year-old white Virginia native and an acting surveyor of customs (manuscript census returns, Norfolk County, Virginia, Jackson Ward, City of Portsmouth, p. 58). This split the Republican vote—661 for Teamoh to 396 for Brownley—and allowed the election of Captain Samuel Watts, the Conservative candidate who got 901 votes. See "Statement of the Whole Number of Votes Cast in the City of Portsmouth in an Election for Members of the House of Delegates of Virginia, Held Pursuant to Law, the First Tuesday after the First Monday in November, 1871," in Office of the Secretary of the Commonwealth Election Returns 1870–1871 (State Delegate) Abstracts. MS No. 3, Manuscript Division, Virginia State Library. Detailed plans for the celebration of Watts's victory by his Conservative supporters were published in the *Virginian*, 8 November 1871, p. 1.

[105]*The Norfolk Virginian*, 14 November 1871, p. 1, reported the shooting death of John F. Wilson, a "colored" policeman, on the night of Saturday, 11 November, and noted that the "other negroes shot were not seriously hurt." "The Register of Deaths, City of Portsmouth, Virginia, 1858–1896" (Office of the Circuit Court, City of Portsmouth), listed Wilson's age as twenty-six at the time of his murder. He was single, and his place of birth was not known. The 1870 manuscript census returns, Norfolk County, Virginia, City of Portsmouth, Jefferson Ward, p. 124, listed John Wilson as a thirty-year-old mulatto, a Virginia native, and a policeman.

The *Virginian*, which was fearful about black reaction to Wilson's death (15 November 1871, pp. 1 and 2; 20 November 1871, p. 1), reported a detailed version of Wilson's murder in its 20 November 1871 (p. 1) issue. According to the paper, a noisy group of Watts's supporters was coming up High Street when Wilson, who was off duty and wearing no visible badge, heard them, borrowed a pistol from a friend, and went from Langhorn's Drug Store (accompanied by other blacks) to meet the crowd. The two groups met at the center of Middle

Street and Wilson began a quarrel. He then drew his pistol, but "somebody" shot him before he could fire it. He fell with his pistol in his hand. As he fell, he exclaimed, "you d___n sons of b___s, you have shot me." The paper concluded this report by asserting that there had been "too much mistaken sentimentality wasted on this case, and that it has about been run into the mud." This account is therefore typical of many stories in the Conservative press that mention violence by whites toward blacks in the postwar South. In this case the black started the trouble, Wilson drew his weapon first, "someone" unknown shot him in self-defense, and no one was arrested and tried for that act.

The *Virginian* (14 November 1871, p. 1) noted the verdict of the coroner's jury—a body headed by James H. Clements—in the shooting. It concluded that Wilson "came to his death by a pistol shot, fired by someone to the jury unknown." Likewise, according to the *Police Blue Book* (Portsmouth: National Printing Company, 1915) 118, it was "impossible to ascertain who did the actual shooting, although the records of the Mayor's Court show that a number of prominent citizens were arrested, charged either with the actual killing or an assessory [*sic*] before and after fact. The parties arrested, however, were given a hearing, and as nothing could be proved on them, they were subsequently released."

In commenting on Wilson's funeral, which took place on the 13th, the *Virginian* (14 November 1871, p. 1) noted that it was attended by a crowd of around 3,000 people, including a group of 1,000 freedmen from Norfolk, and that the hearse was followed by the entire police force. The four white pall bearers were: Mayor Philip G. Thomas, James H. Clements, William G. Hitchings, and Colonel James D. Brady. For detail on Clements, see n. 93. According to the 1870 manuscript census returns for the City of Portsmouth, Thomas (Jefferson Ward, p. 29) was forty-six years of age, a native of Virginia, a cooper, and the mayor of the city. Brady (Jefferson Ward, p. 103) was a twenty-seven-year-old Virginia native and a city clerk. Hitchings (Jackson Ward, p. 61) was a forty-five-year-old boat builder and a native of Virginia. Hitchings was also listed as a captain in the Portsmouth Fire Department (Resolution Fire Company) in *The Norfolk and Portsmouth Directory, 1872–1873* (Norfolk: Chataigne & Boyd, 1872) 328.

The symbolism of Clement's action in placing Wilson's body in the white cemetery is reminiscent of the actions of Radical Pennsylvania Congressman Thaddeus Stevens, who was buried in a black cemetery following his death in 1868. It is interesting that, while a delegate to the state constitutional convention, Clements had corresponded with Stevens, a man whom he obviously admired. See James H. Clements to Thaddeus Stevens, 14 March 1868, in Smith, "Virginia During Reconstruction," p. 90.

[106]See n. 41.

[107]The factionalism to which Teamoh referred was a constant problem for Portsmouth Republicans (see n. 104). The platform he mentioned was probably discussed at a Republican meeting on 1 October 1867. Various factions held meetings during this period: Teamoh and Lee were nominated by Regular Republicans on 1 October, and Clements was nominated by a group that met on 5 October. See the *Virginian*, 5 October 1867, p. 1; 7 October 1867, p. 1. This factionalism was resolved, at least for a time, when a united Republican ticket for the district of the city of Portsmouth and the county of Norfolk (Teamoh, Clements, and Lee) was agreed upon at a Republican meeting on 11 October. See the *Norfolk Virginian*, 12 October 1867, p. 1.

[108]The *Norfolk Virginian*, 29 November 1871, p. 1, noted that some 600 men—black and white—were employed in the Navy Yard. Of these, 350 to 400 lived in Portsmouth; the re-

mainder resided in the city of Norfolk or in the county. Teamoh's interest in the working conditions of these men stemmed in large part from his background. He, too, had worked in the yard as a slave; he would work in there again as a caulker after leaving political office.

There was a good deal of labor unrest in the Gosport Navy Yard during the postwar years, especially in 1869, the year of Teamoh's election to the state senate. Congress had enacted a law on 25 June 1868 (reported in the *Virginian* on 25 May 1869, p. 1) that declared eight hours "a day's work for all laborers, workmen, and mechanics employed by or on behalf of the government of the United States." This did not turn out to be the panacea for which laborers in the yard had hoped. Secretary of the Navy Adolph E. Borie, in fact, responded to this legislation by reducing wages in the shipyard by twenty percent, arguing that the cut was justified by the reduction in the normal ten-hour workday of the laborers.

When this action was announced in Norfolk and Portsmouth on 3 April, a public meeting was held (reported in the *Virginian*, 6 April 1869, p. 1) and a series of resolutions adopted unanimously. They noted that the pay of workingmen in the yard was scarcely adequate and that Secretary Borie's action was unjust and oppressive. The workers thanked Congress for the eight-hour-day law, but asked that it be amended to prevent future misconstruction of its provisions; they further called on friendly Congressmen to support the objectives of those resolutions. (Since Virginia had no Congressmen at that time, those citizens at this meeting could not simply petition their own representative.) A committee of three was also selected to go to Washington and present these concerns to Congress.

This action was followed by yet another meeting on 27 April (reported in detail in the *Virginian* on 29 April 1869, p. 1). Here, friendly Congressmen were thanked for their efforts, and a committee on permanent organization was appointed. This effort was supported with enthusiasm by laborers in New York City, who sent a rousing letter (dated 1 May 1869 and published in the *Virginian*, 10 May 1869, p. 1). It called for working-class solidarity and argued that terms such as *radical* and *rebel* should be dropped from the working-class vocabulary so that laborers north and south could join together "for the emancipation and promotion of labor."

This encouragement led to yet another meeting, this time at Portsmouth's Zion Church on 14 May (reported in the *Virginian*, 17 May 1869, p. 1). Here a report from the committee on permanent organization was adopted, officers were elected, and The Workingmen's Union of Norfolk, Portsmouth and Vicinity was established. As this meeting was about to adjourn, the issue of whether the new union was to be integrated was raised. Corresponding Secretary Daniel Collins and several blacks in the audience endorsed the concept of a biracial union and spoke of "the advantages to be gained by co-operation, regardless of 'class, color or condition.' " A motion to allow membership for both races was then passed.

These actions, and similar ones at other government installations across the country, were effective. On 19 May 1869, President Ulysses S. Grant issued a proclamation directing that wages of government workers should not be reduced "on account of such reduction in the hours of labor." The proclamation was published in the *Virginian*, 25 May 1869, p. 1.

Despite this victory, navy yard laborers continued to face economic difficulties, which they tried to deal with collectively. Economic hard times following the Panic of 1873, however, seemed to retard further organization, causing local laborers to consider more radical methods of dealing with their problems. A number of workers, for example, were evidently willing to support the General Strike movement in 1877, and the yard commander planned to put down any such activity with "guns and howitzers, also marines and sailors armed as infantry." See Emmerson, "Some Fugitive Items of Portsmouth & Norfolk County History," p. 174.

[109]A reference to the platform the Republican party adopted in Chicago on 20-21 May 1868, in the national convention that nominated Ulysses S. Grant for president and Schuyler Colfax (a Congressman from Indiana) for vice president. The three Reconstruction-era amendments—13th (1865), 14th (1868), and 15th (1870) ended slavery, granted citizenship to blacks, and outlawed voting restrictions based on race.

[110]At the start of the war, various northern states and cities offered cash bonuses to encourage the enlistments required to meet state quotas for recruits into the Union Army. The practice continued at the state level through much of the war, and it was adopted in July 1861 by the federal government. It is estimated that the Union's total "mercenary bill"—that is, bonuses paid to enlistees by the local, state, and national governments—ran to something around three-quarters of a billion dollars. See Fred A. Shannon, *The Organization and Administration of the Union Army, 1861–1865*, 2 vols. (Cleveland: Arthur H. Clark Co., 1928) 2:80. This system encouraged the practice known as "bounty jumping," in which a man who had no intention of actually serving in the military would enlist, collect his bounty, desert immediately, and then repeat the whole process under a different name in a new community. In theory, this practice could be carried on indefinitely.

[111]Evidently a reference to John F. Lewis, a native of Rockingham County. Lewis was elected to the Virginia secession convention, where he refused to sign the secession ordinance. Elected lieutenant governor in 1869, he soon went to the United States Senate, a body in which he served from early 1870 to 5 March 1875. He secured a second term as Virginia's lieutenant governor during the early 1800s. See *Directory of Congress*, p. 1288.

[112]Congressman James H. Platt, like Teamoh, had been a member of the 1867–1868 convention, in which he had represented the district of the city of Petersburg. A native of the Canadian maritime region, he was a longtime resident of Vermont, where he had obtained a medical degree. He settled in Virginia after serving as an officer in the Union Army during the war. Elected to Congress as a Republican in 1869, he served two terms in that body before leaving Virginia and moving to New York. He later settled in Colorado, where he was involved in mining and manufacturing. Ibid., p. 1549. The 1870 manuscript census returns for Dinwiddie County, Virginia, City of Petersburg, Second Ward, p. 22, listed Platt as a thirty-two-year-old bachelor from Vermont. He held property valued at $29,000.

[113]George M. Robeson replaced Adolph E. Borie as secretary of the Navy on 25 June 1869, and he held that position for the remainder of Grant's presidency. The son of a well-to-do New Jersey iron manufacturer, he had graduated from Princeton with honors in 1847. An attorney, Robeson was appointed a brigadier general during the war, in which he commanded volunteer troops stationed at Woodburg, New Jersey. In 1867 he was appointed attorney general of New Jersey; he left that post when selected for Grant's cabinet. His administration of the Navy was tainted with scandal, but no action was taken against him following a congressional inquiry into the affairs of his department. After returning to New Jersey, Robeson, whose size and personal characteristics made him a favorite target of cartoonists, served two terms in Congress. See Dumas Malone and Allen Johnson, eds., *Dictionary of American Biography*, 22 vols. plus suppl. (New York: Charles Scribner's Sons, 1928–) 16:31.

Platt served on the House Committee on Naval Affairs (see n. 154) and knew Robeson well. Robeson had even come to Virginia's second congressional district to campaign for Platt. This action did not work out well; it resulted in a major race riot (see n. 155). According to the *Virginian*, 13 May 1871, p. 1, Teamoh's meeting with Robeson, which the paper labeled "The Navy Yard Dodge," was arranged because work was needed at Gosport and the radicals were "afraid if the men are not at work they will be unable to control their votes."

[114]This Republican meeting was reported in the *Virginian*, 29 April 1871, p. 1. At the meeting, Philip G. Thomas was elected president of the local party's executive committee; Teamoh was elected vice president of the committee. Among other items of business, a resolution was passed stating that mechanics and laborers in the Gosport Navy Yard received less pay than did those in other yards. It then went on to request that Congressman Platt introduce a joint resolution in Congress that would bring the wages paid at Portsmouth into line with those paid in the Navy yard in New York City.

[115]*The Great Eastern* was the largest steamship built to that time and remained so for thirteen years following its destruction in 1888. The ship (also known as *The Leviathan*) was built in 1859 and left Southampton 17 June 1860 on its maiden voyage, under the command of Captain John Vine Hall. It arrived in New York City on 28 June, where a group of Norfolk businessmen was successful in arranging its sailing to Virginia. It departed from New York on 2 August 1860 and arrived in Hampton Roads on 3 August. It came into the harbor the following day, and it left on 5 August, after being viewed by some 8,000 people. For details on the ship's Norfolk visit, see Thomas B. Rowland, "Scrapbook," 3 vols., Sargeant Memorial Room, Norfolk Public Library, 1:237. For a detailed and colorful history of the life of the ship, see James Dugan, *The Great Iron Ship* (New York: Harper & Brothers, 1953).

The famous Confederate ironclad *Virginia* was built on the hull of the damaged *Merrimac* at the Gosport Navy Yard in 1862. See Marshall W. Butt, *Portsmouth under Four Flags, 1752–1970* (Portsmouth: Portsmouth Historical Association and Friends of the Portsmouth Naval Shipyard and Museum, 1971) 39-44. As noted in the introduction, it met the Union ironclad, the *Monitor*, on 9 April 1862, in an inconclusive engagement that remains the most famous naval battle of the Civil War.

[116]From the brief account of the Republican meeting (where the issue of pay was discussed) given in the *Virginian*, 29 April 1871, p. 1, it is apparent that the factionalism which had plagued the local party since 1867 was still present. The paper reported that James H. Clements "made a speech, giving an account of the history of the troubles in the camp of the faithful, from the beginning." If the *Virginian*'s later comments (see n. 104) were correct, Republican meetings of this type represented an extremely interesting but eventually unsuccessful attempt to focus on common black-white economic interests to overcome racial tensions within the biracial Portsmouth party. Teamoh and the *Virginian* agreed that the meeting of 28 April 1871 was well attended—a sign of significant black-white effort to overcome factionalism regarding an issue on which, as Teamoh noted, the concerns of blacks and whites were identical. Still, his negative comments about (white) bounty jumpers (n. 110) suggest strongly the continuation of racial divisions within the party.

[117]As a member of the House Committee on Naval Affairs, Platt attempted to promote the economic interests of his district through the introduction of bills such as those to construct an iron plating shop at Norfolk, to construct a lighthouse on the York River, and to survey the Chickahominy and Hampton rivers. See *Congressional Record*, 43 Cong., 2d sess., 1874–1875 vol. 2, pp. 190-191.

[118]The election concerning the new constitution and the selection of new state officials was actually held on 6 July 1869, more than a year after the constitutional convention had adjourned. Teamoh defeated his Conservative opponent, Thomas H. Williams, by a vote of 3,527 to 2,158. See "July 6, 1869 Election Returns Portsmouth and Norfolk," MS Election Record no. 428, Manuscript Division, Virginia State Archives. These complete returns do not give

the race of Teamoh's supporters, but partial returns for Jackson and Jefferson Wards in Portsmouth, which appeared in the *Virginian* on 7 July 1869, p. 1, did offer that information:

	Jackson (Portsmouth) Ward		Jefferson Ward (Portsmouth)	
	White	Black	White	Black
Teamoh	106	268	104	630
Williams	233	0	551	1

These returns suggest that as many as twenty percent of the ballots for Teamoh were cast by whites. If so, that is a surprisingly high degree of white support for a radical black politician. It can, however, perhaps be explained by several factors. The federal employment offered in the Navy Yard clearly attracted significant numbers of Union veterans and other northerners to the community. Portsmouth residents had been slow to support secession, and perhaps this vote also showed some support for the Republican party from native white Unionists. Teamoh was probably an articulate and well-organized campaigner—his diary certainly suggests this—who could appeal for some support in the white community, especially in an election in which Virginians (because of a provision of the new constitution) were voting by secret ballot instead of by the traditional system of *viva voce*. Finally, the biracial Workingman's Union of Norfolk, Portsmouth and Vicinity (organized in May—see n. 108) might have been able to build some degree of black-white cooperation during the eight-hour-day campaign. If this was the case, though, this support was evidently lost by 1871, when white and black Republicans divided between Brownley and Teamoh respectively (see n. 104).

The newly elected state Senate contained thirty Conservatives and thirteen Republicans (including six blacks). The new House of Delegates contained ninety-six Conservatives and forty-two Republicans (including twenty-one blacks). See Richard L. Morton, *History of Virginia*, 6 vols. (Chicago and New York: The American Historical Society, 1924) 3:155. For a listing of the names of delegates and senators, see Leonard, *General Assembly of Virginia*, 508-12. Teamoh represented the Twenty-first Senatorial District (city of Portsmouth and county of Norfolk). The five other black senators were: James W. D. Bland (Charlotte and Prince Edward—14th District), Isaiah Lyons (York, Surry, Elizabeth City, and Warwick—24th District), William P. Moseley (Fluvanna, Goochland, and Powhatan—5th District), Frank Moss (Appomattox and Buckingham—7th District), and John Robinson (Amelia, Cumberland, and Nottoway—30th District). All of these politicians, with the exception of Lyons, had been delegates to the constitutional convention. See Richard L. Hume, "The 'Black and Tan' Constitutional Conventions of 1867–1869 in Ten Former Confederate States: A Study of Their Membership" (Ph.D. diss., University of Washington, 1969) 197-203; Luther Porter Jackson, *Negro Office-Holders in Virginia 1865–1895* (Norfolk: Guide Quality Press, 1945) 143.

[119]Senators Charles Sumner (1811–1874) and Daniel Webster (1782–1852) of Massachusetts.

[120]As noted in the Introduction, Bland died in what the Richmond *Daily Dispatch*, 28 April 1870, p. 2, called the greatest calamity since the burning of the Richmond Theater in 1811. More than sixty people were killed (and a large number injured) when the third floor of the capitol building collapsed.

Born free in Farmville, Prince Edward County, in 1838, Bland was probably apprenticed to Alexander Bruce, the former owner of his mother (his father, Hercules, had purchased her freedom). He later worked as a cooper in his father's shop, making barrels for the packing of tobacco (Jackson, *Negro Office-Holders*, 3-4). Like Teamoh, Bland showed some distrust of the white leadership of Virginia's Republican party. While a convention delegate, he wrote Congressman Elihu Washburne of Illinois to ask advice on the matter of white disfranchisement and stated that "*frankly* I am afraid to follow in the footsteps of the weakest *minds* and *nerves* the world has ever seen in party leaders. They are too changeable." See Smith, "Virginia during Reconstruction," 91. For actions of the Senate regarding Bland's death, see *Journal of the Senate of the Commonwealth of Virginia: Begun and Held at the Capitol, in the City of Richmond, on Tuesday, the Fifth Day of October, in the Year One Thousand Eight Hundred and Sixty-Nine—Being the Ninety-Third Year of the Commonwealth* (Richmond: James E. Goode's Steam Presses, 1870) 362, 365-66, 460, 465, 498, 503, 516.

[121] Lyons's death (on 21 February 1871) was announced in the Senate on 22 February 1871. See *Journal of the Senate of the Commonwealth of Virginia: Begun and Held at the Capitol, in the City of Richmond, on Wednesday, the seventh day of December, in the year one thousand eight hundred and seventy, being the ninety-fourth year of the Commonwealth* (Richmond: James E. Goode, Printer, 1870 [*sic*]) 207, 223, 286, 358, 360-61. The 1870 manuscript census returns for Wyth Township, City of Hampton, Elizabeth City County, Virginia, p. 14, listed Lyons as a twenty-seven-year-old mulatto from New York employed as an apothecary. He held property valued at $200. His wife was also a New York native, and they had a twelve-year-old son who was a native of Virginia.

Dr. James McCune Smith was a well-known black physician. He was acquainted with Virginia blacks who had settled in New York's Franklin County during the 1840s, and with abolitionists such as John Brown and Gerrit Smith. See Willard B. Gatewood, Jr., ed., *Free Man of Color: The Autobiography of Willis Augustus Hodges* (Knoxville: University of Tennessee Press, 1982) xlvii-xlviii. *Wilson's Business Directory of New York City (1851)* (New York: John F. Trow, Publisher & Printer, 1851), p. 252, listed J. McCune Smith as a physician at 55 West Broadway.

[122] Washington L. Riddick (Nansemond, Southampton, and Isle of Wight—22nd District) died in New Orleans on 3 February 1871. In the 1870 manuscript census returns for Nansemond County, Virginia (city of Suffolk, p. 8), Riddick was listed as a lawyer, forty-five years of age, who held property with a total value of $1,500. He was a native Virginian. For legislative reactions to his death, see *Senate Journal, 1870–1871*, 155-56, 164-65, 234.

[123] Moseley (1819–1890) served in the Senate from 1869 to 1871. He was born a slave to the Haden family of Goochland County, and he operated a freight boat on the James River and Kanawha Canal. During and after the war, he ran a similar vessel between Richmond and Lynchburg. Moss served in the Senate from 1869 to 1871 and in the House of Delegates from 1874 to 1875. Born free in Buckingham County, he was employed as a farmer and as a minister. Robinson (1822–1900) served in the Senate from 1869 to 1873. He was a tavern owner and mail carrier who had been born free in Cumberland County. See Jackson, *Negro Office-Holders*, 28-29, 35-36. Moseley and Robinson (both mulattoes) and Moss (Negro) all owned some property in 1870. See 1870 manuscript census returns, Goochland County, Virginia, Byrd Township, p. 1 (Moseley); Buckingham County, Virginia, James River Township, p. 28 (Moss); Amelia County, Leigh Township, p. 87 (Robinson). These returns also indicate that each of these three black senators was literate.

[124] During the early 1870s, the Pennsylvania-Southern Railway Security System gained control of thirteen southern railroads and more than 2,100 miles of track. This holding company, formed in 1871, was the work of powerful business and railroad interests in the keystone state. It was organized by Thomas Scott and was headed by George Washington Cass, a Pitts-

burgh railroad man and the nephew of Lewis Cass, the 1848 Democratic presidential nominee. In addition to Cass and Scott, other powerful Pennsylvanians—most notably, Simon Cameron (President Lincoln's first and somewhat tarnished secretary of war) and his son James, the president of the Northern Central Railway—were involved with this postwar effort to rebuild and consolidate a southern rail system and connect it with Philadelphia and other northern cities.

Scott himself, along with many other lobbyists, was in Richmond in early 1871. He was trying—successfully, as it turned out—to gain control of the Alexandria and Fredricksburg Line, a twenty-six-mile-long road in northern Virginia and an essential connection between Washington, D.C., and Richmond. To do this, he needed to obtain stock in this road (and others) held by the state of Virginia. Such an acquisition was promoted by Scott and his supporters—including Governor Gilbert C. Walker—through a campaign for "free roads," which called for the eventual sale of state stock in existing roads to private interests. This effort was opposed strongly by Scott's rivals, which included the Baltimore and Ohio Railroad and the energetic William A. Mahone, a former Confederate general and a future United States Senator from Virginia, who was trying to piece together his own rail system in the state. The legislative contest between Scott's forces and those of his opponents was thus one to determine which group would gain control of a number of Virginia railroads when and if the state divested itself of its shares of their stock. These railroad matters—perhaps the most explosive question to face Virginia's new legislature—were made even more complicated by various local interests, some of which supported various forms of railroad consolidation, either by Mahone or Scott, while other interests opposed that policy.

Teamoh obviously believed that he represented the concerns of many citizens of the Portsmouth-Norfolk area who feared that the consolidated Pennsylvania Southern Line would destroy their local Seaboard and Roanoke Road. Massive protest meetings took place, on 16 February 1871, in both communities, and concern was voiced against what was called the "great Pennsylvania Central railroad monopoly." The protesters were fearful that Scott's system—which would control roads from Philadelphia to Georgia—would be pieced together in such a way that the 130,000 bales of cotton that moved over the Seaboard road would "pass through our State 80 miles above our port." This arrangement, it was said, would clearly "ruin the interests of our twin cities, and blast their commercial greatness." Despite this mass protest meeting (which was reported on in detail in the *Norfolk Virginian*, 17 February 1871, p. 1), the Alexandria and Fredricksburg Railroad bill passed the Senate on 23 February 1871, by a vote of twenty-one to seventeen, with Teamoh joining the opposition. It cleared the House on 20 February 1871, by a vote of sixty to forty-three. See *Senate Journal, 1870–1871,* 213; *Journal of the House of Delegates of the State of Virginia, for the Session of 1870–1871* (Richmond: Clemmitt & Jones, Printers, 1871) 208. For the text of the bill to amend the charter of the Alexandria and Fredricksburg Railroad—and to change the name of that road to the Washington and Richmond Railway Company—see *Acts and Joint Resolutions Passed by the General Assembly of the State of Virginia, at Its Session of 1870–1871* (Richmond: James E. Goode, Printer, 1871) 141-45. The bill was approved by Governor Walker on 4 March 1871. For a fine, brief discussion of this entire issue, see John F. Stover, *The Railroads of the South, 1865–1900: A Study in Finance and Control* (Chapel Hill: University of North Carolina Press, 1955) 99-121.

[125]Senator Walter H. Taylor represented the 20th District—Norfolk City and Princess Anne County—and he, like Teamoh, voted against the railroad bill. According to the 1870 manuscript census returns, Norfolk County, Virginia, Ward 1, City of Norfolk, p. 53, Taylor was a prosperous merchant (a hardware dealer with property valued at $10,000). He was thirty-two years old in 1870; along with his wife and three children, he was a native of Vir-

ginia.

[126]The letter appeared in the *Norfolk Virginian*, 18 February 1871, p. 1. There were a few spelling and paragraph or punctuation changes made between the diary and newspaper versions, but they are not significant. The letter in the newspaper, however, contained a paragraph that was not included in the diary. This additional paragraph reads as follows:

. . . give us employment.

What would my colored friends in Norfolk, among whom I was born, and those in Portsmouth and Norfolk county with whom I was raised, say, if, per adventure, through my single vote I should, either directly, or indirectly, (for it takes indirection to find direction out) cause to be switched off all the freight that now gives employment to the laboring classes, from Townbridge to Town Point and Kimberly's or Chamberlaine's warf? What could they, what would they, or what ought they to say? Why, sir, billingsgate would be inadequate, and tar and feathers could never reach the case. Certainly this would be so with me were I laboring along shore where I have been; and where I expect to be again.

And having heard arguments pro and con. . . .

[127]Teamoh, who admitted that the debate on the railroad bill was complex and confusing, was somewhat inaccurate there. A black representative, William H. Ragsdale (Charlotte— 20th District), introduced a resolution (not an amendment) which requested that "a committee of three be appointed by the Speaker of the House, whose duty it shall be to communicate and confer with the various railroad presidents in the State of Virginia, and present the policy and justness of providing a special car upon their trains for the exclusive accomodation [*sic*] and comfort of the colored passengers, male and female, who may travel over their routes."

In offering this resolution, Ragsdale was actually voicing black opposition to the then-common practice of requiring all freedmen to ride in railroad smoking cars. He suggested that blacks (although certainly not unanimous on this point) would prefer to ride instead on segregated "regular" passenger cars. There was never an actual vote on this resolution. It was not sent to committee, and it was not tabled for later consideration. This lack of action showed that the majority of the delegates, Conservatives and Republicans, were willing to continue the "smoking car" accommodation for blacks. Teamoh, in contrast, believed that black and white Republican legislators—like blacks and whites in the Workingmen's Union of Norfolk, Portsmouth and Vicinity—should support integrated facilities and oppose the "smoking" or "special" car for blacks. When they did not stand for such a principle by bringing Ragsdale's resolution to a vote, Teamoh evidently concluded that members of his own party were opposed to a policy that would "accommodate equally all persons irrespective of color." See *Journal of the House of Delegates, 1870–1871*, 79; Charles E. Wynes, *Race Relations in Virginia, 1870– 1902* (Charlottesville: University of Virginia Press, 1961) 69-70; Jackson, *Negro Office-Holders*, 35.

[128]For a map showing the Pennsylvania-Southern Railway Security System, and a listing of the thirteen separate roads that constituted it, see Stover, *Railroads of the South*, 106, 118.

[129]See n. 126. Opponents of the railroad bill complained bitterly about bribes, payoffs, and emotional appeals to Republican party loyalty to get the Alexandria and Fredricksburg Bill through the General Assembly. For examples of such charges, see the *Norfolk Virginian*, 21 February 1871, p. 2; 23 February 1871, p. 2.

[130]See n. 127.

[131]Both the Portsmouth and the Norfolk protest meetings of 16 February 1871 (*Virginian*, 17 February 1871, p. 1) had passed resolutions against the Alexandria and Fredricksburg Bill that echoed the points Teamoh mentioned in this conversation. A seven-point resolution had been passed by Portsmouth citizens who met at Oxford Hall before adjourning to join with protesters meeting at the Opera House in Norfolk. This combined group had then passed a six-point protest resolution. The *Virginian* emphasized the size of both of these meetings— despite recent severe storms that might have been expected to discourage attendance—and the fact that these resolutions were supported widely in both communities. At the combined meeting in Norfolk, for example, the paper claimed that all "classes were represented; the capitalist standing shoulder to shoulder with the working men, and the business men of every grade were out in full force." In Portsmouth, the same was the case. Again, according to the *Virginian*, that meeting "was not confined to any branch of our community, but embraced the merchant, the mechanic, and the professions."

[132]In fact, the Pennsylvania-Southern Railway Security System never produced the profits expected of it. It collapsed from problems associated with the Panic of 1873. See Stover, *Railroads of the South*, 120.

[133]*Hamlet*, 2.2.213; Henry Clay (1777–1852) and John Calhoun (1782–1850), American political leaders.

[134]Teamoh noted that this was from George Gordon, Lord Byron, the English romantic poet (1788–1824).

[135]Teamoh attended four sessions of the state senate from October 1869 to March 1871; 5–20 October 1869; 8 February–11 July 1870; 1 October–10 November 1870; 7 December 1870–31 March 1871. See Leonard, *General Assembly of Virginia*, 508.

[136]Teamoh made a valid point. Even so, his literacy was obviously a tremendous advantage to him in furthering his political career. It allowed him to correspond with his constituents (as was the case with his letter in the *Norfolk Virginian*—see n. 126) and with Republican leaders such as Secretary of the Navy William E. Chandler (see n. 179). It also enabled him to learn quickly of the time and place of local Republican meetings, attend them, and inform the masses of freedmen—good Republican voters—of his opinions on important local issues. His literacy evidently also impressed local white Republican leaders, such as James H. Clements, and it undoubtedly encouraged their support of his candidacy for legislative office. General John Schofield, who was often quite critical of the illiteracy of black convention delegates, for example, noted that Teamoh was a man of "some talent." See Lowe, "Virginia's Reconstruction Convention," 347. For comments on literacy and the selection of black leaders of the Reconstruction era, see Richard L. Hume, "Negro Delegates to the State Constitutional Conventions of 1867–1869," in Howard N. Rabinowitz, ed., *Southern Black Leaders of the Reconstruction Era* (Urbana, Chicago, London: University of Illinois Press, 1982) 138-39.

[137]George William Curtis (1824–1892) was not a member of Congress. He was, however, a prominent advocate of civil service reform. This cause—its objective was that of replacing the spoils system with one that would bring into governmental service "a better class of people"—was an extremely popular reform among liberals during the latter half of the nineteenth century. Their campaign began in 1864 and climaxed with the passage of the Civil Service Act (Pendleton Act) on 16 January 1883, shortly after the assassination of President James A. Garfield. In 1871 Curtis had been appointed chairman of a newly authorized Civil Service Ad-

visory Board. On 18 December 1871, that body issued its first report, a document "that rang all the charges on the evils of the spoils system." This was evidently the action to which Teamoh made reference. See John G. Sproat, *"The Best Men": Liberal Reformers in the Gilded Age* (New York: Oxford University Press, 1968) 257-65 (quote, 261); Malone and Johnson, *Dictionary of American Biography*, 4:614-16.

[138]The Grand Army of the Republic held its first national meeting at Indianapolis, Indiana, in November 1866. As a national veterans' organization, it was associated closely with the Republican party, and it functioned much as a present-day pressure group. It glorified the Republican effort to end slavery and reunite the Union, and it argued that its members—veterans of the successful Union military effort—should receive substantial pensions and preference in Federal employment.

Following its organization in the North, the Grand Army of the Republic soon became active in the South, moving into Tennessee, Arkansas, and Louisiana (all states occupied in part by Union forces prior to 1865), and it appeared in Virginia, West Virginia, Florida, Mississippi, and Texas by 1868. Its membership in the South was most often composed of whites working with the Freedmen's Bureau, the postal service, or the Bureau of Internal Revenue. Teamoh clearly believed that this organization advanced the interests of white Union Army veterans to the detriment of those of the local freedmen, and there is evidence that the G.A.R. in his district was made up solely of whites (who were sometimes antiblack) employed in the navy yard. See, for example, the *Norfolk Virginian*, 21 October 1872, p. 1; 18 September 1873, p. 1. For details on the Union League, see Mary R. Dearing, *Veterans in Politics: The Story of the G.A.R.* (Baton Rouge: Louisiana State University Press, 1952) 114-15, passim.

[139]Teamoh was a Union League organizer in the Portsmouth area. The League had its beginning in Philadelphia in November 1862. It spread, during 1863, to more than eighteen northern states and to Unionist groups in the South as well. Initially, the League offered a focus for rallying civilian support for the northern cause: it distributed pro-Union literature; it recruited white and black soldiers to the Union Army; and it raised money for the relief of Union soldiers. However, it soon became an increasingly political organization, working for the reelection of President Lincoln in 1864 and for the success of the radical opponents of President Andrew Johnson from 1866 to 1869. By 1867, the League, complete with a great deal of ritual and ceremony, was well established in much of the South, where its meetings were often used to organize the freedmen as Republican voters. This activity, of course, outraged southern white conservatives, who often justified the actions of the Ku Klux Klan as a righteous response to League activities. For a brief account of the League and its functions, see James G. Randall and David Donald, *The Civil War and Reconstruction* (Lexington, MA: D. C. Heath and Company, 1969) 490-91, 660, 682.

[140]Two "Enforcement Acts"—those of 31 May 1870 and 20 April 1871—were passed by Congress in response to the terrorism of the Ku Klux Klan and other vigilante groups active in the South. The first of these acts provided fines and/or prison terms for individuals who attempted to keep the freedmen from voting. The second act, formulated as a result of an extensive congressional investigation into the "Condition of Affairs in the Late Insurrectionary States," declared certain acts (such as the wearing of disguises while preventing citizens from voting) to be crimes and allowed the president to intervene to suppress "armed combinations" engaged in such activities. In October 1871, President Grant used this act to suspend habeas corpus and to send federal troops to suppress Klan activity in nine upcountry South Carolina counties. See Trelease, *White Terror*, 385-88, 403.

[141]Teamoh was one of many who were disillusioned with the postwar trends in the Repub-

lican party. By 1872, a group that became known as Liberal Republicans argued that the party had become too corrupt and too tied to patronage, tariffs, and political bribery. These dissenters nominated Horace Greeley, publisher of the New York *Tribune*, as their presidential candidate that year. Greeley, who was also nominated by the Democrats, ran on a platform focused largely on the issues of sectional reconciliation and governmental reform, and he was defeated rather easily by Ulysses Grant, who gained a second term as president. Republican problems, however, continued. Stories of corruption in the Grant administration itself, and in Republican governments in a number of southern states as well, combined with a very serious economic panic in 1873 to provide a political upheaval in the 1874 congressional elections, in which the Democrats gained control of the House of Representatives. The fact that Democrats could then block the passage of further Reconstruction legislation in the House—coupled with the loss of reform zeal among Republicans themselves—thus led effectively to the ending of the Reconstruction era.

John Brown, of course, was "martyred. ' He was executed for treason by the state of Virginia on 2 December 1859, following his unsuccessful raid on the Harpers Ferry arsenal that October.

[142]A reference to the Modoc Indians who held out against whites for months (during the Modoc War of 1872–1873) in the natural fortifications of the lava beds south of Tule Lake, California. While attempting to negotiate a settlement of that conflict, General Edward R. S. Canby, who had been in command of the military district of Virginia when the legislature of 1869 first assembled, was killed by Captain Jack (Keintpoos), a Modoc chief. For details on Canby's shooting, which occurred on 11 April 1873, see Keith A. Murray, *The Modocs and Their War* (Norman: University of Oklahoma Press, 1959) 180-89.

[143]A reference to a classical Greek myth involving Halcyone, the daughter of Aeolus. In grief over the drowning of her lover, Ceyx, she threw herself into the sea. Out of compassion, the gods changed both lovers into kingfishers.

[144]A reference to a villain in William Shakespeare's tragedy *Othello*. He convinced Othello that Othello's wife, Desdemona, was unfaithful. Herod was the biblical king who attempted to murder the infant Jesus.

[145]The Virginia Constitution of 1869 provided that judges of the supreme court, the circuit courts, and the county courts be chosen "by the joint vote of the two houses of the general assembly." Supreme court judges were selected for twelve-year terms, circuit court judges for eight-year terms, and county court judges for six-year terms. See Article 6, Sections 5, 11, and 13 of the constitution in Francis Newton Thorpe, comp., *The Federal and State Constitutions, Colonial Charters, and Other Organic Laws of the States, Territories, and Colonies Now or Heretofore Forming the United States of America*, 7 vols. (Washington D.C.: United States Government Printing Office, 1909) 7:3888-89.

[146]Teamoh was a delegate from Portsmouth to the Republican state convention that met at Petersburg (on 9 March 1869) to nominate a Republican ticket for the 6 July 1869 state elections. He was selected as a delegate at a meeting at Snead's Blacksmith Shop on 22 February 1869 (See the *Norfolk Virginian*, 24 February 1869, p. 1). For brief comments concerning his role at the convention, see Eckenrode, *Political History*, 119.

The convention, which met at the Union Street Colored Methodist Church, was even more divided than the factionalized Democratic convention of December 1858, which met in Petersburg and selected John Letcher as its gubernatorial nominee. In this instance, the battle was between supporters of Henry H. Wells (who was successful) and supporters of James H.

Clements for the gubernatorial nomination. In addition, the selection of a black, Dr. J. D. Harris of Hampton, as the party's candidate for lieutenant governor, aroused the ire of more conservative white Republicans. A rumor circulated that William Mahone, who disliked Wells and wished to defeat him, used his influence to get Harris on the ticket to arouse the racial fears of whites and thereby secure the election of Wells's opponent. See Smith, "Virginia during Reconstruction," 146; Eckenrode, *Political History*, 119; Richmond *Daily Dispatch*, 10 March 1869, 1; 12 March 1869, 1. It is clear that Teamoh believed this rumor to be true.

[147]See n. 112.

[148]See n. 96.

[149]A reference to the test oath and disfranchisement provisions of the new constitution, which were incorporated into that document largely through the efforts of Orrin E. Hine. These two measures were voted on separately in the 6 July 1869 elections, in which the constitution was ratified. They were defeated and stricken from that document (see n. 99). "Grant and Wilson" is a reference to the successful 1872 Republican national ticket of Ulysses S. Grant and Senator Henry Wilson of Massachusetts.

[150]The divided Portsmouth Republicans nominated Matthew P. Rue (who was elected) for Teamoh's senate seat in 1871. Teamoh ran for a seat in the House of Delegates and came in second in a three-man race. He lost to white Conservative Samuel Watts; he ran ahead of James W. Brownley, a white Republican (see nn. 104 and 138).

[151]See n. 111. For examples of racial division in the local GAR chapter, see the *Norfolk Virginian*, 21 October 1872, p. 1; 18 September 1873, p. 1. The first reference noted separate steamers for white and black members of the order who visited a soldiers' asylum at Hampton; the second reference noted the control of the local GAR chapter by the white "navy yard element." For an example of additional black opinion critical of Platt's "Republicanism" and his alleged racial prejudice, see the letter of W. J. Reed (black) to the colored voters of Nansemond County in the *Norfolk Virginian*, 11 September 1874, p. 1.

[152]Peoples of the Persian Empire (550 B.C.–330 B.C.).

[153]Dagon was an ancient Philistine deity (1 Chr. 10:10) discussed in the Old Testament. Noted temples to Dagon stood at Ashdod (1 Sam. 5:1-7), Gaza (Judg. 16:21-23), Beth-dagon (Josh. 15:41), and in Asher (Josh. 19:27).

[154]Platt took his seat in Congress on 26 January 1870, and he was appointed to the naval affairs committee on 7 March of that year. He held his position on that committee until he left Washington at the end of the 43rd Congress. Teamoh is incorrect, however, in stating that Platt chaired the committee. Throughout Platt's tenure in Congress, the naval affairs committee was chaired by Representative Glenni W. Scofield, a Republican from Pennsylvania.

[155]Richmond *Daily Dispatch*, 3 November 1870, p. 3; The *Norfolk Virginian*, 2 November 1870, p. 1.

Robeson had come to Norfolk on Tuesday, 1 November, to assist in Platt's 1870 campaign for reelection to Congress. Following his arrival, "hundreds" of whites and blacks assembled that evening at the City Hall in Norfolk, where they were addressed by Governor Henry Wells, Secretary Robeson, and Professor Langston (black) of Howard University. While this rally was in progress, according to the *Virginian*, a procession of blacks carrying Chinese lanterns arrived and took up a position in front of the speakers' stand. When Robeson finished his remarks, a Colonel William E. Cameron of Petersburg asked to speak, arguing that Platt had agreed to give him equal time. Platt refused, and Cameron and his friends left for the National Hotel.

A black named Lancaster then started to speak while some freedmen in the audience attempted to clear out white listeners who "had gathered on the outskirts of the assembly. " According to the paper, two police officers—Lieutenant C. C. Benson and Private W. J. Messick—then drew their pistols and tried to quiet the blacks in the crowd, a "number of whom were armed with sticks." They attempted to arrest someone in the crowd who shouted that he had a revolver, but the two officers were "badly beaten, and in defending themselves, they used their pistols. This brought out other weapons, both from the whites and negroes, and some eighteen or twenty shots were fired, when the latter broke and ran." Although at least four people were wounded seriously in the fracas, the fleeing freedmen rallied again on Bank Street. Lieutenant Benson, in the company of eight to ten other policemen, proceeded to attack them again "and was met by a volley of pistol balls, which was returned, and the negroes broke in the wildest disorder." Meanwhile, the white radicals, "headed by Platt," had sought safety in the courthouse. At least three additional people were wounded during this second violent outbreak, and Robeson ordered a batallion of marines from Washington to maintain order until after the election, which was scheduled for 8 November 1870.

The *Virginian* went on to say that although the Republicans blamed the Conservatives for the riot, it was really "but the natural outgrowth of the insendiary [*sic*] teachings they have been planting in the minds of the negroes for years past." It also reported yet additional casualties and concluded that the riot was "more serious in its consequences than we had supposed." One of these newly reported casualties was Willis Augustus "Spec" Hodges, a black known to Teamoh who had represented Princess Anne County in the 1867–1868 constitutional convention. Hodges, who earned the epithet whites gave him from the fact that he wore large eyeglasses, had allegedly assaulted a white man who "was prepared for such customers, and fired a pistol at Hodges, the ball taking effect in his left thumb, and afterwards gave the doughty Specs, a severe larruping with a hickory stick."

For a better-balanced assessment of Hodges and his political activities than that presented by the *Virginian*, see Gatwood, *Free Man of Color*, lx–lxvii; Jackson, *Negro Office-Holders*, 21.

The *Virginian* finally summed up its view of the riot on 3 November 1870. On its front page that day, it concluded that the people of the Norfolk-Portsmouth region "trust that this little blood-letting may have a salutary effect, and that such disturbances will be no more seen or heard of among us."

[156]The *Norfolk Virginian* noted dissension from time to time on the county board of supervisors, a body containing members from each of the county's townships. For an example of the type of Republican infighting to which Teamoh made reference, see the *Norfolk Virginian*, 19 September 1871, p. 1.

[157]William H. Lyons—master machinist at the navy yard, leader of the GAR, and Teamoh's longtime rival in the local Republican party—had allegedly taken 5,000 cigars worth 300 dollars from the Spanish mail steamer *Ocean Bird* 1 February 1867 and tried to smuggle them ashore. He was first indicted for smuggling at Richmond during the court term of September 1869. No action was taken at that time or during later terms (May 1870, November 1870, and October 1871). The case was dismissed from Richmond, and Lyons was told to report to the district court in Norfolk on 6 November 1871. Unfortunately, there are no criminal docket books for the Norfolk district from 1865 to 1882, so there are no official records showing the final outcome of the case. From Teamoh's comments, however, it appears that

Lyons was never actually convicted of smuggling. Teamoh was a member of the grand jury that failed, in his judgment, to bring Lyons to justice. See the *Norfolk Virginian*, 9 November 1871, p. 1; 13 November 1871, p. 1.

The records of Lyons's legal difficulties are contained as cases 199 and 283 of the U.S. Circuit and District Courts for the Eastern District of Virginia—Richmond and Norfolk Divisions, General Services Administration, Region 3, Federal Archives and Records Center, Philadelphia. A summary of these records was supplied by Robert J. Plowman, Chief, Archives Branch, of the above-noted depository.

The *Norfolk Virginian*, 16 August 1871, p. 1, argued that the case against Lyons was based more on Republican factionalism than on legal principle. It noted that the accused party had served as chairman of the Republican Executive Committee of Portsmouth, until he was replaced in that position by Philip G. Thomas in early May. According to the paper, the Norfolk City and County Executive Committees refused initially to cooperate with Thomas, but some committee members on these bodies were eventually brought into line by promises of navy yard patronage. Even so, the *Virginian* noted,

> they have not succeeded in uniting the influence at Washington, formerly held by the old committee, and the friends of the new committee attribute their failure to Mr. Lyons, and heap upon him all manner of abuse, and in order to crush him out finally, beyond a possibility of a resurrection, they have revived the old charges against him, which he thought settled years ago. Several delegations of the Thomas wing have visited Washington lately upon secret missions. In fact, Mr. Thomas himself returned Sunday, and on Monday Mr. Lyons was arrested, as a means of getting him out of the way, and of destroying the influence which he is said to possess at Washington.
>
> We do'nt [*sic*] know what will be the result, but presume if there was anything in the charge, the United States District Attorney would not have entered a nolle prosequi, but it serves to demonstrate that no one, whether friend or antagonist, is safe from the machinations of the Rads, if he stands in the way of the accompolishment [*sic*] of their ends.

[158]In the last city directory in which he appeared, Teamoh was listed as a caulker living at 404 Green in Portsmouth. See *Chataigne's Directory of Norfolk and Portsmouth, 1883–1884* (Norfolk: J. H. Chataigne, 1883) 447.

[159]Teamoh purchased this property from Nathan B. and Isabella Webster on 11 July 1871 for $2,100. To make the purchase, he paid $1,050 in cash and signed a note for an additional $1,050. He agreed to pay off the note (held by Webster) within twelve months at 10 percent interest. "Deed Book 6," pp. 403–405, Office of the Circuit Court, City of Portsmouth, Virginia. The 1870 manuscript census returns, Norfolk County, Virginia, City of Norfolk, Ward 1, p. 73, listed Nathan Webster as a fifty-year-old New Hampshire native employed as a schoolteacher. He held property valued at $16,000. His wife, Isabella, was a forty-nine-year-old Virginia native. The Webster household also included three children—Ella (also a schoolteacher), John (the photographer cited in n. 160), and Frank (a teenager employed as a retail clerk).

[160]Webster had run a school for boys at the Green Street address. By the time Teamoh made this purchase, however, he had moved that operation, The Webster Institute for Boys, to 45 and 47 Charlotte Street in Norfolk. An advertisement on p. 179 of the *1872–1873 Norfolk and Portsmouth Directory* listed Professor N. B. Webster as a principal of the institute, which

gave instruction in "Scientific, Mathmatical [sic], Commercial, Classical, and Preparatory Studies." The advertisement also noted that applications for admission to the school could be obtained in Norfolk from Webster himself or from J. N. Webster at the Photographic Gallery in Portsmouth.

[161]Teamoh and a group of twenty other Portsmouth blacks purchased this property for $2,500 on 1 September 1870. "Deed Book 6," pp. 359-61. For the names of Teamoh's partners in this venture, see n. 164.

[162]This reference is somewhat confusing. Teamoh first referred to the school Webster opened in Norfolk (see n. 160). Teamoh then referred to the Portsmouth property he (and twenty others) purchased from Webster (see n. 164).

[163]In 1870, the total population of the city of Portsmouth was 10,492, with the city's black population totaling 3,617. Teamoh may have included sizable black populations in surrounding Norfolk County districts (such as Tanner's Creek, Washington, and Western Branch) in his population estimate of seven to eight thousand blacks. See *A Compendium of the Ninth Census (June 1, 1870,) Compiled Pursuant to a Concurrent Resolution of Congress and under the Direction of the Secretary of the Interior* (Washington D.C.: Government Printing Office, 1872) 356.

[164]The deed cited in n. 161 listed the twenty-one shareholders (twelve of whom were women) in this venture. They were David Bailey, Julia Ann Brown, William H. Brown, Thomas Davis, Henry Foster, Sarah Halstead, Mary Ann Hodges, Nancy Hodges, Rose Murray, Sarah Nash, Dave Portlock, Milley Riddick, Martha Sawyer, Richard Silvester, George Teamoh (two shares), Nicy Wallace, Eliza Webb, Mary White, Henry Wilkins (two shares), Caroline Williams, and Joshua V. Wilson.

[165]The Portsmouth public free schools rented the Webster building from 17 August 1871 to November 1879 for $45 per month. Reference to "Portsmouth School Board Minutes," supplied in letter of W. T. H. Galliford, Jr., assistant superintendent for instruction, Portsmouth Public Schools, to Richard L. Hume, 21 April 1983. The nature of the criticism that Teamoh noted could not be established with certainty, but it was perhaps related to factionalism within the local Republican party.

[166]George Peabody was a banker, merchant, financier, and philanthropist. Born in South Danvers (now Peabody), Massachusetts on 18 February 1795, he became a successful businessman and railroad president in Baltimore before 1837, when he moved to Britain and resided in London until his death in 1869. There, Peabody accumulated a considerable fortune through the sale of American securities and through his activities as a money broker. Beginning in 1852, he gave large amounts of money to various causes, including the Peabody Educational Fund (established in 1867) for the improvement of education in the South. The fund (which amounted to some $1,000,000 in 1867 and eventually to some 3,500,000) was dispersed to black and white institutions on a segregated basis. Republican radicals criticized this policy, but it was defended as a necessary concession to southern realities. See Malone and Johnson, *Dictionary of American Biography*, 14:336-38; William Preston Vaughn, *Schools for All: The Blacks and Public Education in the South, 1865–1877* (Lexington: University of Kentucky Press, 1974) 141-49.

Portsmouth did receive money on a regular basis during the 1870s from the Peabody Fund. This money, however, was not categorical, and it apparently went into the general fund, of which it constituted almost half. Although there was no George Peabody school for blacks in Portsmouth during the late nineteenth century, a school of that name was built in 1919, long after Teamoh's day. Letter of 21 April 1983 from W. T. H. Galliford, Jr. to Richard L. Hume.

[167]Joseph Cook (1838–1901) was a native of Ticonderoga, New York, who became a well-known author and lecturer. He graduated from Harvard in 1865, and he then studied for the ministry for four years at Andover Theological Seminary. After extensive foreign travel, he settled in Boston in 1874 and became a pastor of a Congregational church in that city. In 1875, he was invited to speak at a weekly Y.M.C.A. prayer meeting. He began to participate in these meetings (Mondays at noon) on a regular basis, and his popular addresses (on a variety of topics ranging from theology to socialism) eventually attracted crowds of up to 2,500 per lecture. He also traveled again to Europe, where he lectured in Britain, Germany, and Italy. See the *New York Times*, 26 June 1901, p. 7. For the background of Cook's lecture activities, see "Boston Monday Lectures: History of the Lectures," in Joseph Cook, *Marriage, with Preludes on Current Events* (Boston: Houghton, Osgood and Company, 1879) appendix, pp. 1-4. For a hostile evaluation of Cook's approach to scientific questions, such as the issue of evolution, see John Fisk, *A Century of Science and Other Essays* (Boston: Houghton, Mifflin and Company, 1900) 333-49.

[168]The prominent American abolitionist and the editor of the abolitionist newspaper *The Liberator*, from 1831 to 1865 (see n. 82).

[169]*Chataigne's Directory, of Norfolk and Portsmouth, 1882–1883* (Norfolk: J. H. Chataigne, 1882) 552, listed three white Methodist churches in Portsmouth: Methodist Episcopal South—Dinwiddie, corner of Queen—Reverend William E. Judkins; Central Methodist Episcopal South—County, near Washington—Reverend R. J. Moorman; and Methodist Episcopal Church South—Second Street, Newtown—Reverend George Wright.

[170]A native of Accomac County, Henry A. Wise (1806–1876) served for a decade (1833–1844) in Congress and as American ambassador to Brazil (1844–1847). Elected governor in 1855, he served as Virginia's chief executive during the turbulent late antebellum years that climaxed with John Brown's raid on Harpers Ferry. After leaving the governor's office in 1860, Wise served as a brigadier general in the Confederate Army. Following the war, he practiced law in Richmond. See Malone and Johnson, *Dictionary of American Biography*, 20:423-25. By the early 1880s, when Teamoh wrote this section of his manuscript, southern whites were already quite successful in eliminating many of the social and political gains made by the freedmen during the Reconstruction era. This exclusionary effort was justified, in part, on traditional (often religious) antebellum arguments of black inferiority and on paternalistic concepts espoused by many leaders in the conservative governments, which replaced the southern Reconstruction regimes. By this time the work of Charles Darwin, in the popularized form known as "Social Darwinism," was also used frequently as a "scientific" justification for further limitation of economic and political opportunities for blacks within southern society. For a good, brief discussion of this "scientific racism" and its use in matters such as the communion issue of concern to Teamoh, see George M. Fredrickson, *The Black Image in the White Mind: The Debate on Afro-American Character and Destiny, 1817–1914* (New York: Harper & Row, 1971) 228-82.

[171]John Wesley (1703–1791) was an English clergyman and the founder of the Methodist Church.

[172]There is an extensive literature on political, social, and economic objectives of Negroes and mulattoes (at both the leadership and the rank-and-file level) during the postwar years. Some historians see basic differences on these questions between these two groups in the black

community; others tend to minimize these differences and stress instead a growing Negro-mulatto unity in response to the racism of southern whites. For recent examples of the former view, noting racial and class divisions within the black community, see Thomas Holt, *Black over White: Negro Political Leadership in South Carolina during Reconstruction* (Urbana: University of Illinois Press, 1971) 17-18; Leon F. Litwack, *Been in the Storm So Long: The Aftermath of Slavery* (New York: Alfred A. Knopf, 1979) 521-22. For a recent study stressing the growth of black-mulatto cooperation in the face of continuing racial tensions in the postwar South, see Joel Williamson, *New People: Miscegenation and Mulattoes in the United States* (New York: Free Press, 1980) 61-109.

[173]For the classic study of a long-standing debate regarding the relative importance of the biologically inherited and culturally acquired elements of the American black "personality," see Winthrop Jordan, *White over Black: American Attitudes toward the Negro, 1550–1812* (Chapel Hill: University of North Carolina Press, 1968).

[174]Black churches, of course, played an extremely important role in the evolution of the free black community following the war. Ministers, for example, were quite prominent as leaders among blacks during the postwar years. For a positive evaluation of the impact of this group as leaders of the freedmen during the early years of Reconstruction, see Hume, "Negro Delegates," 139-40. For comments on the problems some black ministers faced in changing their ministry from one to the slaves into one directed at the freedmen, see Eugene D. Genovese, *Roll, Jordan, Roll: The World the Slaves Made* (New York: Pantheon Books, 1974) 273.

[175]Hampton Institute was established in 1867, when "Little Scotland," a small plantation on the Hampton River, was purchased as a site for a school. Its founding was the work of General Samuel C. Armstrong, a Freedmen's Bureau official, and it was based on the model of a manual labor school that he had operated in Hawaii. Its most famous graduate, Booker T. Washington, attended Hampton (1872–1875) and advocated Armstrong's philosophy of industrial education for blacks after assuming the presidency of Tuskegee Institute in Alabama (1881). See Henry Allen Bullock, *A History of Negro Education in the South from 1619 to the Present* (Cambridge: Harvard University Press, 1967) 32-33.

[176]This term suggests that Teamoh was aware of the popularized form of Social Darwinism, which was used in part to give credibility to segregationist legislation passed by various southern legislatures during the latter nineteenth century. Unfortunately, some social darwinists predicted the extinction of less "advanced" races—such as the West Indians (Jamaicans)—just as a number of southern whites at the end of the Civil War had foreseen the extinction of southern blacks. Members of the black race, it was argued, were lazy and would not work without the institution of slavery to force their labor. For the standard analysis of Social Darwinism and the hold it had on American society during this period, see Richard Hofstadter, *Social Darwinism in American Thought, 1860–1915* (Philadelphia: University of Pennsylvania Press, 1944). For brief comments on black intellectuals and their reactions to the doctrine, see William Toll, "Free Men, Freedmen, and Race: Black Social Theory in the Gilded Age," *Journal of Southern History* 44 (November 1978): 578-79.

[177]Teamoh, as was the case with a number of American blacks, believed that the British—who had ended slavery in Jamaica in 1833—had pursued especially enlightened racial policies in their West Indian colonies since the 1820s. There was some truth to this view. Sir Anthony Musgrave, governor of Jamaica during the years in which Teamoh was writing this section of his diary (1877–1883), undertook significant educational reforms that benefited the island's former slaves. Teamoh, however, was not entirely accurate in his positive assessment of British

policy toward black Jamaicans. In fact, almost constant racial difficulties existed on the island from 1833 (the date of emancipation) to the mid-1860s, when Britain took direct control of Jamaica as a crown colony.

For an example of another black diarist who noted British racial policies in Jamaica as "enlightened," and contrasted these policies with those of the antebellum American government, see Ray Allen Billington, ed., *The Journal of Charlotte L. Forten* (New York: Collier Books, 1961) 11-12. For a brief history of Jamaica, with a good summary of emancipation and British policy toward the newly freed black population, see Irving Kaplan, Howard I. Blutstein, Kathryn Therese Johnston, and David S. McMorris, *Area Handbook for Jamaica* (Washington D.C.: United States Government Printing Office, 1976) 58-71.

[178]The standard account of northern teachers in the South during the Reconstruction era is Henry L. Swint, *The Northern Teacher in the South, 1862–1870* (Nashville: Vanderbilt University Press, 1941). It is markedly hostile to those products of Yankee culture. For a more sympathetic view, and one that is better balanced than that of either Swint or Teamoh, see Sandra E. Small, "The Yankee Schoolmarm in the Freedmen's Schools: An Analysis of Attitudes," *Journal of Southern History* 45 (August 1979): 381-402.

John Brown, of Harpers Ferry fame, was hanged in 1859; William Lloyd Garrison was almost lynched by a Boston mob in 1835; Wendell Phillips (1811–1884) was a well-known New England abolitionist leader (see n. 83); Senator Charles Sumner of Massachusetts was beaten by Representative Preston Brooks of South Carolina on the floor of the United States Senate in 1856; President Abraham Lincoln was assassinated in 1865; and President James Garfield was assassinated in 1881. Emmanuel is a reference to Jesus Christ.

[179]William E. Chandler (1835–1917) became a leading Republican legislator in his native New Hampshire during the Civil War era. After helping to devise the strategy that secured Rutherford B. Hayes's election in the disputed presidential contest of 1876, he split with Hayes, whom he believed was too lenient toward the South. In 1880 Chandler supported James Garfield for the Republican presidential nomination; following Garfield's assassination, President Chester Arthur appointed Chandler secretary of the Navy, a post he held from 1882 to 1885. He then returned to New Hampshire, where he was elected to the United States Senate, in which he served from 1887 to 1901. See Allen and Malone, *Dictionary of American Biography*, 3:616-18.

Chandler's original reply to Teamoh, with only a few minor differences in punctuation from the version in the diary, is located in William E. Chandler to George Teamoh, 12 March 1883, Miscellaneous letters sent, Record Group 45, Naval Records Collection of the Office of Naval Records, Navy and Old Army Branch, National Archives and Records Service, Washington, D.C. Chandler stated that he had referred Teamoh's manuscript to the Bureau of Construction and Repair. There is a gap in the correspondence files of that office for the years 1870–1886, and Teamoh's original eight-page letter, unfortunately, cannot be located.

[180]Moloch—Canaanite war deity to whom children were sacrificed; Ahiun—perhaps a reference to Ahijuh, an Old Testament prophet who urged rebellion against Solomon; Ashtoreth—Canaanite deity of fertility and war.

[181]The International Order of Good Templars, a temperance organization, was formed in Syracuse, New York, in 1852, and its first annual national convention met in Cleveland, Ohio, in 1855. It held its nineteenth annual convention in Britain (in London—not in Wales, as Teamoh noted) in 1873, and that must be the meeting to which Teamoh referred. The organization was active in Portsmouth (see, e.g., the *Norfolk Virginian*, 9 August 1871, p. 1), and

it held its 1886 international convention in Richmond. For a list of the locations of these conventions (1852–1886), see "Proceedings of the Thirty-Second Annual Session of the Grand Lodge, I.O.G.T. Held at Richmond, Virginia, U.S.A., May 25, 26, 27, 28, 29 and 31" (Milwaukee: Cramer, Aikens & Cramer, Printers, 1886) 61. This document listed a number of current and past officers of the organization in the British Isles, but a "Miss or Mistress Collins" (evidently only a rank-and-file member) was not among those listed.

Teamoh had obviously been interested in prohibition and temperance for his entire adult life. This interest, however, may have been heightened during the postwar years. The Freedmen's Bureau—under the direction of General Oliver O. Howard, who was very interested in this reform—promoted the virtues of thrift and temperance among the freedmen. For interesting detail on this activity at the grassroots level, see Martin Abbot, *The Freedmen's Bureau in South Carolina, 1865–1872* (Chapel Hill: University of North Carolina Press, 1967) 108-109.

[182]See n. 139. The Methodist minister to whom Teamoh referred could not be identified positively.

[183]Jacob E. Moore, who served as minister of the African Methodist Episcopal Church in Portsmouth from 1879 to 1883, was the object of Teamoh's critical remarks here and later (see n. 185). See the list of ministers, 1857–1957, inside the front cover of "Centennial Anniversary Emanuel African Methodist Episcopal Church Portsmouth, Virginia 1857–1957" (n.p., n.d.) in Ester Wilson Memorial History Room, Portsmouth Public Library. Moore was probably the black minister, J. W. Moore, listed as a native of Maryland, thirty-three years of age, with a wife and four children, in the 1880 manuscript census returns, Norfolk County, Virginia, Hall's Corner Voting Precinct, p. 5.

[184]William Mahone (see n. 124) had lost control of his railroad interests during the 1873 depression. He had subsequently become active politically as the most prominent leader of the "Readjuster Movement," an attempt to scale down Virginia's state debt.

A rather modest debt had accumulated to finance public improvements during the antebellum years, but that liability had grown to the substantial sum of more than $40,000,000 by the end of the Reconstruction era. The legislature had attempted to reduce that total by raising taxes and by reducing public expenditures, especially on public schools. By 1879, however, the debt question divided Virginia's voters between "Funders" (who wished to pay the debt in full) and "Readjusters," who wished to pay off only a part (about 2/3) of that obligation. The "Readjusters" carried the state elections in 1879 and 1881, the year in which Mahone was sent to the United States Senate. They then reduced the state debt, lowered state taxes, liberalized voting procedures, and promoted educational reforms. Nonetheless, Mahone's willingness to appeal to the state's black voters (and his alliance with Republicans in Washington) divided the "Readjusters," who lost both the legislature and the governorship by 1885. See James T. Moore, *Two Paths to the New South: The Virginia Debt Controversy, 1870–1883* (Lexington: University of Kentucky Press, 1974) 54-108; Carl N. Degler, *The Other South: Southern Dissenters in the Nineteenth Century* (New York: Harper & Row, 1974) 270-315. Bishop Paine could not be positively identified.

[185]Teamoh had borrowed $940 on 28 July 1882, and he had secured that loan with the home he had purchased in 1871 (see n. 159). When he could not repay that obligation, he lost his property, through a forced sale recorded on 28 March 1883, to the organization he referred to as the "Tide Water Trust Company." That group actually consisted of twenty individuals. In addition to Reverend J. E. W. Moore (n. 183), they were: James Baker, Southall Bass,

Sr., George Colden, Thomas R. Colding, David Council, Giles Cuffee, Samuel Davis, Alexander Gordan, David Graham, Nelson Gray, Sr., John W. Jasper, Peter Jordan, John Johnson, N. C. Norcum, James Norcum, Nelson Proctor, J. H. W. Scott, Joseph H. Smith, and John Warren. Deed Book 14, Office of the Circuit Court, City of Portsmouth, Virginia, p. 346. A restored apartment building with the name "Tide Water Building" and the date 1906 on its facade was still standing on the corner of Queen and Green streets in Portsmouth in the fall of 1988.

[186]John A. Armistead served as minister of the Zion Baptist Church (located at the corner of Green and King streets in Portsmouth) from 1882 to 1925. He was trained in theology at the Richmond Institute of Theology and at Roger Williams Theological Seminary in Nashville, Tennessee. He served as editor-in-chief of the *Baptist Companion*, which was published at Knoxville, Tennessee, and at Portsmouth. He also once served as a member of the Portsmouth City Council. See "Souvenir Program, The Centennial Celebration of the Zion Baptist Church Portsmouth Virginia (1865–1965)" (n.p., n.d.), Ester Wilson Memorial History Room, Portsmouth Public Library. In 1883 William G. Alexander replaced Jacob E. Moore as minister in Teamoh's church. See inside front cover, "Centennial Anniversary African Methodist Episcopal Church." Alexander held that post until 1887.

[187]Teamoh made his last entry in 1883, and his wife was listed as a widow at the time of her death from pneumonia (at age eighty-two) on 2 September 1892. However, a check of spotty records of local cemeteries in the Norfolk-Portsmouth area—by Mrs. Brooke Maupin (of the Ester Wilson Memorial History Room of the Portsmouth Public Library) and Mrs. Peggy Haile (of the Sargeant Memorial Room of the Norfolk Public Library)—failed to establish the exact date of Teamoh's death during the decade of 1883–1892. A search by Sheila H. Musser, deputy registrar, Department of Public Health, City of Portsmouth, Virginia, was also unsuccessful in locating data on Teamoh's death. The death of his wife, Sarah (Sallie), was recorded in "Elizabeth City, County, Register of Deaths, 1853–1896," microfilm copy, Virginia State Archives, Richmond.

INDEX